Hollywood Mother of the Year

HOLLYWOOD
Mother of the Year

Sheila MacRae's Own Story

WITH H. PAUL JEFFERS

A Birch Lane Press Book
Published by Carol Publishing Group

A Birch Lane Press Book
Published by Carol Publishing Group
Birch Lane Press is a registered trademark of Carol
    Communications, Inc.

Editorial Offices: 600 Madison Avenue, New York, N.Y. 10022
Sales & Distribution Offices: 120 Enterprise Avenue, Secaucus,
N.J. 07094

In Canada: Canadian Manda Group, P.O. Box 920, Station U,
    Toronto, Ontario M8Z 5P9

Queries regarding rights and permissions should be addressed to
Carol Publishing Group, 600 Madison Avenue, New York, N.Y. 10022

Carol Publishing Group books are available at special discounts
for bulk purchases, for sales promotions, fund raising, or
educational purposes. Special editions can be created to specifications.
For details, contact: Special Sales Department, Carol Publishing
Group, 120 Enterprise Avenue, Secaucus, N.J. 07094

Manufactured in the United States of America

10 9 8 7 6 5 4 3 2 1

Library of Congress Cataloging-in-Publication Data

MacRae, Sheila, 1926–
    Hollywood mother of the year : Sheila MacRae's own story / with
H. Paul Jeffers.
        p.   cm.
    "A Birch Lane Press book."
    ISBN 1-55972-112-X
    1. MacRae, Sheila, 1926– . 2. MacRae, Gordon. 3. Television
personalities—United States—Biography. 4. Singers—United States–
Biography. I. Jeffers, H. Paul (Harry Paul), 1934– .
II. Title.
PN1992.4.M257A3 1992
791.45'028'092—dc20
[B]   91-44777
                                                          CIP

I have some rights of memory
in this kingdom of ours.
—Shakespeare

This book is dedicated to all Hollywood mothers but especially to the seven of us who in 1953 joined in the founding of Share Happily and Reap Endlessly (SHARE) to help mentally-impaired children and signed ourselves thus: Mrs. Robert Blythe, Mrs. Sammy Cahn, Mrs. Jeff Chandler, Mrs. Gordon MacRae, Mrs. Dean Martin, Mrs. Gene Nelson, and Mrs. William T. Orr.*

*It was a time when a woman was invariably identified by her husband's name. All of us ultimately divorced.

Contents

The Malted Milk Kids

FROM MY DIARY

I've been chosen "Hollywood Mother of the Year." Hurray! For
me! I guess! I guess nobody knows my marriage is a shambles! My
Gordon, my darling, is a total addict. Both liquor and pills. Oh,
God! I've just found out that he's gambled the ranch away to some
cardsharp from Las Vegas. Our beautiful ranch in Oregon is gone!
He took my birthday present from Lucy Ball to pay off a debt to
some guy from Texas. My lovely land next to Lucy's lot at the
Indian Wells Country Club. Lucy says it's forgery! She's totally
mad at him and she's not going to speak to him ever again. He's
given up on AA—and on me, too, I fear. Thank God I have my
children.
P.S. Another miscarriage—three so far.

Jack Warner and a handful of Hollywood insiders knew this truth
about Gordon and Sheila. In keeping the secret, I'd become a
magnificent illusionist.

Movies are a trick of the eyes. There's a quirk in how we see that allows a series of still pictures to spring into motion. In pursuit of that optical illusion, fortunes have been made; lives have been devoted to it, and some have been ruined. The trouble came if you couldn't tell what was legerdemain and what was real, distinguish the magician from the magic, but if you were the magician's assistant as I was, eventually you got to know all the tricks.

Yet I had never expected to become Gordon's partner in his show-business career. All I ever desired was to be his wife. But even that notion had seemed preposterous at first. He and I were as opposite as opposite could be.

Nothing so clearly defined the root of our differences as our mothers. Born and bred in the United States, he was raised by Helen MacRae in the American tradition of Mom, apple pie, and the flag. A transplanted British-born girl with an English accent that never truly left me, I was the daughter of Winifred Baker Stephens and lived a childhood that could only be described as bizarre and baroque and interesting.

Gordon's mother was a talented classical pianist. When my mother touched a keyboard, it was to play jazz. Mrs. MacRae held traditional views. Mrs. Stephens took a more radical turn. Helen hated for Gordon to be the boy who would play hooky from school to go fishing. Winifred urged daughter Sheila to always be a lady and let her have clothes that were grown up and helped her to become an actress.

We lived on Long Island—my parents, my sister Paula, and I. My father, Louis Albert Stephens, was an engineer. A wizard with auto-mobiles, he had designed for Rolls Royce/Bentley before moving his family to the car-crazy America of the 1930s. Our home was an old, brown, shingled house with thirty willow trees on a piece of land jutting into Hempstead Harbor. It had a black and yellow living room. This was my mother's Japanese period. My six-foot-four, acerbic father hated it, but he could deny nothing to the dazzling, clever, five-foot-two Winifred Baker Stephens.

Always sociable, she delighted in having her friends in for her Long Island version of an English tea. With the intention of teaching her daughters the social amenities, Mother allowed my sister and me to serve. On one of these occasions, when I was six years old, I presented tea and cake to a round woman with a prominent bosom. "I think you are ever so lucky to have such a huge front," I said, imitating her high-pitched, nasal way of speaking. "You can put your teacup there and eat your cake with both hands."

Everyone laughed. Except the woman, of course. And Mother.

"Leave at once," she said, pointing to the door.

Later, I pleaded, "Mummy, I don't understand! Everyone laughed."

With a chuckle, my father was on my side. "You must admit, Winnie, that it was a rather good imitation of that woman," he said. "It seems to me that Sheila's a born actress."

Mother was not immediately persuaded, but as my imitations persisted, she announced, "If you're to be an actress, you'll have to have elocution lessons and speak up! Don't mumble!"

Drama coaches were next. One of the first was Miss Francis Robinson Duff, who had taught Katharine Hepburn. I went to see Miss Duff prepared to perform, but she was much more interested in how I looked. Very grand and proper, she put a great store in one's stage presence and physical bearing. Assessing me from all sides as I sat on a stool, she said, "Yes, you have the head of an actress." Because I was in school, I saw her only on weekends. I was ecstatic being in the presence of such a lady. "But do you have the desire to act?" she asked.

How could I have not felt the tug of the stage? Like golden apples, artistic temperaments festooned the branches of my family tree. My aunts said we were related to two of the most illustrious names of the English theater: Sarah Siddons and John Philip Kemble, her brother and frequent costar in Shakespearean productions in mid-nineteenth-century England.

Those who are more familiar with American movies than with the Bard of Avon and the career of Madame Sarah Siddons might recall my illustrious ancestor's name from the opening scene of the classic Bette Davis film *All About Eve*. It's a closeup of a theatrical award in the form of "the Sarah Siddons award," which is about to be given to the unscrupulously ambitious actress Eve Harrington, portrayed so cunningly by Anne Baxter.

Others will recognize my actress-relative as the subject of *Mrs. Siddons as the Tragic Muse*, the masterpiece of the English portrait painter Sir Joshua Reynolds. He, too, was a distant ancestor of a teenager named Sheila Stephens, who was born in England but grew up in the United States, dreaming of filling the immortal Sarah's footsteps.

While in high school I had the great good luck to meet another imposing figure, Christopher Morley, essayist and playwright and one of the celebrated wits of the Algonquin Round Table. He told me about an Englishman and his wife who were going to take a company of players on weekend tours of colleges.

Because I was an excellent student, I was able to take off from school from Thursday night to Monday morning and travel with the Ben Greet players in their station wagon, loaded with costumes, scenery, and props. Our repertoire consisted of all the popular Shakespearean comedies and tragedies. I was Ophelia at matinees and later, three witches.

When I was fortunate enough to be chosen for a small part in William Saroyan's latest three-act play being produced at the Milllpond Playhouse in Roslyn, Long Island, I immediately developed a girlish crush on the renowned author of *The Time of Your Life* and *My Heart's in the Highlands*. With his dark looks and white suit, he was the embodiment of my girlish fantasies but far beyond the reach of a silly English teenager.

It was a summer of heady, sunny days and thrilling nights, and I was ripe and open for all of it, for all the romance my teenage heart could absorb.

My girlish fancies did not go unnoticed by the other young apprentices at the playhouse. On my sixteenth birthday they gathered around me, all giggles and snickers, to present me with a huge card covered with cutouts from magazines of pictures of handsome, eligible young men. Scrawled upon it was: "Sixteen is an engageable age."

Their sentiment turned out to be prophetic, because that day a handsome singer-actor swaggered into auditions on the stage of the Millpond Playhouse and with cocky self-confidence announced, "I'm Albert Gordon MacRae."

My reaction was instant, intense dislike. He struck me as someone who believed the universe turned around him. I did not care for pushy people. I thought he was, in the slang of the day, "stuck on himself." He was twenty years old and much of his life had already been spent in show business, though that had not been his father's plan.

When Gordon was born on March 12, 1921, in East Orange, New Jersey, his father, William Lamont MacRae, a Scottish toolmaker, had looked forward to having his son follow in his footsteps. His father felt even more strongly about it after starting a tool business that flourished beyond his wildest dreams, making the MacRae family quite well off in its new surroundings of Syracuse, New York. But young Gordon showed no interest in taking over a manufacturing firm. He knew happiness could never be found in making things. It had to be achieved by making music.

If ever anyone was born to sing, he believed—and bragged— it was none other than Gordon MacRae. Music appeared to have been bred into him. His mother had taught him piano. But being a realistic woman, she fretted about him, fearing that he did not take life seriously enough. She often lectured him. "Life is not all golf matches and songs," she warned. "It isn't easy. It requires responsibility."

Helen also expressed concern about his easy-come, easy-go attitude toward money. Though the MacRaes did not have to worry about finances, she chided him for pouring his allowance into pinball machines. However, what vexed her the most was Gordon's determination to become a professional singer of popular music.

He sang anywhere and everywhere, to himself and for anyone who cared to listen. He sang while in schools in Buffalo and in Syracuse and in many student productions at Deerfield Academy. A local radio announcer, Jimmy Van Heusen, heard him and encouraged him to pursue singing.

At age eighteen, Gordon traveled to New York City and won a singing contest at the 1939 World's Fair. His reward consisted of a two-week stint with Harry James's band.

Although Helen MacRae's son now made money singing, she doubted he would ever earn a living doing so. If he insisted on pursuing a singing career, she told him, she hoped he wouldn't be a crooner of love songs. She had no taste for popular music. In her view, opera would have been much more suitable for her son. Later, others who heard Gordon sing shared her view. Among them was Rudolph Bing of the Metropolitan Opera, who, years later, invited Gordon to study at the Met.

Helen preferred that Gordon be a radio announcer and was delighted when he got a job as a page at NBC. But Gordon saw the job as a stepping-stone toward his singing career. He scoured *Variety* for casting calls and announcements of auditions and talked to other actors and singers about shows that were looking for performers. In pursuit of one of those leads, he had traveled from Manhattan to our little playhouse on Long Island.

Despite my first assessment of him, he was attracted to me right away—and dogged in pursuit. It soon became clear that he had marriage in mind; I had my heart set on a career as an actress. This was more than a teenage girl's pipe dream. At fifteen, I'd been spotted by Halsey Raines, famous Metro-Goldwyn-Mayer talent scout. He had seen me in a school play and immediately spoken to my mother about offering me a seven-year contract. "I simply couldn't permit her to go to Hollywood," Mother said. "She's only fifteen."

"Naturally, you'd come with her," Mr. Raines replied.

Mother shook her head. "I couldn't possibly live there."

Although my breaking into movies was deferred, I pursued my acting dream through the classes in New York. The school was located in Rockefeller Center, where Gordon continued working as an NBC page and pursuing me romantically. Whenever I went to an actors' hangout at Radio City—the "Redhead Café" (because of the actresses who hoped to be discovered there)—I found him nursing a milk shake and keeping an eye on the door while waiting for me to appear.

By now my opinion of him had changed dramatically. I'd seen through his braggadocio and caught glimpses of a sweet, charming, earnest young man. Dislike had warmed into friendship. Then, over milk shakes at the Redhead Café, friendliness toward him turned into a fondness rooted in admiration. Traits that seemed lacking in me abounded in him—self-confidence and optimism and not a shadow of a doubt that a successful career was just around the corner. That he wanted to share his bright future with me was thrilling. Realizing I was loved, I found myself loving back.

I also discovered that he had a sense of humor, so when April Fool's Day came, I met him at the Redhead Café expecting some kind of prank.

We both liked grapefruit, and as I was about to plunge a spoon into mine, he whispered, "Wait a minute. I think there's something funny about that grapefruit."

Not knowing what to expect—it was April Fool's Day, after all— I looked down anxiously. An engagement ring sparkled there.

"It's so little, I was afraid you'd gobble it up," he chuckled.

He had paid fifty dollars for it—a lot of money for somebody working as a page until "the big break" came along.

The break happened in an NBC men's room. Singing at the top of his voice and, no doubt, luxuriating in the superb acoustics that bathrooms somehow always provide, he heard another voice. "Say, you're pretty good. You ought to go over to see Horace Heidt. I understand he's looking for a singer for his band. Big tour."

What Horace was looking for was a fourth man for a quartet. "Can you sight-read music?" he asked.

"Hell yes," Gordon replied.

"Good," Horace said. "The tour starts in Akron."

Gordon was upset. I was crushed.

"Akron?" I cried. "It might as well be the moon!"

Gloomy and dispirited, I kissed him good-bye. Resigned to my fate and already counting the days until I would be with him again, I sulked and made myself a nuisance to my mother and sister, but my glum mood vanished with a phone call. "Sheila, you'd better get yourself out here to Akron right away," said a desperate-sounding Horace Heidt.

I was so fearful that something had happened to Gordon, I could not speak.

"This young man of yours is driving us crazy," Horace continued. "You'd just better come out here and marry him and put him out of his misery."

If life were a movie script, my decision would have been obvious— hop a train and dash off to my love—but life is never that simple. The call had come at a moment when my dream of being an actress seemed to be within my grasp. I'd been offered and had signed a contract to be the lead in a play in New York. I had to choose.

I chose Gordon.

Furious with me, the agent, Louis Shurr, who had arranged the role warned, "This is the end of your career."

Thrilled at becoming Mrs. Gordon MacRae, I rushed to Ohio. I was not eighteen and could not get married without permission in Ohio, so Horace's wife, Adeline, and the lead tenor of the quartet, Larry Cotton, became my legal guardians and gave the necessary permission.

The transition to Mrs. MacRae did not go as smoothly as I had expected. Not having had the experience of traveling with an orchestra, I was hardly prepared to be a girl—and I *was* a girl!—in the midst of "the boys in the band." Musicians have always been a breed apart. They have their own lingo, which has always been at the leading edge of language, contributing such slang as "jazz," "jive," "take it from the top," "bop," "one-night stand," "hip," "cool," "with it," and "square." A worldly and cynical group, they can be rough on the naïve and the innocent, a category to which Gordon and I clearly belonged, being neither cool nor hip.

Horace gave Gordon the afternoon off for the ceremony, but Gordon had to work that evening. When he joined the band, the musicians were eager to know everything that happened. "How was it?'" they asked.

"It was fine," Gordon answered. "We walked around and took in the sights."

"The hell with that" came the reply. "How was the sex?"

Because both Gordon and I naïvely believed that sexual intercourse must be performed only at night, Gordon blithely answered, "Oh, we'll be doing that after the show."

We had not slept together before our wedding night.

Traveling through the American heartland in a series of one-night stands, the couple cuddling on the train became fair game for Horace's "Musical Knights." They were especially amused when we passed the time by my telling Gordon the plots of the great works of literature. I was a reader and always had been. Gordon was not. He boasted to me that he had never read a book, never had a headache or a dream.

"I don't believe it," I said. "How'd you get through school without reading a book?"

"How do you suppose?" he said, grinning. "On my looks!"

Whether he was teasing or not didn't matter. I loved relating what I had read. I especially adored recounting the plays of Shakespeare and acting the parts. But as I read to him, I began to realize what different individuals we were. I made a list of the things we loved.

He loved singing, golf, gambling, and me.

I loved Gordon, images, ideas, words, and facts. At the time, I had no inkling that our differences held the seeds of future troubles and I rejected any suggestion that I had made a mistake. The first person to say so was Larry Cotton, a singer with the band.

"You've married the wrong guy," he said, sidling next to me in the wings as Gordon was performing. "He's uneducated, coarse and crude." He drew closer, pressing against me. "You need a man who will treat you right. I'm that guy."

With a gasp, I lurched away from him. "Horace says Gordie is just a diamond in the rough!"

"Yeah? Well, diamonds are hard. They cut," he said, pushing close.

"Someday when you're scratched and bleeding, maybe you'll call me."

I jerked back. "Horace says I'm Gordon's anchor."

"Believe me. It isn't going to work," Larry said. "The day will come when you'll realize that you want more out of life than spending all day in bed with Gordon MacRae."

Horace and Adeline Heidt were more encouraging. "When he does things that upset you," Horace advised, "say nothing. Be available to him. Learn the wifely ways."

"Men will always have something else to do," Adeline said. "It's your job as a wife to be there for him when he needs and wants you. You're part of his life now. But you must accept the fact that you are *not* everything in his life."

The pattern of that life became apparent immediately. From Fort Wayne to Texas to Arkansas to Kentucky, up and down the middle of America, we traveled with forty-four people, five shows a day with no day off, breakfast in our room, meals in roadside diners, and making love at night.

There were also long absences when he played golf, always accompanied by his betting on the outcome. Almost always he lost money that we could not afford to do without. Every week we had to wire home for money.

At Springfield, Illinois, the agent who had pronounced the demise of my acting career got in touch me with and offered what he called a "second chance." "There's an opening on a soap opera in Chicago," he said excitedly, "and it pays $750 a week."

Gordon was delighted. He was making $65 a week. "Do it, Sheersie," he said. "You can come and visit me on weekends. Look at all the money you'll be making."

"I want to be with you," I said, crying. "I don't care about the money."

"Well, I care about it," he said, taking me into his arms and kissing me. "With that dough I could buy a Cadillac."

Because he wanted me to go, I took the train to Chicago for the audition, arriving at the studio in tears. Understandably concerned, the producer of the program, Hyman Brown, asked what was wrong. He listened patiently as I explained that I really didn't want the part and that I wanted to be with my husband, but when I mentioned Gordon's remark about buying a Cadillac, Hy was noticeably upset. "Let me tell you something," he said. "This guy's not going to make it. He sounds like a loser. You're going to meet a lot of guys. Great guys. Take my advice and go back to New York. Dump this guy before he dumps you."

Offended and shocked, I could not go through with the audition. I rushed back to Gordon with the bad news that there'd be no $750 a week and no Cadillac. "Don't worry about it," he said, holding me close. "It won't be long until we can have all the fancy cars we want. I'm going to be a huge success. All you need to get to the top is the help of God and a good infield. With you on my team, Sheersie, how can I lose?"

During that 1942–43 cross-country tour, it became obvious to me that Horace was very fond of Gordon and his bride. He was like a father to us and very concerned about our future. He encouraged Gordon to save money and went so far as to match the amount that Gordon put in the bank. He also admonished him about gambling, much as Gordon's mother did, but, unfortunately, with as little effect. Money that Gordon was expected to be setting aside was often lost in card games.

When Horace found out, he was furious, yet he did not give up. Instead, he told Gordon he would give him a raise and double his matching funds so we could buy land. It was a futile gesture. Relations between Gordon and Horace grew more strained. But it wasn't the issue of money that stretched Horace's patience to the breaking point.

Always blunt and outspoken in his opinions, Gordon went too far one day with a comment on a dress Horace's wife was wearing. "It's awful," he blurted. "She doesn't have the shape for it."

Flushed with anger, Horace snapped, "Gordon, you're fired."

There was no patching it up. Our tour with Horace Heidt was ended there and then. As we headed back to New York, I was sick with worry, but Gordon brimmed with his usual confidence and inborn optimism. "Don't worry," he said soothingly. "Everything will be okay."

Amazingly, things did turn out well. I ran into an old friend, Beth Shea. We'd been cheerleaders together in school. An actress, she told me that her husband was leaving a show being produced by Moss Hart in which there was a part for a seventeen-year-old that Gordon could play perfectly. Moss liked what he saw but was concerned about Gordon's status in the draft. World War II was a cloud hanging over us and everyone else in the country. Gordon was 1-A in the draft and likely to be called up soon.

Moss suggested that he could arrange for Gordon to go into the military in Special Services and perform in a show that Moss was producing called *Winged Victory*. Gordon would have none of it. He had made up his mind he was joining the Army Air Corps.

He began training in 1944 as a navigator-bombardier at Ellsworth Field outside Houston. Because no wives and families were allowed to live on the base, we found the best accommodations available, a converted garage. We were lucky to have it. Our wallpaper, pasted up by Gordon and me on the one day he had off every two weeks, consisted of navigation maps. They were colorful and bright and the most unique wall coverings I have ever had.

While he was occupied in training, including flights that carried him hundreds of miles away, I was pregnant and doing my best to cope with the heat and dust of Texas. When he could, he telephoned, always brightening the lonely hours with his cheerful boyishness as he recounted the day's adventures in the wild blue yonder.

For Gordon the days when he was flying were filled with adventure. For me they were endless hours of worrying. I knew that those dashing young men in their flying machines could be killed or injured during training, so it was always with great relief and often with tears that I heard Gordon's beautiful voice on the telephone in the evenings saying, "Hi, Sheersie!" calling from wherever he might be.

One hot afternoon when he was away on a training mission, the familiar gnawing anxiety which filled all my days suddenly seemed quite different, horribly so. "Something's wrong," I thought as a chilling fear stabbed into me. In panic, I dashed from the apartment, screaming for our landlady. "Mrs. Fitzgerald," I cried, "something's happened to Gordie! I know it!"

"Calm down, darling," she replied soothingly as she wrapped me in her snug, comforting arms. "Come in and have some nice iced tea and tell me all about it."

Tell her what? How could I explain what I felt? The apprehension, the awful premonition of disaster.

"You're a Christian girl," she said quietly. "Have faith in God. Say a prayer and everything will turn out fine."

Out of the memory of my Christian Science Sunday School classes I recalled my teacher telling us that in times of fear comfort and help would be found in the words of the Ninety-first Psalm. "I will say of the

Lord, He is my refuge and my fortress.... Thou shalt not be afraid for the terror by night; nor for the arrow that flieth by day.... For he shall give his angels charge over thee, to keep thee in all thy ways." I began to feel a sense of peace.

The phone rang at six o'clock. It was Gordie, more excited than I'd ever known him to be. "Sheersie, you won't believe what happened today," he blurted. "We were flying an A-26 and everybody got a chance at the stick. Well, this nervous guy froze at the controls. He wouldn't let go. The lieutenant was beating his hands to get them loose. The plane started to go into a spin. Then the lieutenant ordered everybody to bail out. Most of 'em did. But at that moment—and I can't explain it—I heard the words of the Ninety-first Psalm. And the next thing I knew, I was reciting it. Suddenly, the guy at the controls let go of the stick and the lieutenant and I were able to pull the plane out of the dive."

Determined not to let flying divert him from singing, he entertained at the officer's club at every airfield to which he was sent. To my great relief he was not called to go overseas and into combat.

Money was a problem, of course. There wasn't enough of it. But a chance to earn some came my way in the form of a job on the radio station in Houston owned by Howard Hughes. It was a job that later would be called "disc jockey." The program manager was looking for a girl to give his station a different sound. "With that English accent of yours," he said, "you'll certainly be different. You'll also make radio history, because, as far as I know, you'll be the first girl ever to spin records on the radio."

I proposed a show in which I would pretend to be talking on the phone to recording stars. The idea was people phoned to ask me to play the latest hits. I called the show *Penthouse Serenade*. The audience loved it. But I had not forgotten that I was a wife and mother. I nursed Meredith at work and was prepared to support Gordon in renewing his singing career after his discharge from the Air Force.

As the discharge date neared, Gordon returned from duty one day to announce that he had decided to stay in the service. "I can go to Officer's Candidate School," he said, "and in a few years I'm sure to make *major*. I hope to be assigned to Japan. How's that sound to you?"

It sounded awful. I was horrified. So we went to live with my parents in New York.

With the war over, he was ready to resume the promising career which had been interrupted almost before it had begun. Unfortunately, there was no job awaiting.

Eager to be helpful, I scanned all the show business papers as well as the entertainment pages of the newspapers looking for leads to jobs. The search paid off in the form of an item in the *Times*. It quoted William Paley, owner of CBS, promising jobs to those had had a contract before the war. The article also noted that he was looking for program ideas.

I phoned CBS immediately. Claiming to be Gordon's agent, I proposed to Mr. Paley a show like *Penthouse Serenade* but with the girl on the phone talking to Gordon, as the show's star, and setting up his songs. He asked us to come to the studios for an audition.

Loving what he heard, Bill added *Penthouse Serenade* to the schedule and hired me to be the girl who introduced the new CBS singing star. What he did not know was that Sheila Stephens was Gordon's wife and pregnant again. Only when he casually remarked to me that I seemed to be "putting on a lot of weight" did Gordon and I tell him that the "girl" was Mrs. MacRae.

Another man might have fired us for deceiving him. Bill laughed it off, and the show became a hit.

Ironically, soon after shedding his Air Force uniform, Gordon found himself in another, playing a military policeman in Ray Bolger's 1946 revue, *Three to Get Ready*. The part called for a seventeen-year-old but Gordon was so young-looking, the fact that he was in his twenties was overlooked.

On opening night, Gordon became a star, though not because of his good looks and great voice. He burst into the front page headlines of newspapers from coast to coast because of something he did on stage that was not in the script.

A scene in the musical called for Gordon and Ray Bolger to fight. Because the faking of the fisticuffs required precise timing, they had rehearsed it again and again. "You take the swing at me on the count of three," Ray explained. "It goes one, two, pause, and on three you throw it."

But on the tense and anxious opening night, when the crucial moment for Gordon to lash out arrived, he simply forgot to pause between the two and three count. He decked Ray, sending him to the stage as limply as if he were once again the Straw Man in *Wizard of Oz*. It would be six minutes before Ray came to.

With their attention drawn to Gordon in such a spectacular way, the press quickly discovered his talent as a singer. Critics raved. Newspapers and magazines, including *Life*, trumpeted this "new found talent."

Gordon was in demand to perform in theaters all over the country. This was a time when the price of admission to a movie also meant a stage show. During an appearance in Chicago, he was noticed by William Orr, a Warner Bros. talent scout and son-in-law of Jack L. Warner. Bill invited Gordon to make a screen test.

Even before the results were made known, Gordon boasted, "Sheersie, it looks like you and I are going to be raising our babies in Hollywood!"

The offer of a contract came a few days later. Not long after that, in 1948, we found ourselves in Hollywood searching for a place to live. We wanted a home that would better accommodate our growing family than a small house the studio had arranged for us on a temporary basis. Gordon decided on a large home on Magnolia Boulevard. By every measure it was a real bargain, ideal for children. There were four bedrooms, an outside playhouse, an orange grove, walnut trees—forty acres in all. The owner, a family man who had to leave California because of his business, was even willing to include in the sale two small horses and a pony.

But the moment I stepped inside the house I felt ill. Although I was pregnant at the time, this feeling of illness was quite different from any discomfort I had experienced before. It grew worse as I wandered through the sprawling house listening to the real estate woman extolling its obvious virtues. It was a cold, terrifying sense of anxiety that soon took the form of an inexplicable presence.

Entering the kitchen, I observed a woman in a breakfast nook. Seated at the table, bending over a glass in her hand and smoking a cigarette, she was in a swirling gray mist. "Oh, I didn't know anyone was here," I said apologetically. But when the real estate woman turned to look, the figure in the nook was gone. "No, no, this won't do. I can't live in this house," I cried, hurrying outside.

Naturally, the real estate agent was annoyed. In the car, she kept saying, "I'm sure if Mr. MacRae looks at the house, he'll see what a bargain it is."

A few hours later, when she telephoned, I expected her to try again to make a sale. I gave Gordon the phone. He listened for a moment, then gasped, "You've got to be kidding!" Putting down the phone, he turned to me with a ghastly expression. "That house you said you couldn't live in?" he asked. "It burned down two hours ago! They're all dead. The man, his wife, the animals—all gone."

Gordon delighted in telling the story, relating it when he was interviewed for fan magazines like *Photoplay* and *Movie Life*. As a result, I received an invitation to meet with a group of scientists at Duke University who were studying parapsychology and episodes of extrasensory perception. Not wanting to be associated with matters that at that time were seen as weird and generally associated with fortune-tellers, gypsies, and tea-leaf readers, I declined. I didn't mind being known in Hollywood as Gordon MacRae's wife, but the last thing I wanted to be known as was Gordon MacRae's *strange* wife!

When we first bounded onto the Warner Bros. lot in 1949, Hollywood and its cottage industry were at their peak, and we were wide-eyed and awestruck innocents, marveling and thrilled. So very, very young we were. Still opposites in every way, we were very much in love.

While Gordon made movies, I went to the studio every day to have lunch with him. I would enter the cold, dank atmosphere inside a soundstage, where there were only men: high up in the spider-webbing catwalks, wrestling with the lights, ghostly silhouettes working on sets and adjusting the microphones, grips, best boys, sound technicians, lighting men, makeup men, writers, producer, director, actors. Men, men, all men. Except for the star! The leading lady. The actress!

"I like you, kid," whispered Jack Warner, the genius who ran Warner Bros., as he slyly switched place cards so that I and not Vivien Leigh would sit next to him at his prized antique dining table. "What I love about you," he went on, giving me a gentle hug, "is that you don't want to be an actress. An actress will kill her grandmother to get a part. Even if she has to eat through wolf! Take my advice! Don't ever become an actress."

At that moment I had no dreams of acting. I was blissfully content to be Mrs. Gordon MacRae. But—if there's to be a good story there must always be a "but"—what the reigning monarch of Warner Bros. did not know was that I had taken the halting steps in that direction I have described. Of course, I uttered not a peep about it to Jack.

Although Gordon had been contracted for the movies by Warners because of his talents as a singer, his first picture was not a musical. *The*

Big Punch put him in the role of a boxer who is falsely accused of murder and finds refuge with a former fighter who has spurned the ring for the pulpit (played by the film's star, Wayne Morris). In 1950, Gordon made *Backfire*, a tale of mystery that had him searching for a missing friend through a maze of murder and romance. This film marked my movie debut. I played a corpse! That same year he was in a Western, *Return of the Frontiersman*. Gordon's roles in all of these pictures were meant to season him as a screen actor before he started making the musicals for which he had been hired.

The MacRaes arrived in Hollywood before television was to rise up in the 1950s and wrest movies from the hearts of most Americans. We got there in the midst of the golden era of Hollywood's great musical stars—Fred Astaire, Ginger Rogers, Gene Kelly, Bing Crosby, Frank Sinatra, Ann Miller, Debbie Reynolds, Kathyrn Grayson, Donald O'Connor—too many to list; and, of course, there was James Cagney. When Gordon was cast with Jimmy in 1950 in *The West Point Story*, he was thrilled. The story seemed silly—Broadway director goes up the Hudson to the U.S. Military Academy to stage a musical revue—but so what? The star was Cagney, "Yankee Doodle Dandy" himself.

Immediately, Jimmy became a close friend. He was generous with advice on all the things about performing that he had learned since his first appearance on a stage as a teenager looking to pick up extra money to support his family. It was a revue in a small theater in the Yorkville section of New York. Jimmy performed as a female impersonator.

Jimmy liked Gordon very much and believed he had a bright future in the movies, but one evening, he drew me aside at a party we were attending. "There's something about Gordie that puzzles me," he whispered, looking worried. "It's a thing he does with his hands." He raised his as if studying them and then began picking his fingers with his thumbnails. "He does it all the time," he went on. "Now, I'm not an expert in these things, but it looks to me as if it's a nervous habit. It's as if behind that calm exterior, something's eating at him. It's not good for a man to bottle things up, Sheila."

Later that evening, I watched Gordon closely and saw that Jimmy was right. He was doing exactly what Jimmy had shown me. I was shocked at how raw his hands were, but when I mentioned it, he just shrugged and said it was nothing. "Don't be such a worry-wart," he said with a laugh.

I never mentioned the habit again. Only years later was I able to recall that conversation with Jimmy and realize that he had spotted the first outward expression of something deeply troubling in my husband.

Jimmy's advice was also available on love and sex in the film capital. "Never get involved in an affair with anybody who has less to lose than you do," he advised.

Flustered, I blurted, "Jimmy, I would never have an affair, and neither would Gordon."

"I know you wouldn't, my darling," he said, chuckling and patting my hand.

Realizing he had been teasing, I turned bright red with embarrassment.

The full-fledged musical debut of Gordon MacRae had occurred the year before he had the privilege of working with Jimmy. *Look for the Silver Lining* was very loosely based on the biography of the chanteuse Marilyn Miller, played by June Haver. Ray Bolger, Charles Ruggles, and Rosemary DeCamp were also in it.

Because Jack L. Warner was convinced that music had to be an essential part of the motion picture business, the studio pioneered musical films. Jack and his brothers introduced the first synchronized film score in 1926 in *Don Juan*, which starred John Barrymore. Then Warners made the first talking-singing picture, *The Jazz Singer*, in 1927, starring Al Jolson. Next came the first sound operetta, *The Desert Song*, in 1929, and the grandaddy of movie musicals, *42nd Street*, in 1933.

Jack hadn't become the champion of music in movies because he personally liked music but because he knew that the moviegoing public liked it. Musicals were good box office, and Jack Warner was a businessman—the prototype of the Hollywood mogul. "Don't be an actor," one of his brothers had advised him during his own youthful acting days. "Pay actors! The money is where the customers are. Don't act in movies. *Produce* movies!"

Loud, wisecracking, a flashy dresser, with a pencil-thin mustache and slicked-back hair, Jack liked to be called "the Colonel" in recognition of his rank during the Second World War when he used the studio's facilities to aid the war effort. Because he was notoriously rough on actors, his tenure as head of production at Warners was marked by historic battles of will with top stars, among them Bette Davis, Errol Flynn, Humphrey Bogart, Paul Muni, and Jimmy Cagney.

When I naïvely mentioned that I had heard he was an ogre, Jack laughed. "Not me! Actors are just ingrates! Ninety percent of them are thrilled when I take them from poverty, as I have done for so many of them, and give them a big fat contract. Then it all goes to their heads! By the fourth year they can't understand why I won't let them direct, write the story, and do the costumes."

The remark that was most revealing about Jack Warner's attitude toward actors was uttered in 1955 when he learned that James Dean had been killed. "How could he do this to me after all my work to build him up into a star?"

Once, in a moment of wounded self-defense, when Lauren Bacall was complaining about his treatment of her, he led her to the window of his office and pointed to the sprawling Warner Bros. studios. "Would all that be there," he asked, "if I didn't know what the fuck I was doing?'

Of course, Jack did not do it alone. The studio belonged to the Warner *brothers*. The eldest was Harry, the president of the company. A short, wiry, gray-haired man who many in Hollywood thought resembled George Arliss, one of the studio's early stars, Harry was the overall head of the company and the court of last resort when problems arose. But, he once complained to *Fortune* magazine, "they never bring anything to me until it's already wrong." He was once described as a producer who asks a question, gives the answer, and then tells the other person he's wrong. During the war, Harry had been given the rank of major and took pride in being addressed as Major Warner.

When Gordon first met the major, he thought that Major was his first name, "Say, Major," he said, "You have the same name as my boss, Jack Warner."

"Young man," the major thundered, "I'm his brother, and *I* am *his* boss!"

A similar misunderstanding involved Harry Warner and me, except that this time it was the major who got an identity mixed up. The occasion was a visit to Warner Bros. by General Dwight D. Eisenhower, fresh from victory in Europe. Like hundreds of others on the lot, I stood on my toes and craned my neck to get at least a glimpse of everybody's hero.

Suddenly, Harry grabbed my arm. "What are you doing here?" he demanded.

"Ike, I'd like you to meet Warner Brothers' greatest star," Harry said, beaming. "Allow me to introduce Miss Doris Day."

I found myself staring into the disbelieving eyes of the general. But neither of us corrected the major.

Albert Warner was stunned. Referred to as Honest Abe, he was treasurer and head of sales, and he liked to say that Warner Bros. was "the Ford of films."

As I walked away, he shook his head.

In the gorgeous Technicolor fifties musicals that the Warners made, there was no bigger star than my husband. In his masculine world of movies, I was thrilled to be the wife of the person *Time* magazine called "God's Chosen Boy."

Devoted to one another, we were a disappointment to gossip-crazy Hollywood, which both doted on and feared the newspaper columns of Louella Parsons and Hedda Hopper. These two could make or break a star, often through innuendo, but there was never a shadow of a doubt about Mr. and Mrs. Gordon MacRae. Because we drank milk shakes rather than liquor, we soon became known as "the Malted Milk Kids." On many evenings when we played charades, I had the tag "Mother Goose" pinned to my back. Or "Mother MacRae."

At one of those parties, Rocky Cooper, Gary's wife, informed me she had been approached by one of the Hakim brothers, foreign movie producers, in a brazen attempt to arrange a tryst with me. I was shocked. "You may tell him that I have several good reasons not to accept," I replied. "My children, Gordon, my wonderful life."

As a handsome newcomer, Gordon became a prime target of those who looked on sex as a sport. He would come home from the studio and tell me of blatant attempts to draw him into sexual relationships. With each new story, I was disturbed. He was amused.

"I don't see why it bothers you," he said. "It's the way things are out here. The whole place runs on sex. But don't worry. I've got more than I can handle."

That the leading man should have an affair with his leading lady was to be expected. That a leading man would decline the opportunity and the invitation was a rarity. But that was Gordo in those days.

Dancing with Barbara Stanwyck, one of the great and elegant beauties of all time and recently divorced from Robert Taylor, he was aswim in her intoxicating aroma and asked her the name of it. Missy, as she was known to her friends, cocked her head in that foxy, quizzical tilt so familiar to her millions of fans. "Why do you ask?" she inquired, teasingly.

"It's sexy," he replied with boyish eagerness.

In her sultriest manner, Missy whispered, "That's the idea."

"Yeah," Gordon sighed. "I'd like to get some for my wife, Sheila."

The next day, from the renowned Beverly Hills jeweler Ruser, a chauffeur delivered a gold decanter with my name engraved upon it. The decanter contained a generous supply of the expensive perfume. With it, Missy had sent a note:

> He's blind to everyone but you.
> Keep your love alive.
> You're a lucky lady!

Warner Bros. was a movie factory, cranking out hundreds of films, good, bad, and awful—and some of the lushest, grandest, and most enjoyable musicals ever made. The Warner lot was magificent. The gracefully arched roofs of its giant hangarlike sound stages sprawled along Burbank's Olive Avenue. They glistened under the flawless California sky that had been deemed perfect for moviemaking when pioneers like the Warners, Cecil B. DeMille, and Louis B. Mayer invented the motion picture business in open-topped tents.

Gordon was the new face at Warners, a handsome, dark-haired, brown-eyed, golden-voiced baritone, the heartthrob star of lavish musicals that warmed the hearts of moviegoers and filled the studio coffers in those heady, optimistic, lilting days just after the war.

Like Gordon, Doris had come to the movies with the momentum of a singing career in radio and with several bands. Born Doris von Kappelhoff in 1924 in Cincinnati, she was the second child, inheriting her theatrical bent from her mother, who named her after the actress Doris Kenyon. It was bandleader Barney Rapp who changed her name to Doris Day after hearing her sing "Day by Day" on a local radio station. She told Rapp, "I'm glad I wasn't singing *Götterdämmerung*." Soon she was singing with the big bands of Bob Crosby, Fred Waring, and Les Brown.

In 1947, Al Levy, a talent agent for Century Artists Agency, fell in love with Doris and arranged an interview for her with director Michael Curtiz, who was looking for a "name" singer for *Romance on the High Seas*. While making the movie, Doris promptly demonstrated a penchant for crying that was to be a hallmark of her Hollywood career.

Gordon found it infuriating. "That gal thinks acting is crying. I never saw anyone who could cry like her. If she loses at volleyball, if the lighting isn't right, if she can't sing the damned duets in her key all the time—she cries!"

His opinions could be terribly blunt and at times wounding, to the point where Oscar Hammerstein II would say to me, "Sheila, your husband has a lot to learn about how to treat his friends."

Yet I do not believe Gordon meant to be mean. Raised as a Christian Scientist, he was taught to be himself. To him, being himself meant being honest. To others, that sometimes made him seem completely insensitive.

Actors play characters on the screen and off, but Gordon was Gordon. Some of his remarks have become classics of Hollywood lore. At a dinner party at Samuel Goldwyn's home he told Goldwyn that his wife's dress looked awful, adding, "She doesn't have the right ass for it." On the set of *The Desert Song*, he griped to bosomy costar Kathryn Grayson, "Your boobs are getting in the way." He once told Doris Day, "Your teeth are too buck and your chest too flat."

To me Dodo brought to the screen, in addition to her teary eyes and a great voice, a "golden girl" image that Jack L. Warner desired in the musicals he chose for her. The "Golden Girl" and the "Chosen Boy" were together in *Tea for Two, The West Point Story, On Moonlight Bay*, and its sequel, *By the Light of the Silvery Moon*. America's moviegoers adored these boy-next-door, girl-next-door pictures.

At the start of the 1950s, Americans were still a moviegoing people, and when they went to the movies it was a family night out. The stories that filled the screens were wholesome fare. No pairing of stars was more wholesome than the handsome and dashing Gordon MacRae and blond, blue-eyed, honey-voiced Doris Day. They were a sweet screen couple ideally suited to the mood of a country that had won a great war.

Gordon found her maddeningly difficult, often returning home furious with her. He came home outraged one day because she had refused to pose with him and several handicapped children for an Easter Seals poster. She had to decline, she explained, because she was a Christian Scientist and Christian Scientists didn't believe in cripples.

As a Christian Scientist himself, Gordon was insulted and furious. "Hell and damn it," he said to me that evening. "She's giving my religion a bad name."

To me, Dodo was always one beat off. She never seemed to have an appreciation of her success. She appeared to be scared, loving nothing about it.

Gordie said one night, "She thinks you're so lucky to have three kids and a home—her mom is raising her son, you know. But I told her you were lucky 'cause I was a hot lover!"

The truth is, Gordon and I never had been able to get enough of making love. We had had sex everywhere, under a blanket in Long Island Rail Road coaches when we were young aspiring actors, in a map-decorated makeshift garage apartment during the war, on airplanes, on boats, and in stolen moments in recording studios and in his dressing room at Warners, where making love to him during his lunch hour was like being in an all-male dormitory.

He referred to me as "my wife the nymphomaniac." He wasn't far from the truth. Looking back, I can now see that I was so obsessed with having sex with him that it can only be described as an addiction as overwhelming and enslaving as that which eventually became apparent in Gordon. Suddenly and shockingly, that dark cloud appeared in the lucky lady's blue sky.

I received a phone call from the studio. On the line was Jack Warner. "Sheila, come to the studio right away."

He sounded quite frantic. I thought there'd been an accident and Gordon was hurt. Barely able to speak, I muttered, "Is it Gordie?"

"Yes," Jack said gruffly. "He's drunk."

"My Gordie?" I gasped. "No!"

Sex and Scandal on the Hollywood Merry-go-round

GORDON DRUNK? Impossible! I had never seen him take a drink. We were the Malted Milk Kids! Over and over again as I rushed to the studio, I told myself that it couldn't be, but why would Jack Warner say so if it weren't true?

Praying that there'd been some silly mistake but dreading the truth, I knocked on the door of the dressing room where Gordon and I had made love so often, oblivious to the voices passing the window and blissfully unconcerned about where we were—the very heart of Jack Warner's domain. Opening the door, Jack greeted me with a look of utter anguish. "Sheila, I never expected this from Gordon," he said in a tone of deep disappointment. "When he came back from lunch, he was so polluted he could hardly walk straight. This has made me a very unhappy man, Sheila. If he ever does this again in the middle of a day's shooting, I'll personally kick his ass and then I'll suspend him."

"Jack, I am so sorry," I said, brushing away tears.

"Why are you apologizing? He's the one who got drunk."

Because my father had been a heavy drinker and because I'd seen plenty of drunks while traveling with Gordon when he was on the road with the Horace Heidt band, I knew what a drunk looked like. I saw all the signs in Gordon—the blotched skin, the odor of his breath, the bloodshot eyes, disheveled clothing. He was making *The Desert Song* and was still costumed as the Red Shadow, a sheik. In an open shirt and boots he looked as handsome as ever as he took me into his arms. "Don't worry, Sheersie," he said, almost in tears. "Everything's going to be fine. It will never happen again."

It would be many, many years before I would understand what Jack Warner meant, that it wasn't my fault. In the decades to come, I would go on apologizing for Gordon, making excuses, covering for him, putting up with his drinking and accepting his apologies to me. But on that terrible, heart-wrenching day, I could not know that when he said, "It will never happen again," it was a promise he wouldn't keep.

Because I had no alternative, I accepted his pledge, but in the innermost recesses of my heart I was gripped by a chilling and unshakable fear rooted in the knowledge that he and I were in an industry and living in a professional and social atmosphere fueled by alcohol and driven by duplicity.

While I recognized the ugly side of Hollywood, Gordon did not. The idea that someone could pat another on the back one minute and plunge a knife into it the next was incomprehensible to him. If I saw the dangerous twists and turns in the road we were on, Gordon looked out at a broad highway that would always be sunny and straight. Now, here I was, faced with an aspect of him I had never seen before.

I looked to see if there were other actors and actresses with similar problems. I had as little trouble finding them as Ray Milland had had. In preparing for his Oscar-winning role as an alcoholic in *The Lost Weekend* he had studied drunks. "I didn't have to go far," Ray said. "Half my friends were boozers." I found heavy drinkers everywhere as well, but I discovered that nobody cared, unless, of course, a star's excessive drinking threatened to cause a scandal by becoming public. At that point the studio would step in—not to help the star deal with the cause of the problem but to cover it up.

Studios were terrified of scandal and the effect one could have on the box office. Still vivid in the minds of the moguls was the Fatty Arbuckle case. One of the comedy stars of the silent era, 320-pound Roscoe "Fatty" Arbuckle was accused of raping starlet Virginia Rapp. When she died, he was charged with manslaughter. Despite two trials that ended in hung juries and a third that acquitted him, the panicked film industry, shuddering before the public's outrage, stopped showing Arbuckle's pictures and forced him out of the business.

The studios promptly created a system of self-censorship—the Motion Picture Producers and Distributors of America, headed by Will Hays, a former lawyer, chairman of the Republican National Committee, and postmaster general. The "Hays Office" wrote a Motion Picture Production Code that molded the content of films and the image of Hollywood for four decades, until a more liberal code was adopted in the 1960s to reflect the changed mores of the American public in the "anything goes" era.

As fearful as the studios were of offending the moviegoing public with what was shown on the nation's screens, they were just as feverishly worried about how the public perceived movie stars' private behavior. Guarding those images was the job of studio publicity departments. "It's amazing how small-town Hollywood is," said Donna Reed, whose image was that of the wholesome all-American sweetheart—Jimmy Stewart's wife in *It's a Wonderful Life*—until she managed to break the mold as a whore in *From Here to Eternity* in 1953.

"In Hollywood everyone knows everyone's business," she said. "Let a man be seen with the same girl twice, and tongues start wagging about them being lovers."

While the public was kept from knowing what was going on behind the scenes, the gossip at parties was filled with sexual antics and escapades. Soon after we arrived, Gordon told me a scandalous tale about Vera Hruba Ralston. She had come to Hollywood from Czechoslovakia after being runner-up to Sonja Henie in the ice skating events of the 1936 Olympics and had starred as Vera Hruba in *Ice-Capades* in 1941 and *Ice-Capades Revue* in 1942. Then she added "Ralston" to her name for a string of Republic Pictures. Gordon told me that what the public didn't know—though everyone in Hollywood did—was that thirty-year-old Vera skated nude daily for the much older Herbert Yates, head of Republic—then her boss and later her husband.

Other escapades weren't so discreet. At a New Year's Eve party at which I was the hostess (Gordon was away), I discovered Eartha Kitt and Arthur Loew, Jr., heir to the Loew fortune, making love behind one of the couches. I was so embarrassed that I phoned Miriam and Jack Meyers and demanded that they come get me. Rescued, I spent that New Year's Eve with them at an ice cream parlor. As they gobbled up huge bowls of every flavor of ice cream available, I cried.

Hardly a week went by without my hearing of some new scandalous activity, all of them hushed up by the studios in their obsession with protecting their stars' images. I heard all about Gary Cooper's affair with Anita Ekberg. I listened with amazement as our secretary told me Dean Martin was surprised at the golf course by the statuesque beauty Ursula Andress popping out of the bushes, naked. I heard about Doris Day and the baseball player Maury Wills and then of Doris singing in the choir at Maury's Los Angeles church. The grapevine brought me the story of girls performing sex acts together during a Christmas party at the home of choreographer LeRoy Prinz while carols played on the phonograph. I heard it all—as did everyone else in town—but not the public.

No actress's screen image of purity exceeded that of Ingrid Bergman. A nun in *The Bells of St. Mary's*, the victimized wife of *Gaslight*, a saint in *Joan of Arc*, and Paul Henreid's nobly self-sacrificing wife in *Casablanca*, she was built up by the Hollywood publicity mill as being in real life exactly as she appeared on the screen. Unfortunately, that image exploded in 1949 when she deserted her husband and daughter in favor of Italian movie director Roberto Rossellini. How America's moviegoers felt about the shattering of their illusions was reflected on the floor of the United States Senate when she was denounced as "Hollywood's apostle of degradation." The studios' answer was to ban her from their films for seven years.

Sexual scandal also touched the career of our pal Errol Flynn, although the effect was the opposite of what happened to Ingrid. Having been boosted in his publicity as a great lover, in keeping with his screen image, Errol was not expected to be anything in real life other than what the public saw on screen. How could the dashing hero of *Captain Blood, The Charge of the Light Brigade,* and *They Died with Their Boots On* be anything but a rake? Of course, he was also a man.

Therefore, he was unaffected professionally when he was charged in 1942 with the statutory rape of a pair of teenage girls on his yacht.

Acquitted, he did not find himself banned from the movies. Instead,

Warners discovered that box office receipts went up. Offscreen escapades only reinforced the public's conception of Errol as a devil-may-care character who had a yen for young girls. The most famous of these was the teen bombshell Beverly Aadland. Her mother wrote a biography of Beverly that began with one of the most arresting lines in the history of telltale books: "My daughter was a virgin before she met Errol Flynn."

Ultimately, Errol's potentially ruinous incident with the teenage girls gave the American language a new phrase—one that is still in use—"In like Flynn."

Errol was our friend, so Gordon and I were quite familiar with his offscreen life. He adored the Andrews Sisters and loved playing bocci with their father and eating their mother's food.

Because they called him the Count, so did Gordon and I.

We frequently played poker at his home. A most unusual house by ordinary standards, it was exactly what one might expect of a man with his sexy reputation. I recall the mixture of pride and devilish delight in his eyes when he showed me a little room with a big bed that he made available for friends to use for sexual liaisons. Little did they know that the large mirror above it was two-way and that people could watch through it. One night he tried to shock me, stocking a large fish tank with the testicles and penises of bulls.

Despite the man-about-town image, Errol was earthy in the true sense of the word. He was quite proud of his farm in his native New Zealand.

I introduced him to his last wife, Patrice Wymore. Joy Orr and I saw her as a dancer at the Strand Theater in New York and recommended to Jack Warner that he take a look at her. He did, and immediately gave her a contract.

Spotting her in the Warners commissary, Errol asked me for an introduction. As perceptive as she was pretty, Patrice gave Errol a birthday present that could not fail to impress him—a tractor for his farm.

Although scandal could not destroy Errol, drink and drugs did. His increasing abuse of substances eventually showed in his face. When he died in 1959 at the age of fifty, the doctor who performed an autopsy remarked that he believed he was examining the body of a much older man.

After his death there were stories that he'd been a Nazi spy and a homosexual. I don't believe any of it. Of course, had these stories surfaced when he was alive, his career might very well have been destroyed, no matter whether they were true or false.

It was the public's perception that the movie studios feared. The wrong kind of story could be disastrous.

It now seems ridiculous that Robert Mitchum's career should have been jeopardized because he was caught with a bit of marijuana, yet that is what happened to Bob in the 1940s.

It would be years before Hollywood drug abuse and alcoholism would be acknowledged by the industry or its stars and accepted by the public.

About his alcoholism, Spencer Tracy said, "Anyone who stayed drunk for twenty-five years as I did would have to be in trouble. Hell, I used to take two-week lunch hours!"

A constant drinker of vodka, Lana Turner had been warned by her doctor about her drinking. "If you want to live," he told one of the most glamorous beauties in the history of motion pictures, "give up the booze."

For my friend, handsome leading-man Robert Walker, whom I remembered so fondly from the playhouse in Roslyn, New York, liquor was an escape from the torment of breaking up with Jennifer Jones. "I got to thinking about 'poor me,'" he told me. Turning to drink was his answer. Clark Gable once told director Edward Dmytryk that if he couldn't drink he'd just as soon die. "The only friends I have in this town," said the legendary stage and screen actor John Barrymore, "are Haig & Haig."

It was accepted that heavy drinking was harmless, not only in Hollywood but everywhere. Boozing and boozers were the butt of jokes. Laughter at the quips of W. C. Fields on the subject were shared by millions, as were gags about bandleader Phil Harris's propensity for being drunk and, a few years later, Dean Martin's. Humphrey Bogart made light of the subject as Rick, the saloon owner, in *Casablanca*. When the Nazi major asked his nationality, Rick replied, "I'm a drunkard." That was on the screen. In real life Bogie said, "The trouble with the world is that everybody in it is three drinks behind me."

Did these fabulously successful people drink because it was the fashion? Or did they need to? Were these difficulties with alcohol inherent in the nature of their work? Despite the obvious benefits of acting in the movies—the fame, the money, the opulent way of life—did the method of making movies in some way leave them unsatisfied?

Movies did not provide the instant satisfaction and gratification that a stage actor enjoyed. It was quite common that after spending months working hard on a movie, more months and as long as a year could go by before the finished picture was screened. When a film was completed and the director declared, "That's a wrap," there would be a party on the set (with liquor flowing abundantly), but there was nothing to come close to the glorious instant sense of achievement that the stage or even a nightclub provided.

"Why, if nothing else, there's applause," sighed Anne Baxter as the crafty would-be actress Eve Harrington in Joseph L. Mankiewicz's brilliant screenplay, *All About Eve.* "I've listened backstage to people applaud. It's like waves of love coming over the footlights and wrapping you up. Imagine, to know every night that different hundreds of people love you. They smile. Their eyes shine. You please them. They want you. Just that alone is everything."

I wondered if the lack of immediate acclaim caused Gordon's despair, for which his only answer was to drink. I'd noticed that when he worked on a movie for six or eight weeks, he would suddenly lose interest in the picture and long to get away to the golf course. If I told him that the screenings of a day's shooting, known as rushes, were great, he would reply, "The rushes aren't the movie." There were moments when I felt that he resented being in the movies and that the work they required was an intolerable intrusion upon the manly activities he loved so much—golfing, fishing, camping.

In observing the atmosphere for self-destruction through drinking that enveloped so many performers, I noted that the phenomenon did not reach into the top echelons. I knew of no studio head who ever had a problem with alcohol, yet they had the same and often worse pressures. Nor did I find composers with booze problems. Perhaps actors were susceptible because we were, at our core, narcissistic and required approval, acclaim, and love, or at least the appearance of it.

The problem with feeding on those things in Hollywood was that no one really could be sure that all the adulation, the fussing over hair and makeup, the concern that one got the proper lighting, the plushest dressing room, and the reserved parking space—that is, star treat-ment—were genuine. Many jokes were cracked about the shallowness and insincerity of Hollywood.

"If you look beneath the fake tinsel," jibed Oscar Levant, "you'll find the real tinsel."

The claim to the most cynical put-down of Hollywood has been attributed to one of its major moguls. "The most important thing is sincerity," said Sam Goldwyn. "Once you've learned to fake that, you're in."

There certainly was a lot of phoniness to be put up with in being a movie star. For many in "Tinseltown," fame was a trap. "Celebrity scars you," Charlton Heston said. The downside of celebrity, he added, is the damage to your character. "After a taste of stardom," said the alluring Hedy Lamarr, "everything else is poverty."

Gordon looked at fame differently, perhaps naïvely. He had little tolerance for those who tried to push the trappings of stardom on him. He hated all the fuss. If he was taken to task because his hair was deemed too short and made his ears stick out, he would grumble, "Who the hell cares?"

The studio cared. Jack Warner cared. While Gordon had been contracted by Warners for his voice, Jack also recognized that he had a quality that was highly valued in the movies—sex appeal. (His nickname for Gordon was "Muscles.") Consequently, Jack expected great care to be taken to make Gordon look as good as possible. Gazing aghast at Gordon after a weekend of golfing that left Gordon sunburned, Jack exploded. "God damn it, Muscles," he yelled, "stay out of the sun! And if you can't, wear a hat."

"I won't wear a hat," Gordon said. "It interferes with my putting."

"Listen, Muscles," Jack replied, calming down, "you're in the movies now. You've got responsibilities."

"What about my life?" Gordon said.

"You don't have a life," Jack snapped. "You have a Warner Brothers contract."

Except for his unabashed appreciation of the uniqueness of his voice, Gordon was not vain about being in the movies. The emphasis on image and physicality puzzled and exasperated him. That an actor could have a "good side" and a "bad side" as seen by the camera seemed not only unimportant but silly. "I don't care what side they shoot me from," he said to me. "All I want is for them to just shoot the scene and get it over with."

"As a matter of fact," I said, "you do have a good side—the left."

"Okay, my good side is my left side," he grumbled. "So what?"

"It's important for you to know."

"I don't see why."

"You will," I said, laughing, "when you find yourself in a scene opposite somebody who's good side is also the left!"

Throwing up his arms, he pleaded, "What about my *talent?*"

Paired with some of the screen's most image-conscious actresses, he couldn't escape the demands they made of the camera and him. This was especially true during the making of *The Desert Song* with Kathryn Grayson. Day after day, he came home with complaints. "I can't hold her this way." "She doesn't want me to put my hand on her waist because she thinks it makes her look too thick." "Don't hold her too tight because your arms obscure her boobs." "I don't know how long I can put up with all this."

Things that Gordon would not put up with invariably found their way onto lists. He compiled many, even when he was a child. One containing names of directors he divided into columns listing those he liked and did not like working with.

A list of writers he disliked was quite lengthy. Unlike me, who admired writers, Gordon found little in common with people who made their living putting words on paper.

There was a compilation of names of people whose parties he did not want to attend. He preferred to socialize with "good old boys" like Gable. Despite a shaky start in getting to know Louella Parsons, he put the gossip columnist on a list of favored people along with Lolly's chief competitor, Hedda Hopper.

He could not stand Joan Crawford but he did like her various husbands. He liked Tyrone Power but found Linda Christian, his wife, to be a little on the tough side. He loved Bette Davis and her husband Gary Merrill. Ethel Merman was on a preferred list, as were two of her husbands, especially Bob Six, president of Continental Airlines, who later married Audrey Meadows.

Humphrey Bogart was high on the list of likable actors with Jimmy Cagney and Gary Cooper, each viewed by Gordon as a man's man.

I teased him about the list-making, asking him if he kept a record of all the women he had made love to, as did Mickey Rooney and, I had heard, Frank Sinatra.

"Sure, I have a list," Gordon answered. "But it's got only one name. Yours."

From time to time, Jack Warner's name switched from the favored list to the unfavored, depending on how Gordon viewed his treatment by Jack. Their relationship could become quite testy.

There was a skating scene in *By the Light of the Silvery Moon* with Doris Day. Having been raised in the ferocious winters of Syracuse, Gordon was an expert on the ice and a terrific hockey player. He looked forward to director David Butler (on the approved list) calling "Action!" so he could show off his skating abilities.

But when the scene was barely underway, Jack Warner bounded forward yelling, "Cut, cut, cut! Jesus, Muscles, you're doing it wrong!"

Gordon fumed. "Wrong? I've been skating all my life, so I damned well know how to do it."

"No, no, no," Jack insisted. "It's all wrong. You're squatting down."

"When you skate," Gordon growled, "you *squat*!"

"For this shot to work, you've to stand straight! When you squat like that, you look ridiculous! And so does Doris."

Gordon wasn't the first, nor the last, to learn that image was all and that resisting the one the studio created for you was futile. "It is not true I was born a monster," Boris Karloff lamented. "Hollywood made me one."

Irene Dunne's image was that of a lady. "There are worse things you can be called," she said resignedly, "so I gave up the fight." Ann Sheridan was called "the Oomph Girl." Lana Turner was "the Sweater Girl." Lauren Bacall was "the Look."

Thanks to a studio publicity shot of her in a bathing suit that soldiers hung in their lockers and pup tents during the Second World War, Betty Grable became "the Pinup Girl" and deplored it. "Guys who go to see my pictures are truck drivers and soldiers," she said, "so they put me in whorey-looking parts."

How a star looked off the set was also important. There, too, Gordon rebelled, not out of perversity but simply because the rules seemed foolish. Dressing to the nines was not for him, but there were times when it was required, often on orders from Jack Warner. One of those occasions was a formal dinner that Joan Crawford gave for Jack. Because

I liked parties, and none better than a fancy one with dancing, I splurged on a pink tulle Dior gown. Resplendent in it, I waited for Gordon to come home from the studio with a new tuxedo. For weeks I had nagged him to buy one. To my horror, he had not done so. Instead, he borrowed a tux from the Warners wardrobe department. A white dinner jacket, it had fancy piping on the lapels and looked like something from another era. "Isn't this great, Sheersie?" he beamed. "It used to be Al Jolson's."

It was awful, but it was too late to do anything about it.

The invitation was for seven o'clock, which to Gordon meant seven o'clock. It also meant that there would be lots of cocktails before we sat down to eat. Because he had never in his life not been on time and didn't understand the practice of being "fashionably late," we rang Joan's doorbell at seven on the dot—and were greeted by the most glamorous star in Hollywood sans makeup and wrapped in a terry bathrobe.

I'm sure that had it been anyone but Gordon MacRae catching her off guard, Joan Crawford would have stricken that person's name from her guest list forever. But Gordon was so natural and unassuming that no one could be angry with him for long. Joan was practicing Christian Science. In a champagne town she found him to be a sip of clear, refreshing spring water. Behavior that might have been considered rude in others was accepted as charming honesty from him, which is exactly what it was.

Of course, this trait was basic to many of his film roles. Onscreen he was the winningly innocent boy next door. That he truly was the same offscreen often came as a surprise to those who had long since learned to carry their invented onscreen roles into everyday life.

Jack Warner arrived at eight. He saw Gordon's vintage tuxedo, and his jaw dropped. That it was Jolson's suit and from his own costume department notwithstanding, Jack was appalled. "Christ, Muscles, this is embarrassing," he groaned. "People will think I don't pay you enough."

Blissfully missing the point, Gordon replied, "Well, it doesn't make sense to shell out five hundred bucks just to have a suit to wear to dinner at Joan Crawford's."

"There'll be lots of other occasions when you'll need a tux," Jack answered. "And I sure as hell don't want to see you in that getup again. I'll make an appointment for you with my tailor and by Jesus you'll be there." He paused, then cracked a forgiving smile. "Since you're obviously a skinflint Scot, I'll pay for it!"

Because entertainers are compelled to entertain, even if it's just for their friends, there seemed to be a party every night. Initially, when Gordon and I were the Malted Milk Kids, I'd loved being invited out. Since the wrenching experience of being summoned to the studio and seeing Gordon drunk for the first time in my life, every invitation to a party where I knew liquor would be served now provoked dark forebodings.

Jack Warner and his wife, Ann, were legendary party givers, and because they liked Gordon and me, we were frequent guests. The focus of one of these opulent gatherings was the unveiling of a portrait of Ann by Salvador Dali. Jack hated it.

"Dali made her look like she was an embalmed wop," he complained to me as he took my arm to escort me in to dinner. "And the house that's behind her looks like a dump."

He felt especially put out about that, because the house the Warners lived in was a palace. "He's made it look as if it's falling into a ravine after a mudslide," Jack groused. "He's made it look like Jeeter Lester's shack in *Tobacco Road*."

Honestly, Dali's portrait was a masterpiece. I believe he caught Ann Warner's tenuous position as a "second wife" in Hollywood. A Latina, uneducated and married into the rich Jewish upper echelon of Beverly Hills, Ann had been married at sixteen to Don Alvarado-Page, an actor in silent films. She was an extra in silents when Jack discovered her. Now she was not only the hostess of some of the most glittering parties in Hollywood but one of moviedom's most powerful women. That power lay in her ability to influence Jack in the intimacy of their bedroom—the power of pillow talk!

Being Jack Warner's dinner partner entailed listening to his bawdy jokes. Of this insistence on entertaining his guests, Jack Benny once jibed, "Jack would rather tell a bad joke than make a good movie." Despite the jokes, I found Jack's party demeanor to be a refreshing change from the contrived "civilized" attitudes of many of the movers and shakers of the film capital, and what an optimist!

At these soirees, Gordon gritted his teeth at the flattery, cozying up, sycophantic smiles, and glad-handing that was the grease that kept the machinery of movies running. It was a custom that rankled, especially when he felt he was being forced to engage in it. During our first Christmas in Hollywood, Jack Warner informed Gordon that he had to give a present to the gossip columnist Louella Parsons. Gordon was furious. (The Scot in him was coming out again!) "Why the hell should I give her a present?" he argued. "I don't even knew her!"

Because, Jack explained, Louella was syndicated by the Hearst newspapers and listened to by millions who tuned in to her Sunday night radio network broadcast. She had become Hollywood's most influential and powerful gossip columnist. "She could hurt your career," Jack pointed out solemnly.

"How can she hurt my career?" Gordon demanded. "I'm the world's greatest singer!"

"There's no getting out of it, Muscles," Jack replied. "You have to give Louella a gift."

Grudgingly, Gordon said he'd send one.

"You don't *send* it," groaned Jack. "You *take* it to her in person."

Incredulous, Gordon reluctantly complied. We arrived at Louella's home and were admitted to a living room literally piled to the ceiling with Christmas offerings. "How nice of you to come see me," Louella said in a distinctive, high-pitched, singsong voice. It sounded as if she spoke while holding her nose, but it held her radio listeners on the edge of their seats waiting for her to announce, "And now, my first exclusive" (pronounced *eck-SKLOO-sive*).

A small, middle-aged woman, "Lolly" did not look to me like the feared reigning queen of the Hollywood publicity mill. She looked like somebody's aunt. Yet she could, if she wished, break a career. Or, if she liked, she had it in her to give a newcomer a boost. In our case, I was "a very nice girl" and Gordon was "a very cute boy."

"It's very important for a movie star to have a wife who looks good, who can dance at parties and make conversation," she declared regally. (That a movie star's wife might also have a mind of her own was not mentioned.) Delighted to see for herself that all she'd heard about the Malted Milk Kids was true, she claimed to be charmed by my "tony" English accent and promptly decided that I had to appear for an interview on her radio show. I was scared to death but got through the broadcast with what Louella judged to be "flying colors."

Hedda Hopper had become Louella's serious rival in the gossip business. Having started her career as a Broadway chorus girl, Hedda married matinee idol William DeWolfe Hopper and moved to Hollywood as her husband shifted his career from the stage to movies in 1915.

Although they had a son (William, Jr., whose acting career culminated in the role of Detective Paul Drake in the *Perry Mason* television series), Hedda worked as an actress, initially in vampy roles and then as a featured player. Following her divorce in 1922, she continued acting until 1936, when she started a gossip show on radio that launched her on a twenty-eight-year career as a Hollywood reporter. Her hallmark was outlandish hats.

Of the rivalry between Louella and herself, Hedda told me, "Louella Parsons is a reporter trying to be a ham; Hedda Hopper is a ham trying to be a reporter."

Perhaps because she was an actress (she continued to take movie roles into the 1960s) and a Christian Scientist, I became quite friendly with Hedda. I found her to be fair, although she carried on bitter running feuds with Joan Bennett and Elsa Maxwell and, of course, Louella. Unlike Lolly, however, you were not expected to treat Hedda as if she were an empress. Louella might be invited to parties because she was feared. Hedda was invited because she was genuinely liked, although not by everyone. Finally fed up with the treatment, Joan had a live skunk shipped to Hedda's house. But Hedda had the last word—as journalists always do. Acknowledging receipt of the gift in her column, Hedda announced that she had named the skunk Joan.

In our fledgling years in Hollywood Gordon was easily shocked by the behavior of others at parties we gave in our home. I can vividly recall one Halloween costume party. Naturally, having many studio wardrobe departments and costumers to choose from, the guests arrived at our door in a dazzling variety of disguises and getups. The exception was Hunt Stromberg, Jr.

Showing up without a masquerade, he saw the disappointment in my eyes. He kissed me lightly on the cheek and with a chuckle said, "Never mind, my darling Sheila, I shall wear one of your delightful dresses." He paused for thought. "That stunning striped number," he declared with twinkling eyes. "The one with the matching turban."

As we were sitting down to dinner, Joan Crawford nodded toward Hunt and whispered, "Sheila, that looks like your dress."

"It sure as hell does," grumbled Gordon. "Who is that?"

"Hunt Stromberg," I answered.

"A man in a dress?" Gordon gasped. "He shouldn't come to our house in a woman's clothes, even if it is Halloween."

"Oh, Gordon, Hunt dresses like that all the time," Joan laughed. "He's a transvestite! Didn't you know?"

Of course, we didn't. Neither Gordon nor I had ever seen a transvestite.

Although I loved going to big parties and giving them, Gordon hated them but stoically agreed to attend them. He preferred to spend evenings with close friends Peter and Mary Hayes and Bill and Joy Orr, playing poker.

Large gatherings liberally sprinkled with people whom he recognized as phonies were not his idea of a good time. With the most festive parties going at full tilt he could be relied upon to look at his watch and yawn, "Well, we've got to be going. I have to be up at six o'clock."

Rather than going out, Gordon preferred to go to bed early, and at our own parties he was known to plead, "Don't you think it's time for everyone to go home?"

With so many parties being thrown, hosts and hostesses vied to be different. Some gave theme parties. Others worked hard to come up with unusual entertainments. One of the most unusual was Humphrey Bogart's "mouse party." It featured an after-dinner race between white mice on a racetrack set up on top of Bogie's pool table. The betting was spirited, sparked by Gordon, who, I was beginning to notice, never passed up a wager.

Much of the time, however, the entertainment came from the invited guests—Red Skelton with his hilarious comedy routines and mimes, jokes by Jack Benny and George Burns, and songs by Frank Sinatra, Bing Crosby, Judy Garland, and, of course, "the world's greatest singer," Gordon MacRae.

Gordon's burgeoning fame in movies was exceeded by his success on radio as the star of one of NBC's musical shows. Not everyone went out to the movies, but all of America listened to the radio. Millions tuned in for *The Railroad Hour*. Part of the network's "Monday Night of Music," the show alternated with *The Voice of Firestone* and *The Bell Telephone Hour* and featured operettas adapted by scriptwriters Jerry Lawrence and Robert Lee. The musical director was Carmen Dragon. The choir was under the direction of Norman Luboff. Gordon was the star.

Beginning with the blast of a locomotive whistle, the hiss of steam, and announcer Marvin Miller's intoning "Here comes our star-studded show train," the program seemed to promise travel, but it really had nothing to do with trains, except for the sponsor, the Association of American Railroads, "the same railroads that bring you most of the food you eat, the clothes you wear, the fuel you burn, and all the other things you use in your daily life." In fact, the shows were musical stories that brought to life the fantasy characters suggested by the music of the great composers—George Gershwin, Victor Herbert, Jerome Kern, Sigmund Romberg, and others.

During the six years the show was broadcast, Gordon always played the male lead, appearing opposite the greatest women singers: Lucille Norman, Dorothy Kirsten, Victoria de los Angeles, Vivienne Della Chiesa, Patrice Munselle, Nadine Connor, Mimi Benzell, Gladys Swarthout, Jane Powell, and many others.

These roles came close to achieving Helen MacRae's hope that her son would lend his vocal talents to more serious music and not become just another crooner. Unfortunately, whatever pleasure Helen felt as a result of the radio show did not last long. While Gordon was making *The Desert Song*, we learned she had not been feeling well. A lifelong Christian Scientist, she was praying about her illness. Then, after a day spent at Jones Beach with grandchildren and Gordon's sister Jane, she said wearily, "I'm so tired. I just want to take off this body." A few minutes later, after praying, she died.

A young doctor summoned to remove the body for an autopsy as required by law drew back the sheet that covered her and asked Jane if her mother might have taken an overdose of medication.

"She wasn't taking medication," Jane replied.

Incredulous, the doctor said, "This woman was in the advanced stages of cancer. She must have been taking painkillers."

"She was a Christian Scientist," Jane answered.

"It's amazing," the doctor said. "By every measure, she ought to have died long ago. How could she be in the ocean today?"

I believe women are most deeply affected by the deaths of their fathers; men, their mothers. When I tried to get Gordon to talk about his mother's death, he said, "I don't want to talk about it." And he never did.

While his mother's passing was not the only factor contributing to Gordon's drinking, I believe the loss provided the impetus to undoing the delicate balances of his life. From that moment on, he moved inexorably onto the long, destructive slide into alcoholism. For a man so imperiled, we were in the wrong place at the wrong time. There was no way of avoiding Hollywood's chief means of socializing, going to parties or throwing them.

We gave many, some of them memorable, such as a little dinner in Palm Springs for Rita Hayworth. She welcomed a chance to get away from the gossip that she was pregnant by the notorious international playboy Ali Khan and was quite willing to become a princess. She was hiding out from photographers. What a beauty she was! To me, Rita typified the international glamour girl. Born Margarita Carmen Cansino in New York City, she was the daughter of entertainers. Her mother, Volga Haworth, came from a long line of English actors and had been a Ziegfeld Follies girl. Her father, Eduardo, was a vaudeville headliner with his sister. The family had settled in Los Angeles in 1927, where Rita took dancing and acting lessons, making her stage debut at the age of eleven in a school play.

Her professional bow took place in 1932 and her first screen appearance in 1935. Stuck in low-budget "B" movies and determined to make a major assault on stardom, she cut and bleached her hair, raised her forehead by electrolysis, and changed her name to Hayworth, inserting a "y" in her mother's maiden name.

But it wasn't until 1941 when she was cast opposite Fred Astaire in *You'll Never Get Rich* that she became a star. *Time* declared, "Rita Hayworth really knows dancing." She had wed Orson Welles, with whom she starred in *The Lady From Shanghai*, but that often stormy marriage ended in 1948 only to be followed by the sizzling, headline-grabbing affair with Ali Khan that had even Hollywood talking.

As we entertained Rita that evening, she seemed to prove my rule that the more beautiful women are, the less difficult they are to get along with. When I mentioned this to Ali Khan, he laughed scornfully. "Women who think they are undeserving are easy," he said, cynically, "and I have never met a beautiful woman who didn't feel undeserving."

Ali Khan was from a far different world than that which Gordon and I had known. Observing Gordon happily presiding over a barbecue grill and delightedly cooking hamburgers in the yard, Ali shook his head in disbelief. "Sheila, how does a man like Gordon MacRae lower himself to do this woman's work?" He just didn't understand that in America, the outdoor barbecue *was* man's work. Of course, Gordon loved it!

I avoided dancing with Ali Khan because he was notorious for having erections. Ann Warner was greatly amused. "My darling," she said, "for some women, Ali's erections on the dance floor are the closest they'll ever get to sex."

The Racquet Club in Palm Springs was the scene of many parties, many marriages, many divorces, and more liaisons between gorgeous screen people than were ever counted. It was a great spot for observing stars in their private moments, offscreen, off guard, stars like Greer Garson and June Allyson.

What is a star? Humphrey Bogart had his definition. He growled, "Joan Crawford, as much as I dislike her, is a star." Someone else trying to define stardom said, "A star is when someone says, 'Let's leave the dishes in the sink and go see Joan Crawford.'" However a star might be described, Joan knew it fit her.

"I worked my tail off to get where I am," she told me. "Who I am is the only thing that counts." Now I was looking at her. With a white sweater around those famous squared shoulders, she knitted while keeping possessive eyes on tall and good-looking Greg Bautzer, a fabulous tennis player, a lawyer, and Joan's current lover.

Some years later, noting that some actresses will sacrifice anything to become a star, Joan Hackett, whose career was much too short, said, "I just don't want the gold ring on the merry-go-round that much. All I want is for the merry-go-round to play *my* song."

Gordon was that way. For him, the Hollywood merry-go-round's song of stardom was a tune he would sing only if it were in his key.

There was one star I was eager to meet. I had adored him since I was a child—Spencer Tracy, the finest actor ever to grace the movie screen. When, at last, I did meet him, I told him about my ancestors and waxed poetic about the art and craft of acting. Spencer heard me out to the end, then said, "I don't think acting's an important job in the scheme of things. Plumbing is."

That crack notwithstanding, Spence appreciated billing. He was asked by Garson Kanin why he was always listed first in the credits of the pictures he made with Katharine Hepburn.

"You're the man," said Garson, who coauthored the Tracy-Hepburn hit *Adam's Rib*. "Why not ladies first?

Spence answered, "This is show business, not a lifeboat."

The people at Warners who fascinated me most were writers. I arranged for Gordon and me to eat lunch at the writers' table in the studio commissary. While the writers at Warners were highly respected for their talents, making movies was a big business. Jack Warner insisted that the writers keep business hours: nine to five.

When Jack caught the Epstein twins, Julius and Phillip, arriving at the studio in midafternoon, he promptly advised them to read their contracts. "You are to punch in at nine o'clock in the morning just like everybody else, just like any president of any bank," he fumed.

Following a particularly nasty critique of one of their scripts, Julius put Jack in his place. "Well, this was written at nine o'clock in the morning," he said. "So why don't you get a bank president to do it?"

Another outstanding writer at Warners said of their tyrannical boss: "Jack Warner has oilcloth pockets so he can steal soup."

The Epsteins had collaborated on the script for *Casablanca*. What was Jack Warner's attitude toward the esteem in which that classic film was held? I asked him at a dinner party. "I wasn't making art," he cracked. "I was making a living." Then he shared with me his secret as a moviemaker. "If the American public wants pullover sweaters," he said, "I'm not going to give them cardigans."

When I repeated the line to Humphrey Bogart, the star of *Casablanca* said, "I always knew Jack had a talent for pulling the wool over people's eyes, only I never thought he'd admit it."

Bogie was a truly fascinating man, and Gordon and I were often in his and beautiful Baby Bacall's company. On the screen Bogart was the hard-as-nails tough guy that he had created with his Broadway portrayal of the insane gunman Duke Mantee in *The Petrified Forest*. The role brought Bogie Warner Bros. stardom in 1936. Like Spencer Tracy and Gordon, Bogie could put his livelihood in perspective. "I hate myself for choosing a profession that gets me up at dawn," he said. "I hate myself all the way to the studio and into the makeup room. There we sit, the glamour boys waiting to be made beautiful and feeling like a snail's grandmother."

Then why did he do it?

"Because," he said, chuckling, "I want Jack Warner to have to look at my sour puss for the rest of his life."

As Sam Spade in *The Maltese Falcon*, Bogie had defined the meaning of the hard-boiled private detective. But being typecast as a tough guy had not pleased him. "I'm sick to death of being a one-dimensional character," he griped. "I'm just a guy in a tight suit and snap-brim hat."

As the mysterious and romantic Rick Blaine in *Casablanca*, he broke out of that mold forever.

As an admirer of the film, I took the opportunity to praise it to Jack Warner while we were lounging at his Mediterranean villa. "It was so good, Jack," I said. "So real."

Jolting upright on his chaise, he blurted, "Real? Hell, there wasn't one moment of reality in it."

While Gordon accepted the studio's demands that he show up at parties, benefits, and other social events, he was happiest when he could get away from Hollywood for trips into the countryside. He loved outdoor sports—hunting, riding, fishing—with his pals Bill Orr and Solly Baiano. A discoverer of talent, Solly brought the Warner brothers Bogie, Errol Flynn, Bette Davis, and Ida Lupino. William Orr had discovered Doris Day and Gordon. He and Gordon were close friends, but Bill was Jack Warner's son-in-law, so he went along on outings and not just out of friendship. He was also there to make sure nothing bad happened to one of Jack Warner's stars.

On one of these ventures into the wilderness I had no idea that the cabin was going to be one room and the privy would be outdoors. Struggling up the rocky slopes of the High Sierras on a mule, I found my spirits flagging. Suddenly, Gordon looked back at me and grinned boyishly, enveloping me with a blanket of warmth and encouragement. It turned out to be a wonderful four days away from the suffocating life of a company town, but I couldn't help wondering if there could be danger here, too. Was it possible, I asked myself, that Gordon's immersion in this "man's world" of hard play and hard drinking contributed to his sudden, terrifying difficulties with booze?

Because of the protective shield of Warners and our guarding group of friends who knew the truth, the public heard nothing about Gordon's drinking. Outwardly we still were the ideal Hollywood couple, the perfect marriage.

Elsa Maxwell, the flamboyant party-giver and unabashed lesbian, found the Malted Milk Kids hard to believe. She thought she saw something more than friendship between Jack Warner and me. "How lucky you are," she whispered, unwilling to believe that Jack liked to be with me for no more complicated reason than that I didn't want to be an actress. Soon even she gave up looking for scandal.

A short, stout woman with a booming voice and a boisterous laugh,

Elsa could be an intimidating figure to someone as shy as I was, but she turned out to be quite a sensitive woman. She had much to teach me about surviving in Hollywood—and in life generally. One of the first of her little lectures came at a dinner party. I had been seated between two businessmen with whom I had nothing in common and to whom I had nothing to say. At the earliest opportunity, Elsa drew me aside and said, "You're bored."

Boredom wasn't allowed at one of Elsa Maxwell's parties. She was one of the most aware people I ever knew. She could put together the biggest mélange of people and make it work. She stirred up a party and kept it moving, like a big tugboat.

"No, I'm not bored," I lied. "Really I'm not."

"Yes, you are," she insisted. "You mustn't permit it. Don't be polite. Get up and move." Boredom is death!

Truth to tell, I was often bored. The talk at Hollywood dinner tables was unrelentingly focused on the movie business. However, I was happy to discover that I wasn't the only one who found it dull. That same Anne Baxter who'd voiced the paean to applause and the glories of show business in *All About Eve* confessed to me, "Most conversation in Hollywood has a boring sameness. After working in it all day, it bores me to go to a dinner party and hear nothing but talk about movies."

At one of the Warners' parties. Hedda Hopper also gave me some timely advice. "Don't be harsh on your husband, ever," she warned. For a moment I feared that she had found out about Gordon's drinking, but she had something else in mind. "Keep in mind that he doesn't want to come home after twelve hours on the set when he's been surrounded by all the glamour of the movies to hear about the damned washing machine breaking down or that one of the kids pulled the cat's tail or the baby ate the tickets. Actors bleed a lot, and they need someone to bandage them. When Gordon bleeds, it ought to be you to comfort him."

I wanted to ask her, "Who is there to comfort me?"

THREE

Curly, Billy, and Me

AFTER A CURLY-HEADED cowboy leapt a fence on the stage of the St. James Theatre on the evening of March 31, 1943, and sang "Oh, what a beautiful morning! Oh, what a beautiful day!" the Broadway musical was never the same.

"The show changed fashions in musicals for two decades," noted Gerald Bordman in his chronicle of the American musical theater. "It is hard to say if Rodgers and Hammerstein consciously planned so dramatic a turnabout, although they clearly understood they were attempting something uncommon."

Heaped with praise by contemporary theater critics, it ran for five years, 2,248 performances. Virtually every song in its brilliant score made it onto the hit parade. This show business landmark was *Oklahoma!*

Despite its triumph and the moviegoing public's hunger to see *Oklahoma!* on the silver screen, seven years would go by after the show closed on Broadway before Hollywood would grant celluloid immortality to Curly, the love-struck cowhand, and the girl he courted, Laury Williams. This delay was due in large measure to the show's creators being so busy creating new hit musicals. In rapid succession Richard

Rodgers and Oscar Hammerstein II gave us *Carousel* (1945), *Allegro* (1947), *South Pacific* (1949), *The King and I* (1951), and *Me and Juliet* (1953).

By the time they turned their attentions to making a movie of *Oklahoma!* a technological revolution had occurred in Hollywood. In part a reaction to the challenge of television and its small, black-and-white screen, the movie industry introduced spectacular wide-screen processes such as Fox's CinemaScope and Paramount's VistaVision. Attempting to turn Technicolor movies stereoscopic, there had been dabblings in 3-D, requiring special glasses, and Cinerama, which created realistic depth with a screen that all but wrapped itself around the audience. All of these innovations were accompanied by stereophonic sound.

Another technique being developed was Todd-AO, whose master-mind was flamboyant show business entrepreneur Mike Todd. Born Avram Goldenberger in Minnesota in 1907, Todd was bitten by the show business bug early and was producing Broadway shows in his early twenties. He turned his hand to movies in 1945, forming Michael Todd Productions. One of the founding partners of the Cinerama process, along with news commentator Lowell Thomas, he sold his interests in it in 1953 and announced the birth of the Magna Corporation. The purpose of this enterprise was development of a 65-mm film process called Todd-AO.

The first film to be shot using the system was to be the long-awaited *Oklahoma!* But because only a few theaters would be equipped for Todd-AO, the movie was going to be simultaneously filmed in CinemaScope, thus ensuring nationwide distribution. Rodgers and Hammerstein were to be intimately involved at every step. The producer was to be Hollywood veteran Arthur Hornblow, Jr. The director would be Fred Zinnemann, fresh from his stunning achievements directing *High Noon*, *The Member of the Wedding*, and *From Here to Eternity*.

Gordon was not an immediate unanimous choice for the big screen's Curly. Mike, Dick, and Oscar wanted him from the start, but Fred Zinnemann hoped to give the role to James Dean. Yes, the surly and rebellious star of *East of Eden, Rebel Without a Cause* and *Giant*. Although only one of those films had been seen by the Hollywood community, Jimmy was already being hailed by the Warner publicity department as a major new screen talent. Press releases left no doubt that Jack Warner had a big new star on his payroll. What they didn't say was that the temperamental Jimmy also showed signs of becoming a major headache in the 1950s for "the Colonel," who had wrestled with headstrong Warner Bros. superstars of the thirties and forties.

James Dean had come to Hollywood in March 1954, along with director Elia Kazan, from the world of the Actors Studio to make *East of Eden*. When they promptly turned their dressing rooms into permanent residences, Jack Warner found out and quickly gave them the boot. Jack was always against people staying on the lot.

"He didn't ban taking up residence at the studio out of meanness," Bill Orr explained. "We had no insurance to cover that, and there'd been a fire not long before after some party that caused a lot of damage."

Out of the blue, Barbara Hutton invited Gordo and me to dinner in her bungalow at the Beverly Hills Hotel. James Dean was there—we found him charming and a little sad. Barbara was bizarre and had one suitcase with her own sugar! The other one contained her jewelry! What a Felliniesque night! Barbara, the heiress to the Woolworth fortune, was twice Jimmy's age. She had met him at Schwab's Drugstore—where Lana Turner was discovered. I wondered if Barbara knew that Jimmy Dean shared digs with Clifton Webb, a known homosexual, and that Ursula Andress and he had lived together.

Hedda Hopper was quick to succumb to his magic. After a private screening of *East of Eden*, she wrote, "In the projection room I sat spellbound. I couldn't remember ever having seen a young man with such power, so many facets of expression, so much sheer invention as this actor."

Little wonder, then, that Fred Zinnemann thought that James Dean, Hollywood's hottest new star, might become Curly in *Oklahoma!* I was one of the few people who had seen Jimmy's screen test, and I found his performance as Curly to be fabulous. He was a fine actor who brought an engaging vulnerability to Curly that was, frankly, far beyond anything which Gordon could have achieved. Of course, had Jimmy been signed to play Curly, the singing parts would have had to be recorded by a trained singer and dubbed onto the sound track, a common practice when musicals starred someone who was not a singer. Ultimately Oscar and Dick prevailed, and Gordon got the part.

Tragically, Jimmy was killed in a crash while speeding along a California highway in September 1955. He had made three films, and for his performances in the first and third, he was nominated for the Academy Award as Best Actor. At the time of his death, *Oklahoma!* was being released.

Fortunately, when Gordon was offered the role of Curly, he was sober and great, so we packed up and headed for Nogales, Arizona. The area around the small town that straddled the Mexican border had been chosen for its close resemblance to the flat, open prairie of nineteenth-century Oklahoma Territory. Modern Oklahoma had been deemed unsuitable because it was filled with the trappings of the twentieth century. Hard by the Arizona-Mexico border in May 1954, movie-set builders created a yellow clapboard house, red barn, windmill, weathered fences, and a smokehouse half-buried in the earth, along with haystacks and a cornfield. I wanted to live in it forever.

Two years earlier Rodgers and Hammerstein had decided who would inhabit the farm as Laurey. Her name was Shirley Jones. Born in Smithton, Pennsylvania, Shirley had an immediate connection to show business—her mother named her after Shirley Temple. By the time she was five, she was singing in church. Recognizing their daughter's talents, her parents arranged for her to study with Ken Welch, a Pittsburgh vocal coach. In school, she appeared in student musicals and won top prize in a statewide singing contest. Soon after graduation, she took second place in the annual Miss Pennsylvania beauty pageant. Then came a year of drama study at the Pittsburgh Playhouse and roles in Pittsburgh Light Opera productions of *Lady in the Dark* and *Call Me Madam*.

By now a pretty, petite twenty-year-old strawberry blond with a sweet soprano voice, she set out for New York, where Ken Welch had arranged for her to audition for Gus Schirmer, a theatrical agent. Shirley so impressed Schirmer that he set up an audition with a casting director for Richard Rodgers and Oscar Hammerstein II. Equally impressed, but believing that Shirley needed some more professional experience, they placed her in the chorus of *South Pacific* and, later, in the chorus of *Me and Juliet*. When that show went on tour, she moved up to the role of Juliet. Meanwhile, what Shirley didn't know was that Rodgers and Hammerstein had their eyes on her to be their film Laurey.

First, however, she would have to make a screen test. When she was informed that she would be making it with Gordon, she was thrilled.

She had listened to Gordon on the radio and seen all his movies back in Pennsylvania. Now, introduced to him in the flesh and in western costume on a lavish movie set, she was terribly nervous.

"You just relax, Shirley May," he said with a smile as she blinked in amazement that he had taken the trouble to find out her middle name. Nearly forty years later, recalling their first meeting, she still spoke with wonder about it. "Don't worry about a thing," he went on. "You're perfect for the part."

Directed by Fred Zinnemann, the test involved two scenes that would be in the movie. The first was the moment when Curly asks Laurey to marry him. The other was when they sing "People Will Say We're in Love."

Gordon liked Shirley immediately and wanted her to meet me right away. "You've got to meet Sheila," he insisted. "She's pregnant with our fourth kid and she's still gorgeous."

That the handsome star of her first movie was not a man who was going to be like many actors she'd known and would not be making romantic advances came as a great relief to Shirley.

Laurey's Aunt Eller was to be played by the truly remarkable Charlotte Greenwood. Born in Philadelphia in 1893, sixty-two-year-old Charlotte showed no sign of slowing down in a career that had begun in the 1915 silent film *Jane*. Tall and energetic, she achieved fame in speakeasies and nightclubs of the Roaring Twenties and then on the stage as a zany acrobatic dancer capable of exceptionally high kicks of her long legs. In the 1940s she had been featured in peppery and kooky roles in a string of musicals and comedies at Fox.

Her most recent picture had been 1953's *Dangerous When Wet*, starring Esther Williams and Fernando Lamas. Perfectly cast as Laurey's spunky maiden aunt, she had no trouble keeping step in lively dances with young and vigorous Gene Nelson.

Portraying the love-smitten Will Parker with a burning yen for Ado Annie, the farmer's daughter played so funnily by Gloria Grahame, Gene had debuted in the movies in 1947 after a success as a skater in Sonja Henie's ice show. He demonstrated his skills as a dancer on film in *I Wonder Who's Kissing Her Now*.

I was not happy to see Gene on the picture. Although he had been a close friend to Gordon and me, I had recently turned sour on him because he had divorced. I'd been very close to his wife, Miriam, and I had brought to Hollywood a deep belief, stemming from my childhood.

that divorce was wrong. It was, I believed, nothing less than the sin the Bible said it was. In addition to having this strongly held principle, I looked on Gene's divorcing Miriam as an example of unforgivable ingratitude. I knew that Miriam had been instrumental in shaping Gene's career as a dancer by providing him with some very creative choreography.

Once, I had gone so far as to point this out to Louella Parsons. On one of her occasional visits to a shooting set, Lolly was gushing in her praise of Gene's dancing. Directing her attention to Miriam, I said, "She's the person who created this dance that you like so much."

My break with Gene took place at our house in 1953 when he and Gordon were making *Three Sailors and a Girl*. Also in the picture was Jane Powell. Seated beside me on an elegant antique Mormon bench, Gene said, "You know, Janie and I are great in this picture. We're a terrific team. We're going to put together an act. We'll be the greatest nightclub act you've ever seen. I wanted you to be one of the first to know because it means that I'm going to leave Miriam."

I was stunned. I knew that Miriam adored him. She was also pregnant. Horrified, I leapt to my feet. "Get out of my house!"

That evening when Gordon came home, he immediately noticed that the Mormon bench was gone. I had it moved to the guest house.

"So what the hell's that got to do with the bench?" Gordie asked.

"I don't want it reminding me," I replied tearfully. "So I will not have it in my house."

"Sheersie," Gordie laughed, "you are a piece of work!"

Not long after the divorce, Gordon had come to break the news that Gene was to be in *Oklahoma!* Greeting me with a nervous smile, he said, "Hey, Sheersie, guess who's going to play Will Parker?"

Startled, I said, "I thought it was going to be Eddie Albert."

"They decided he's too old, so he's getting the part of the peddler. Will's to be Gene Nelson."

"Well, there's nothing I can do about that," I said, "but I want you to know that I won't socialize. I'll be polite, but that's all."

A wonderfully dextrous actor, Eddie Albert proved to be excellent as the wily Persian peddler-man Ali Hakim, who wants nothing more than to whisk Ado Annie to a hotel room and into bed "over to Claremore." Born Edward Albert Heimberger, he was a graduate of the University of Minnesota, former circus trapeze flier, and veteran of radio and stage. He had been in films since 1938, making his debut in *Brother*

Rat, which he had done on Broadway. Most recently, he'd been in *Roman Holiday*

James Whitmore would play the cranky, suspicious, and shotgun-toting father of Ado Annie Carnes, doing a comedic turn that was a sharp contrast to the roles that had made him one of the most promising actors of the new generation that had come to Hollywood after the war.

In a bold selection that also went against type, in that it called for singing and a bit of dancing, the part of the sinister and brooding Jud Fry was given to Rod Steiger. One of the most imposing exponents of Method acting as taught by Lee Strasberg at the Actors Studio, Rod had been nominated for an Oscar as Best Supporting Actor for his role as Marlon Brando's treacherous mob-connected brother in *On the Water-front*. He would portray Curly's sinister nemesis in a famous duet.

At the same time menacing and funny, "Poor Jud Is Dead" was to be filmed almost entirely in closeups within the tight confines of the smokehouse. As if that were not challenge enough, the picture was being shot in the new Todd-AO process and wide-screen Cinemascope, and its giant projections would further magnify the interplay between Rod and Gordon. Bill Orr recognized that this performance would become a severe test of Gordon's acting skills. He suggested that he seek assistance from a drama coach.

The person Bill suggested was Elsa Schreiber-Shdanof. She had coached Gregory Peck, Jennifer Jones, Robert Walker, Patricia Neal, Leslie Caron, and many others. Married to a Russian actor, she was steeped in the Stanislavski techniques that were the basis of Rod Steiger's Method. Elsa had a remarkable talent for coaxing exactly the right reading of a word, a phrase, or a line. She also had an instinct for coming up with little pieces of business, for suggesting mannerisms, and for subtly employing an actor's physical traits to command a role and master a scene. For his portrayal of the monarch in *Anna and the King of Siam*, she had given Rex Harrison a hissing laugh that revealed the humanity behind the intimidating demeanor of a petty Oriental potentate.

Gordon balked. "What the devil do I need a coach for? If I need any help, that's Fred Zinnemann's job."

"Gordie, Fred's got a complicated picture to direct. He's not going to have time," Bill Orr argued.

After thinking it over, Gordie agreed—reluctantly, and probably only to please me.

We had little time for Elsa to do her work—barely six weeks. "I will do what I can in that time," Elsa said. "I cannot be present during the filming. That means, Sheila, that you must come, too, while I work with your husband so that you may assist him when the film is being made."

She began with a stern lecture. "This is going to be a very important film for you, Gordon. It is not like any other you've made. I know you've made many pictures, but I must tell you that in them you made many mistakes. You didn't know what you were doing. You were not challenged. This time you must study your character. Unless you know exactly who your character is, you won't succeed in the role of Curly. It will be a disaster."

Not surprisingly, Gordon refused to go back. He had accepted the idea of being coached only to please me. Now he was hurt and offended. Except for his mother, no one, not even Jack Warner, had ever spoken to him that way. I knew what he would say. "Why should I put up with this bull? I've made fourteen pictures and nobody ever said I couldn't act. Why the hell must I take this? I'm a great singer. This is a musical, isn't it? To hell with coaching, I'm going golfing!"

"Gordie, I know this is very hard for you," I pleaded, "but Elsa is *right*. This is an important chance for you."

It was, to me, vital that Gordon do well in the film. His reputation had sunk quite low in Hollywood. Tales of his drunkenness were being whispered where they hurt most—among the men who made decisions on casting, each with a wary eye on budgets and in no mood to take risks with him. "You can't afford to mess this up, Gordie," I said.

Gamely, he returned. Sensing his mood, Elsa was far more gentle than the previous day. "In this picture," she began, "the most important scene for you is in the smokehouse."

"No problem," Gordon bragged. "I've got it down pat. Want to hear me sing it?"

"Darling, I know you can *sing* it," Elsa retorted. "We are talking about acting, not singing. You will be playing this scene in a tight two-shot with a great dramatic actor. That means that *you* must become a great actor, as well. To achieve this, you need to appreciate what the crucial scene in the smokehouse conveys."

"Hell, it's just a song."

"No, no, no," Elsa answered, throwing up her hands. "It is good versus evil. You must communicate this truth. It must come from within you. The audience must not only hear the words as you sing them. They must grasp what you are *thinking*."

"And just what should I be thinking?"

"In your mind must be a conviction that Curly represents everything that is good. Jud is the incarnation of evil. The materialistic side of the world. On his wall he has dirty pictures. He has what is called a pigsticker. You look in it to see a dirty picture but it conceals a knife for stabbing someone in the chest. Jud is a despoiler. Curly would never go to bed with Laurey unless they were married. Jud would go to bed with her for the fun of it. He wants to corrupt her because in doing so he will also destroy Curly and all Curly stands for. He hates Curly, you see, because deep within himself he wants to be like Curly."

"Jesus, I figured he was just a guy looking for a little fun."

"No. He is, as Curly says, a rattlesnake. When you speak that line, you must make the noise of a rattlesnake."

"Oh, hell, I can do that," Gordon boasted.

"Show me," Elsa said.

Gordon hissed.

"Wonderful," Elsa exclaimed. "Now, listen to me. Because this scene is almost entirely in close-up, the key to success for you must be in effective use of your eyes."

Elsa was exactly right, and her absolute sense of character becomes apparent in the movie. Simply by moving his eyes—slyly, narrowing, mockingly, challengingly, sidelong, and directly—Curly dominates the scene. Even when Rod Steiger is singing, the audience's attention remains riveted on Gordon. The words of "Poor Jud Is Dead" are intended to be an ironic lament on the imagined death of Jud, but it's through the expression in Gordon's eyes that the audience understands Curly's unspoken wish that Jud Fry really were lying dead, "peaceful and serene," in a coffin illuminated by candles at the head.

We took our small children on location with us. Meredith, Heather, and Garr were under ten years of age, and Robert Bruce was five weeks old, the youngest child in the history of moviedom to go on location. Oscar Hammerstein took one look at him and saw "a formidable resemblance to Winston Churchill." From that moment on, Ockie, as he preferred to be called, was like a doting grandfather.

Bruce's birth in 1954 had been quite dramatic, worthy of a scene in a movie melodrama or, perhaps, a comedy. It was April 6, and the baby was a month overdue when, late in the afternoon, as I was looking forward to joining Gordon for dinner and then catching the new Peggy Lee show at Ciro's, I began having contractions at two-minute intervals. I phoned my doctor. "There's no time for you to get to Cedars-Sinai Hospital," he said. "Get someone to drive you to St. Joseph's in Burbank." Except for my small children and two maids, who didn't know how to drive a car, I was alone. There certainly was no time to call Gordon at his golf club or to call for a taxi, so I phoned to the home of our next-door neighbors, the Von Der Ahes, owners of the Vons supermarket chain. Their son, fifteen-year-old Charles, answered. "No one's home but me, Mrs. MacRae," he said.

"Can you drive a car?" I asked.

"I don't have a license," he said, "but I can try."

I met him in the driveway beside our station wagon. "Tie a white handkerchief on the radio aerial and don't stop for signs or red lights, Charlie," I said breathlessly, "because I think I'm going to have the baby on the way."

Sure enough, Bruce arrived en route—ten pounds, two ounces. "You're damned lucky," said the emergency room physician as I was wheeled into the hospital. "Now we've got to stop the bleeding."

It was easier said than done. As the hemorrhaging continued, the doctors worried that I might have cancer. Bone marrow tests were ordered. They proved negative for cancer but *positive* for arsenic. "Has someone been trying to poison you, Mrs. MacRae?" asked the doctor, jokingly.

Now the question was, where did the substance come from? To find out, every aspect of my daily life was explored—my makeup, the food I ate, household furnishings, the chemicals used in our garden and on the lawn, everything that came to mind. Looking at my blond hair, one of the doctors asked if I used anything to lighten it.

Like many fair-haired California women, I was conscious of the damage that relentless sunlight could do, but I had relied on the judgment of my hairdresser. What I did not know was that he routinely applied a special cream that contained a small amount of arsenic. It had accumulated in my bloodstream, having been absorbed through per-spiration as I spent a lot of time out of doors, whereas others whose hair had been treated with "silver blonde" were actresses working out of direct sun in the coolness of sound stages. Of course, this was the 1950s, when there were far less stringent regulations regarding the potentially hazardous contents of cosmetics.

While this medical mystery was being resolved and Gordon and I were living in Palm Springs, he learned he would be playing Curly in *Oklahoma*! and that filming was to start in five weeks in Nogales.

Shooting did not begin immediately. Fred Zinnemann wanted everyone to become thoroughly familiar with their surroundings and with one another. Gordon did not like horses and so he spent part of this period getting to know the mottled gray named Blue that he would ride over the plains or through the cornfield. The stalks were to be "as high as an elephant's eye," but the weather was so hot, the specially planted field withered, requiring constant replacing.

Gordon's hair also needed attention. Although he played a man who got his nickname because he had curly locks, he had few waves in his dark hair. Unhappy with the curls being produced by the movie's hairdresser, Ockie suggested that Gordon should have a permanent.

"The hell I will," Gordon grumbled.

"Well, we've got to do something," Ockie said, turning to me with pleading eyes.

"Finger curls!" I said decisively. "Leave it to me."

So each morning I curled Gordie's hair.

The remainder of my mornings I spent in a comfortable house Mike Todd had provided, taking care of the four children. Afternoons, when Gordon worked, I left them in the care of two nannies so that I could be with him on the set to remind him of all he had learned from Elsa.

This could have led to a problem. Thanks to Rod Steiger, it didn't. After a few days of shooting, he sidled up to me and whispered, "Sheila, are you *directing* Gordon?"

"Whatever do you mean?" I asked innocently.

"C'mon, Sheila," he said, cracking an impish smile. "I've noticed the little hand signals. You know that's not allowed. If the Director's Guild found out, there could be trouble. It's no skin off my nose, but I thought I ought to say something. For your sake. And Gordie's. Be careful, okay? And now that I've got that off my chest, there's something else I have to ask you. It's obvious that you know what you're doing..."

"Thank you. But it's not my work. I..."

"Gordie wouldn't be doing any of the good things he's doing without you," Rod continued. "So, tell me. How come you know so much? And why is it that you, a beautiful and talented woman, are having babies and staying with a man who's so determined to drink himself right down the drain?"

"You're wrong," I gasped. "He's just upset. His mother died last year, you see, and —"

"No. I think it's more than that," Rod said. He flashed a knowing smile. "I ought to know. I've been going to psychiatrists all my life for my drinking problem!"

Shooting had barely begun when Gordon showed up drunk. With a sinking stomach, I looked on in horror and dismay as he was brought back from location, staggered out of the car, surly and defiant, and fell heavily to the ground. Rod had to help me get him into our house.

The lapse was devastating to me and a real threat to the picture. When Gordon drank, the effects on him were evident. His face turned red and puffy—totally unacceptable in ordinary close-ups, let alone in Todd-AO. They had a lot of trouble with the opening scene, in which Gordon rode through the cornfield as he sang "Oh, What a Beautiful Morning." His face was blotchy from drinking, requiring much time- and money-consuming reshooting. He gained weight, an intolerable situation in the movies; scenes are shot out of sequence, often days and weeks apart, so that differences in an actor's looks become obvious. Mike Todd, Dick Rodgers and Oscar Hammerstein, Spiros Skouras (the head of Twentieth Century-Fox, which had invested in the film), and, of course, Fred Zinnemann were furious.

While I appreciated their concerns, I was worried about Gordon and trying to grasp the why of it. How had this happened? Was it possible, as I'd said to Rod, that this terrible situation had been caused by the death of Gordie's mother? Was that why, in the space of a few months, he'd gone from nondrinker to the pitiful lost man I saw before me?

Going over it in my mind, I recalled that at the funeral he'd acted strangely. He had laughed a lot. I had wondered if he was having a slight nervous breakdown. When we returned to California, he refused to be drawn out about his feelings. I never saw him cry. The most heartfelt condolences from Jack Warner, Bill Orr, and all of his closest friends left him unmoved. He had missed days of work. And he drank even more heavily.

Lucy Ball had tried to sound an alarm. "Gordie's becoming a drunk," she said. "You've got to watch him."

"He's just feeling down because of his mother," I insisted. "He'll get over it."

But, obviously, he had not, and now he was in real danger of losing *Oklahoma*!

Charlotte Greenwood helped. A Christian Science practitioner, she prayed for him daily. "You've got to tell the truth to yourself, Gordon," she told him.

They were words that, sooner or later, every alcoholic hears, but the brutal fact is that words from someone else are never the solution. Ultimately, the only person who could help my husband was Gordon himself—by admitting that he had a serious drinking problem.

Unfortunately, he had not reached that point of clarity and self-discovery. He continued to drink on location, and when we returned to Hollywood for further work, he was even worse. He often showed up late and occasionally did not show up at all.

Everyone involved with the picture was very upset, but none more than Ockie and his wife, Dorothy, both of whom adored him.

Rod Steiger was more concerned about the effect all this was having on me.

"I want you to know that I don't think you should stay in this relationship," he said. "I want to take you and little Winston out of it."

As he paused, searching for words, I sat in stunned silence.

His next words came explosively. "Sheila, I really want you. I know you're not happy."

I could not deny that I was attracted to Rod. On an outing across the border into Mexico I learned just how pragmatic he could be. In the straightlaced 1950s, when the slightest hint of scandal could ruin a person's life, he had an acute sense of propriety. He grasped that I was uncomfortable in the situation. "Knowing you as you are," he said, "I know that the only place we could do what I want to do is in the shadow of the Eiffel Tower."

After we were back in Hollywood, a phone call from Gary Cooper surprised me.

"I usually don't meddle in other people's business," Coop said. "Do you know that Rod Steiger's been telling anyone who'll listen that he's crazy about you. He stood up at dinner the other evening and said, 'I am in love with Mrs. Gordon MacRae and I'm going to marry her.'"

I spoke to Rod: "I know you're joking. But Gordo needs everything we can all do for him. Don't tease him. Let's just have fun together. The film's almost over." Rod smiled, "You think that will change him?"

In September 1955, *Oklahoma!* opened to rave reviews. Those for Gordon's performance were no less glowing. "In Gordon MacRae [director Zinnemann] has a Curly, the cowboy hero of the tale, who is wonderfully relaxed and unaffected," wrote Bosley Crowther in the *New York Times.* In Shirley Jones, he went on, the film had a strawberry-blond newcomer "so full of beauty, sweetness and spirit that a better Laurey cannot be dreamed."

What had happened during the making of *Oklahoma!* that the reviewers and the public couldn't know about was a heartbreaking, apparently inevitable, transformation of the Gordon MacRae who had retained enough of the Malted Milk Kid to play Curly in *Oklahoma!* into a perfect Billy Bigelow, the dissolute carnival barker of Gordon's next film, *Carousel.*

He desperately wanted to make that film. "All those great songs." he said, "and I'm just the guy to sing them!"

Between the two pictures, he played a lot of golf and tried to stay sober by keeping busy. To no avail.

He had a bad accident while driving drunk in Bel Air, going over a wall and wrecking Gene Nelson's car and injuring himself badly enough to be taken to the hospital.

The story was kept out of the newspapers.

The following month he ran a stop sign and crashed into four cars, injuring several people, including a pregnant woman who lost her baby. This tragedy could not be kept quiet.

The story ran in all the Los Angeles newspapers and had a devastating effect on our daughter Meredith. At school she was teased terribly by classmates.

Coming home in tears, she told me, "I wish Daddy weren't famous. If he weren't a movie star, they wouldn't have put it in the newspaper."

Having a famous father was to be difficult for Meredith and our other children throughout their lives.

I stayed to myself as much as I could. I was embarrassed and scared and often physically ill enough to seek medical help. When I went to a psychiatrist to seek help for Gordon, he asked, "Where is the patient?"

In the midst of these nightmares, Gordon won the role of Billy Bigelow in the film of *Carousel*. That proved an unexpected development, even a miracle.

Henry Ephron became the producer of *Carousel*. With his wife, Phoebe, he had collaborated on the 1934 Broadway hit *Three's a Family* and many screenplays in the 1940s. Although he worked with Gordon on *Look for the Silver Lining* in 1949, he did not choose Gordon for the role of the carousel barker. For Billy Bigelow, Henry and Twentieth Century-Fox initially signed Frank Sinatra, fresh from his Academy Award-winning triumph in *From Here to Eternity*.

The role of Julie was to be played by Shirley Jones. Most of the songs had already been recorded by Frank and Shirley in Hollywood. The exterior scenes would be filmed in Maine. Like *Oklahoma!*, the picture was going to be made in two processes, ordinary CinemaScope and the newer CinemaScope 55. The location was the idyllic seaside setting of Boothbay Harbor, Maine, and Shirley called to say that Frank was not happy there.

This remote, rock-bound region was quite a change of locale for Frank; there was no place for him to go after work in Boothbay Harbor or a plane to fly him to Portland or any other place where there might be some kind of nightlife. He had arrived in a black limousine on location where everything was ready for shooting the rambunctious "June Is Bustin' Out All Over" that morning.

Waiting nearby in makeup and costume, Shirley looked on in puzzlement as Frank stepped from the car, spoke with the film's director, Henry King, and then had words with Henry Ephon. "All of a sudden, Frank got back in the car and slammed the door and the limo took off," she recalled. "Henry Ephron turned and tears were streaming down his face."

Shirley rushed to him. "Henry, what's going on?" she asked. "Why'd Frank leave?"

"Something about not wanting to do it twice," Henry answered with dismay. "What's it matter? He quit the picture." Grasping Shirley's hands, he was desperate. "Where's Gordon MacRae?"

"I have no idea," Shirley replied.

"You made *Oklahoma!* with him, didn't you?" Henry said, nearly hysterical. "Why *don't* you know where he is?"

At that moment, Gordon and I were at Lake Tahoe where Gordon had just begun a three-week nightclub engagement. Now, suddenly, Oscar Hammerstein was on the phone begging Gordon to cut it short to take over as Billy in *Carousel.*

Gordon had a typical reply. "I'm making good money here, " he said. "Tell the Ephrons they'll have to wait."

"Use your common sense, darling," I told him. "You can't keep *Carousel* waiting. You simply can't risk losing your favorite role."

Four days later, we arrived in Maine.

He would costar again with Shirley, which delighted him and me. Shirley and I had become friends. I thought she and Gordon were much alike—outdoorsy, independent, natural singers, both from small towns and with happy dispositions. It was just that all-American quality that had endeared her to Dick and Ockie and to the people who came to see *Oklahoma!* These traits that were fundamental to Laurey were also basic to Shirley's character in *Carousel,* Julie Jordan. Much of the advance publicity for the film was to feature Shirley's sweetness. A photographer and reporter from *Life* were coming to Boothbay Harbor for pictures, an interview, and a shot of Shirley as Julie for the cover.

This intense focus on Shirley's innocent image led to a big problem. In the eyes of Dick, Ockie, and the others in charge of making the movie, that problem had a name: actor Jack Cassidy. Shirley was in love with him, and Jack was head over heels in love with her. Immediately after completing *Oklahoma!,* Shirley had gone on a tour of Europe with the stage production, costarring with Jack. While there would not have been anything wrong with Jack being around during filming under any other circumstances, his being there while *Life* was doing a story sent shivers down the backs of some people on the picture who regarded Jack with disdain.

First, he was divorced and a father. Second, he was seven years older than Shirley. Third, he was said to be a bit of a rogue and roué. With his dimpled, rugged, Irish good looks and wit, he seemed to be almost a real-life Billy Bigelow. Last, some people thought that the only reason Jack was interested in Shirley was because she was a movie star who might help him in his own career. All of which was plain nonsense, in my opinion. And in fact, I was captured by his personality instantly.

By the time he appeared in Boothbay Harbor to the consternation of his detractors, Jack already had a fine career going. He had made his first appearance at age sixteen in the chorus of Mike Todd's *Something for the Boys*. It was 1943 and the war was on, so Mike was thrilled to find someone who was under draft age who could act, sing, dance, and get laughs. In 1948 Jack had a small part in *Small Wonder*, and the next year he was in *South Pacific*. In 1952 he was in *Wish You Were Here*. For the Phoenix Theater, he'd played in *The Sandhog* in 1954. That was followed by *The Importance of Being Earnest* and *Witness for the Prosecution* in 1955. Along the way he'd married and divorced Evelyn Ward, a television actress. They had a son, David.

I liked Jack. Gordon always liked a man's man—especially one who could drink—so they got along famously. Shirley loved Jack. So, paraphrasing of one of Ockie's *Carousel* lyrics, "that's all there was to that." *Life* paid no attention. It wanted Shirley for its cover and that's who it got. Readers, though, didn't know that under her Julie Jordan frock she was wearing a pair of decidedly un-Julie-like, un-Laurey-like blue jeans.

Carousel, adapted for Broadway from Ferenc Molnar's *Liliom*, was a fitting follow-up by Dick and Ockie to their *Oklahoma!* The bittersweet love story of rowdy Billy's futile attempts to change his ways out of love for Julie, the show contained some of the most enduring songs ever written for Broadway—"If I Loved You," "June Is Bustin' Out All Over," "What's the Use of Wondrin'," and the inspirational "You'll Never Walk Alone."

Everyone discovers something personal in a song. That is the gift and the glory of music. It melds into memory and then stirs it. Its touch can be tender or wounding, a gentle tug upon the heart or a knife plunged into it. How could I not be affected by the words I heard on the set of *Carousel*? I was a girl again, gazing at Gordon as he swaggered into the Millpond Playhouse: *"If I loved you, time and again I would try to say all I'd want you to know..."* It was wartime again and I was a young mother: *"When the children are asleep we'll sit and dream the things that ev'ry other dad and mother dream..."* The countless times I'd forgiven him: *"What's the use of wondrin' if he's good or if he's bad? He's your fella and you love him. That's all there is to that."* Through Ockie's uplifting lyrics, Gordie also renewed my faith: *"At the end of the storm is a golden sky and the sweet silver song of a lark."*

In all the bad times I had known with Gordon, after all the heartbreak and disappointments, there had always been exactly what Ockie's words promised—the golden sky of Gordie's love, the sweet silver song of Gordie's voice.

When Dick and Ockie wrote *Carousel*, they created one of the most daring numbers in Broadway musical history. In it Billy Bigelow was alone onstage for an unprecedented eight minutes. Having just learned that Julie is going to have his baby, Billy ponders his fatherhood in "Soliloquy." He sings proudly of a son: *"I bet that he'll turn out to be the spittin' image of his dad, but he'll have more common sense than his puddin'-headed father ever had."* Suddenly struck by the possibility that his child might not be a son, Billy cries, *"What if HE is a girl?"*

Striding the rocky Maine seashore in a truly masterful film performance of Ockie's poetic portrayal of fatherhood, Gordie was already the father of two boys and two girls. Over a span of four years we had had Meredith, Heather, and Gar. The next three years saw the tragedy of three miscarriages before the birth in 1954 of Bruce, in whom Ockie had detected the remarkable resemblance to Churchill. When *Carousel* was being made, Bruce was two and hadn't known the father whom Meredith, Heather, and Gar knew before he started drinking. The bouts with liquor, the absences, the happy family occasions that were marred because Daddy didn't show up—all these began around the time I was pregnant with Bruce.

A few years later, when Gar and Bruce were having a quite ordinary and normal brotherly spat, Gar glared at Bruce and shouted, "It's your fault that Daddy's the way he is. He didn't drink before you were born."

Children observe things through their young eyes and speak the truth as they see it, but the idea that our having another child might have contributed to Gordon's drinking devastated me. I couldn't dismiss the possibility. Bruce's birth occurred after the three miscarriages and around the same time as the death of Gordon's mother. I even let myself believe that perhaps his birth had been a factor. Did all of those pressures turn Gordon to drink? Could anyone be *driven to drink?*

Supposing so, I was gripped by guilt. Feeling partly culpable, I held Gordon blameless. Feeling responsible, I believed I owed it to him to

stand by him. Loving him, I hoped and prayed that I could save him. In
every way, I understood the fatalism of *Carousel*'s Julie: *"Common sense
will tell you that the endin' will be sad, but what's the use of wondrin' if the
endin' will be sad? He's your fellow and you love him. There's nothin' more
to say."*

By the time *Carousel* was released, television was forcing Hollywood
to reconsider the kind of pictures it made. The audiences that used to
flock to the movie musicals in which Gordon had achieved stardom
were staying at home to watch TV. The era of big-budget musicals was
coming to an end.

Gordon made one more film in 1956, a musical, *The Best Things in
Life Are Free*. Directed by Michael Curtiz, it was the biography of the
songwriting team of DeSylva, Brown, and Henderson, with Gordon as
DeSylva. The cast included Dan Daily, Ernest Borgnine, Tommy
Noonan, and Sheree North. At the conclusion of shooting, a "wrap"
party was held at Dan Dailey's house.

What ought to have been a happy occasion became a nightmare
when, for the first time in our lives, my husband ignored me for another
woman. Sheree North had been signed by Twentieth Century-Fox to be
groomed as a platinum-blond bombshell who might serve as a replacement for the temperamental Marilyn Monroe. Sheree had a reputation
as a sexpot that stemmed from both her personal and professional past.
She had been a dancer at the age of ten, married at fifteen, and a mother
at sixteen. She had drawn some notice for a wild dance in *Hazel Flagg* on
Broadway and the movie version, the Martin and Lewis comedy *Living
It Up*. Now here she was, falling all over Gordon and apparently
meeting little resistance.

Whatever Sheree may have had in mind for herself and my husband
was thwarted by Gordon getting sick from drinking and throwing up all
over the food while I sat in a corner in shame and disgust and quiet
dread. During the long, silent drive home, I couldn't get the sight of
Sheree and Gordon out of my thoughts. Had he grown tired of me?
Didn't he love me anymore? What would I do if he left me? What could
I do? I was a mother with four kids. I had no skills of my own to fall
back on. Looking at him as he slept off the booze, I wept. For him and
for me.

When he came to, I immediately began questioning him. I was doing
then, I was to learn later, what the terrified wife of every alcoholic does,

reaching out in desperation for some kind of understanding of what went wrong and frantically trying to keep us together. I was out of control.

At first, he was angry with *me*. Then he was apologetic and remorseful. In tears, we dumped all our wine and liquor down the drain while he vowed to change. "Please, please forgive me, Sheersie," he begged. Of course he loved me! Of course he wanted us to stay together.

As television forever changed Hollywood, drinking brought Gordon's film career to a halt. He now was considered unreliable. Roles were not offered to him. "God's Golden Boy" was thought of as a pitiable drunk unworthy of Hollywood stardom. After eight years in Hollywood, I was a terrified wife and mother of four small children fighting to keep our relationship alive, to maintain appearances, and to hold my family together—and not to tell him I thought I was again pregnant!

Lucy and Me

ONE DEAR FRIEND in my first year in Hollywood was Lucille Ball. This was well before the whole world learned to adore her through *I Love Lucy*. It was she who forced me to come to grips with the fact that Gordon was an alcoholic. She knew all about alcoholics because she was married to one, Desi Arnaz.

Of course, I knew quite a lot about Lucy before I actually met her. Like everyone, I had seen her in the movies since the 1930s and admired her for the stunning good looks that carried her from Broadway chorus line to Hollywood screen. From bit parts initially as a Goldwyn Girl, she rose in the ranks of contract players to comedic roles opposite Bob Hope and Red Skelton. While working at RKO in 1940, she met Cuban bandleader Desi Arnaz. They were married that November.

Desiderio Alberto Arnaz y de Acha 3d was born in Santiago, Cuba, the only child of the mayor of the city and Lolita de Acha, a Latin beauty. While Lucy had grown up in a family of modest means, Desi's family was quite well off, owning three ranches, a town house, an entire island in Santiago Bay, a racing stable, and lots of fast cars. While acting lured Lucy, music was Desi's love. He started out as a guitar player in

64

Cuba. By 1936, he was the featured vocalist with "Rumba King" Xavier Cugat's orchestra.

Before we all wound up in Hollywood together, Gordon and Desi met in 1947 as they toured the country. Desi was traveling with his own band. From time to time, Lucy left Hollywood to join him, and on one of those occasions in New York, Gordon took me to see Desi teamed up with Peter Lind Hayes at the Copacabana. After the show they introduced me to Lucy and Mary Healy. We were to become best friends, the six of us.

"What a beauty you are," Lucy exclaimed. "Look at those eyes, that hair, that body! Look at you! How come *you're* not in the movies?" This was high praise, indeed, coming from one of the reigning Hollywood beauty queens. To my great delight, she liked me from the start.

"Jesus, she's such a good kid," Lucy said to Gordon more than once. She and Desi had been trying to have children but with no success. "You don't know how lucky you are to have kids," she said enviously.

During one of these discussions about babies, I discovered how much Gordon and Lucy really had in common when it came to humor. "Lucy, if you want to have a kid," Gordon blurted, "you have to be in the right position when you and Desi fuck." While I turned beet red with embarrassment, Lucy roared with the earthy laughter I was used to in Gordon. Having come from rural areas, Gordon and Lucy had a kind of simple, often barnyard sense of humor that is very open, deeply rooted in reality, straight from the shoulder and from the heart.

Batting her eyelashes, she turned to me, saying, "You can take the boy out of Syracuse but you can't take Syracuse out of the boy! Face it, Sheila, your husband's a hick—just like me."

Like Gordon, Lucy was born and raised in upstate New York. Her hometown, Jamestown, was a manufacturing community surrounded by farm country in the Chautauqua region southwest of Buffalo. Her father had been a telephone lineman who died when she was four. Her mother was a talented pianist. Like Gordon's strong attachment to his mother, Lucy's relationship with Desiree Hunt Ball would be one of intense lifelong loyalty and love.

As Gordon's mother saw her son as an announcer rather than a singer, Lucy's mother hoped that her daughter would be a pianist. Indeed, Lucy spent two terms at the Chautauqua Institute of Music. But above all else she wanted to be an actress, a fact she had demonstrated as a schoolgirl.

At the beginning of each summer, she would start the trek to New York on foot until somebody came along to pick her up and take her home.

At last, at the age of fifteen, she made it all the way, enrolling in the John Murray Anderson dramatic school, only to be advised by a teacher to choose another occupation. Undaunted, she landed a job as a dancer in a road company of Ziegfeld's *Rio Rita*, lasting through five weeks of rehearsal before being told, "You're not meant for show business. Go home!" One can only wonder what that teacher and the Ziegfeld man thought twenty years later when the entire country was going crazy over the star of *I Love Lucy*.

At the height of her success in television it was said by many that Lucy could be a difficult person, that she was sharp-tempered, irascible, and hard to get along with. To me she was a small-town girl who really didn't care much for Hollywood, and I missed the East, too.

"It's too damned hot here," she complained. "I hate heat! So why am I here? I don't like the sun. I don't like swimming. I don't fish. I don't golf. I don't play tennis. I miss the change of seasons! So what the hell am I doing here?"

Of course, she knew why she remained in Hollywood, the place that gave her work. But despite all the success that she earned, she remained, at heart, the girl from Jamestown. That inherent simplicity was most apparent when she was a wife at home. While working at MGM, she became the embodiment of the glamorous showgirl in costumes that revealed her long, shapely legs and flaming red hair topped by elaborate headdresses.

In her house she was likely to wear baggy slacks and a sweatshirt, and have her hair pulled back with a bandana. She loved to cook and bake, meaning that much of the time she was spattered with flour. Of course, neither I nor anyone else, including Lucy, had any way of knowing in 1949 that she was about to turn that crazy mixture of the showgirl and housewife who was married to a Cuban bandleader into the theme of the most popular television show in history.

Although she'd been making pictures for years, when I met her, Lucy was not a major star, "not on the A list" for parties, as the columnists put it. To be on the A list you had to be billed with your name above the title. She was a wonderful contract player, nothing more. That's the way it is, she explained to me. It was the pecking order. "It's how the town works," she told me, "so don't worry about it."

"I really feel so shy going to parties," I confessed.

Flashing a smile, she gave me a comforting hug. "You're pretty," she said. "You'll do fine."

"I have nothing to talk about," I said. "Everyone wants to talk about the business. I know nothing about it."

"What do you want to talk about?" Lucy asked.

"Poetry."

"Darling," she said, blinking those big blue eyes and pinching my cheek tenderly, "don't talk poetry."

Soon after Gordon and I arrived in Hollywood, I met Ginger Rogers. Thrilled, I told Lucy about it. Her response was a shock. "Don't talk to me about her," she groaned. "I don't like Ginger Rogers."

This seemed odd to me because I found Ginger to be friendly and outgoing. Furthermore, I knew that Ginger and Lucy had much in common. They had come to Hollywood about the same time and had worked together in *Top Hat, Follow the Fleet*, and *Stage Door*. Later, Gordon explained to me that Lucy was convinced Ginger was having an affair with Desi.

"That can't be true," I said to Gordo in bed.

"Well, everybody's talking about it," Gordon said with a shrug. "So it must be true."

"Does Desi say it's true?" I asked.

"I didn't ask him," Gordon said.

I did not know Desi very well at first. Because of his heavy Cuban accent, I couldn't understand most of what he said. But he and Gordon were great pals with a lot in common. Especially cards. And gambling. And drinking. They were also avid golfers.

When they were out on the links, Lucy and I sat with the kids, playing the games that Lucy adored—Scrabble, backgammon, word games, and dominoes—and comforting one another over our beloved husbands' alcoholism. We also consoled one another about their dangerous need to gamble, playing cards all night at the Thunderbird Country Club in games in which thousands of dollars were lost.

The two of them had been playing poker the night before while Lucy and I chatted. "Sheersie, come over here," Gordon called.

"What is it?" I said. "Lucy and I are talking."

"Ah, you two are always gabbing," he said. "C'mere. This is important."

"What is it?" I asked, going to the poker table.

"Desi and I have a bet," Gordie replied.

"You two always have a bet," Lucy said, standing beside me.

Gordon said excitedly, "I've just bet Desi seventeen thousand dollars that the next card in the deck is the ten of clubs. Go ahead, Sheersie, draw the top card."

Lucy groaned. "Guys, this is nuts."

"C'mon, Sheers," Gordon said. "Turn over the top card."

"Lucy's right," I insisted. "I won't do it."

"Okay," he said, "then I will."

He drew the four of spades.

"Darling, you know I love you and Gordon," Lucy said the next day as we watched our kids romping around the Thunderbird pool. "So I have to tell you, hon, that it looks to me as though Gordo has a real problem with this gambling thing. I think it's just as bad as his drinking. Maybe even worse."

Years later I looked at the "home movies" made that day. They show delightful scenes of the little MacRae and Arnaz kids cavorting. Heather is doing her best to unseat Desi, Jr., from his bicycle. Little Lucy Arnaz is romping and Meredith is mugging before the lens. Garr hurls himself from the high diving board at the pool and splashes Brucie. But Gordon and Desi are not in any of the shots. They were off golfing and drinking. The glimpses of Lucy and me reveal a pair of bewildered wives in love with their husbands, with careers that were booming, with money pouring in, but afraid that their marriages were falling apart.

One afternoon, in an effort to cope with our plight, Lucy invited me to join her and the Reverend Norman Vincent Peale to pray. Although I had read Dr. Peale's inspirational books, I felt a little foolish kneeling before the huge stone fireplace of Lucy's home. "Let us pray," said Reverend Peale. Kneeling with my hands clasped and my eyes shut, I saw Gordon as a ship on a perilous course of its own while the children and I were flimsy, tiny boats adrift on the poet Homer's "wine-red sea, a sea full of blood."

Even more distressing than seeing Lucy's concerns about Desi's drinking and gambling was her obsession with his being unfaithful. More than once I watched in shock as she turned on him to demand, "What were you thinking when that girl went by?" She had just cause, but, clearly, I suggested to her, Desi wasn't sleeping with *every* girl. "He would if he could," she said, wounded to the point of tears.

The most innocent remark could trigger her suspicions. At a luncheon of us "Hollywood wives" given by Lucy at the Thunderbird Country Club, Desi walked in. Gazing at us, he declared, "Hey! What a harem!" It seemed to me to be a harmless remark, but when he left, Lucy announced, "The only person in this room who has not gone to bed with Desi is my friend Sheila MacRae. And I appreciate it."

The idea of me sleeping with Desi was ludicrous. Despite his bouts with booze and the gambling, I was madly in love with my husband. No other man existed. I looked at all men as if they had no penises. I laughed, hoping to brush aside the shock that was so evident in the others. I thought she had made the remark in hopes of flushing out the truth. But in doing so, she had put her friends in a terrible spot. Later, I said to her, "Everybody that was there loves you, Lucy."

Just how much Lucy could be loved by millions of people became apparent with the premiere of *I Love Lucy* on October 15, 1951. An immediate smash hit, the show ran for six years and never ranked lower than third in the ratings. Yet it was a program that had some difficulty getting on the air. Based on the premise of Lucy's successful radio program, *My Favorite Husband*, the show envisioned for TV had problems in the eyes of CBS executives. According to them, no one would believe Desi was her husband—never mind the fact that he *was*. To prove that they could be accepted as husband and wife, Lucy and Desi took the show on tour, performing before audiences in theaters. No one found anything unusual at all about the couple.

Besides this, the network wanted the show to originate before a live audience in New York City. Having no desire to commute from coast to coast, Lucy and Desi argued that the program could be filmed in Hollywood in front of an audience. To prove their case, they produced a pilot, paying for it with five thousand dollars of their own money. Gordon and I attended the filming, howling with laughter along with everyone else.

Faced with incontrovertible evidence that the show worked, CBS gave in on both points and Philip Morris signed on as sponsor for a reported $30,000 a week. I was thrilled and happy for Lucy.

The show made Lucy and Desi millionaires. In one of the delicious ironies of Hollywood history, they eventually bought the RKO studios where Lucy had started out, changing the name to Desilu. The studio's annual income was reported at the time to be $25 million, and when Lucy sold it to Gulf and Western in 1960, it was for a reported $10 million.

That same year, she and Desi divorced.

A star of unmatched magnitude who could have done anything she wished in movies and TV and could dictate her terms, Lucy yearned to go back to the stage, and starred on Broadway in *Wildcat*. A rough-and-tumble show perfectly suited to her unique talents, it provided her with a hit song, "Hey, Look Me Over."

In 1961 she married Gary Morton, a nightclub comedian. Funny, cute, and reliable, he seemed to me to be perfect for her. He laughed at her. And he made her laugh. Jack Carter had introduced them. I was overjoyed at knowing that my dear friend was no longer alone. Now she wouldn't have to stay home from parties because she had no one to go with. It was a feeling I had experienced so many times when Gordon was drinking and didn't come home or show up in time to escort me.

I wanted to do something to express my happiness for her, so I persuaded Gordon to set aside his natural aversion to going to or giving parties and to have one for Lucy and her new husband. It was Christmas time, so a seasonal motif seemed a good idea. But what might it be?

Mulling over ideas, I recalled the old song "The Twelve Days of Christmas" and decided that our party would focus on the fifth day of Christmas, when the suitor in the song gives his beloved five gold rings. Gold would be the color, I decided. Even the trees were sprayed to give them a golden hue. And as a keepsake, I decided, what would be more suitable than to give Lucy five gold rings? Her gift to me, of course, was infinitely more valuable than gold—laughter, friendship, and love.

Lucy also was largely responsible for shy Sheila MacRae becoming a performer. As television had forever changed Hollywood and spelled doom for lavish movie musicals, Gordon's problems with drinking had made him unemployable in films because he was deemed unreliable. He turned to working in television, in clubs, and in theaters, while I was the silent, worried wife and mother fighting desperately to keep our relationship alive and to hold our family together.

In those difficult days, Lucy was a constantly available comforter and friend, as I tried to be to her. Sometimes, all we could do was laugh. Of course, she was a natural wit and comedian with many years of experience. I was a neophyte. But I did have an ear for voices, a talent for impersonation that I felt free to express with Lucy. I entertained her with impressions of Lena Horne, Carol Channing, Tallulah Bankhead, Red Skelton, Marlon Brando, and Lucy.

"You know, hon," she said, " you're hiding your light under the Bible's proverbial bushel. You should be getting paid for your talent. You should be part of Gordon's act."

Such praise coming from the person whom I considered the greatest comedian in the world was heady stuff. But I had no idea how deeply Lucy felt about her suggestion until she turned to Gordon at one of our parties and declared, "Gordo, you ought to put Sheila in your act!"

Gordon blinked with astonishment. "What would she do?"

Lucy fixed him with her big, blue but now-steely eyes. "What the hell do you mean, 'What would she do?' Her impressions! She's *funny*! This is a really funny lady!"

FIVE

Lady in Disguise

BEFORE GORDON'S STAR began dimming because of his drinking, he had made his first inroad into television by way of NBC's popular *Colgate Comedy Hour.* A weekly variety show, it debuted in September 1950 on Sundays opposite *The Ed Sullivan Show.* Alternating hosts were Eddie Cantor, Martin and Lewis, and Fred Allen. In 1952, the format was changed to allow occasional productions of musicals. On April 10, Gordon starred in *Roberta,* the show that had been a Broadway success for Bob Hope before he made it big in Hollywood. It had been one of Jerome Kern's last Broadway offerings (1933), with a score including songs that were to become timeless—"The Touch of Your Hand," "Yesterdays," and "Smoke Gets in Your Eyes."

In 1954, Gordon was part of a galaxy of stars appearing on *The General Foods Anniversary Show.* A genuine extravaganza, it was simulcast by all four TV networks (ABC, CBS, Dumont, and NBC).

Two years later, I wrote and produced his own show on NBC. It was a fifteen-minute program with an informal, relaxed mood that went on the air live at 7:30 P.M. eastern time (4:30 in Hollywood, where the show originated), just before the network news. Appearing with Gordon, and occasionally featured in a number of their own, were The Cheerleaders. The orchestra was conducted by Van Alexander.

The setting was a replica of our living room, with a picture window looking out on a scene appropriate for the songs. The idea was to have a unifying theme, which meant that the program had to have a writer. Gordon insisted that it be me.

Ideas sprang from the songs themselves. A weathered gazebo and wind-blown branches, for example, set the mood for "Autumn Leaves." Gordon's picking up a cowboy hat was the cue for "Oh, What a Beautiful Morning." Though *Carousel* was still in his future, the inspirational "You'll Never Walk Alone" was exactly the sort of song for Gordon as he gazed thoughtfully out the window. There were plenty of love songs, some of them sung with guest stars such as Jane Powell and Patrice Munsel. Remembering how he had been forced to accommodate Doris Day and Kathryn Grayson in their movies, Gordon's rule in choosing his TV guests was simple: "They have to sing in *my* key." When someone suggested Dinah Shore, he growled, "Hell, she can't sing at all!" an opinion I thought ridiculous.

The show ended on August 17, 1956, but Gordon was not off television long. His next vehicle was *Lux Video Theater*, which he hosted for a year, also on NBC. I told Marty Melcher that we ought to do three specials plus a video adaptation of a Warner Bros. film, starring Peter Lind Hayes, Mary Healy, Gordon, and Sheila Stephens!

The first problem I had to cope with was Gordon's unwillingness to learn lines. My answer was a gimmick. I had his lines put on cards that were clipped to a prop that suited each song and lowered on wires. Gordon simply read the words.

I also thought it would be a good idea to have guests on the shows. There wasn't a singer in the country who would turn down a chance to sing with Gordon MacRae. Among those who appeared were Ethel Merman, Merv Griffin, Dolores Gray, Gene Kelly, Dorthy Dandridge, Billy Daniels, Nelson Eddy, and Jeanette MacDonald. Our dear friends Peter Lind Hayes and Mary Healy came on with their unique brand of humor. Miriam Nelson did the choreography.

One of the specials included two of our favorite people, Shirley Jones and Jack Cassidy. It was Jack's first time on TV. "Wow, look at that," he said with twinkling eyes, "my first pay check from television!" (It wasn't a lot of money.) Shirley's compensation was a fur coat, her first. The show was *America's Sweethearts,* a format that allowed Gordon to step out of his role as host and sing. Of course, the reuniting of the stars of *Oklahoma!* assured a large audience, much to the delight of the makers of Lux soap.

Perhaps the most popular show was a musical adaptation of O. Henry's *The Gift of the Magi.* Appearing with Gordon in the Christmas classic were Sally Ann Howes and Bea Arthur. The 1958-59 television season also saw Gordon starring in a television adaption of the hit radio show, *The Voice of Firestone.* One of the longest running musical programs in broadcast history, it had started on radio in 1928 and debuted on TV in 1949. The radio show had featured classical music. But the television show was revamped to accommodate the rapidly growing mass audience of the new medium.

One of the talents Gordon teamed with was Jo Stafford. It was such a lovely blending that the combination carried over onto an album, *Memory Songs,* consisting of twelve songs ranging from Cole Porter's "Wunderbar" to the inspirational "Whispering Hope." As a single, "Hope" sold over a million copies. With that exception and those of "original sound track" recordings of *Oklahoma!* and *Carousel,* Gordon's recordings never sold in sufficient numbers to credit him with continual hits. Why he never had more Number One hits has always been puzzling to me. For appreciation of the voice for the voice's sake, recordings were the thing.

Van Alexander, whose orchestra backed Gordon on more than a dozen records, including arrangements of rock and roll hits, thought that Gordon's voice was simply too good for the pop market. Of course, Gordon believed so much in his voice that he thought the voice was all that really mattered in any medium.

It would be impossible to imagine Gordon performing without Van and his orchestra. They had been working together for six years both on the road and in the recording studios of Capitol Records. Brought together by Marty Melcher, Nick Dorso, and Al Levy, who had a booking agency called Century Artists, Gordon and Van had formed not only a brilliant professional relationship but a real friendship that Van considers the most pleasurable and profitable relationship of his career.

Because Gordon liked Van, it was inevitable that Gordon would include both families in the relationship. In a business and town in which the prevailing attitude was "What have you done for me lately?"

such openness was a rarity. At times for Van, his wife Beth and their children, Gordon's warmth and generosity were a little overwhelming. Just how far Gordon was prepared to go on behalf of a friend and his family was demonstrated shortly after he and Van began working together. In negotiations for a "Sail With the Stars" cruise to Hawaii, Gordon insisted that the sponsor, the Lureline company, also provided passage for the Alexander and MacRae families and my mother—an entourage that included Shirley Vaughn, Oscar Hammerstein's secretary.

Gordon was just as generous with his own money. On Christmas when he and Van were appearing at Las Vegas, his gift to Van was a check for $500 so the latter could go home to see his family. Being the early 1950s, when inflation was something that pertained only to balloons and a dollar was worth a dollar, Van was dumbfounded. Years later, with tears brimming, Van told me that no one had ever given him so much at Christmas.

In the sixties, Van Alexander's devotion was stretched beyond the limits of endurance by Gordon's drinking. That awful moment happened for him at the Monticello, a very popular nightclub in Framingham, Massachusetts. "It was our closing night at the club," Van recalls, "and I'd invited a very dear friend of mine to come see the show. That night, Gordon's New York fan club also came—lots of adoring girls. The place was packed. Gordon had been out playing golf, and when 6:30 came around and Gordon hadn't shown up to get ready for the first show, I began to get a little edgy. When he did arrive he was drunk. He said he'd be all right, but when he came out onstage, he couldn't sing. He apologized to the audience and walked off. Naturally, the owner of the club was furious. He was in the embarrassing position of having to give back the cover charges. He told Gordon, 'I'm docking you thirty-five hundred dollars.' That set off a shouting match. Gordon was very belligerent. Later that night, I sat down and wrote Gordon a letter. I said 'Gordie, I don't know where you're going, but I can't take this any more. It's too rough when someone you love is destroying himself. I hope you can get straightened out.' I left the next morning."

While starring on television, Gordon was still a top-notch nightclub draw.

Just as Elsa Schreiber had to teach him that in the movies he had to act as well as he sang, Gordon had to be shown that there was more to a performance in a nightclub than simply belting out songs. Even while he made movies for Warners, Gordon was appearing in clubs. The studio encouraged him to do so, believing that those who saw Gordon MacRae in person at a Las Vegas club, even though they rarely went out to a movie, might decide to plunk down the price of admission to watch him on the silver screen. Following a warm-up act by a brilliant unknown comedian named Buddy Hackett, Gordon offered a straightforward act brimming with big songs that would allow him to show off his voice.

Sammy Cahn, the Oscar-winning songwriter whose tunes sprinkled the tops of the record charts year in and year out, took Gordon to task for his nightclub repertoire with all the sassy vigor of Elsa lecturing Gordon on the importance of using his eyes in his dueling duet with Rod Steiger. "Jesus, Gordie, you can't sing all closers," Sammy said. "Don't feel that you've got to blast the people out of their seats all the time."

Orson Welles caught the act and offered similar sage advice. Noting that Gordon was starting the show with one of his best numbers, Orson said, "You're throwing it away, don't you see? When you come onstage, nobody's paying attention to what you're singing. They're not *listening*. They're *looking*. Every woman in the club is poking her friend in the ribs and saying, 'My, isn't he handsome!' Or, 'He looks just like he does in the movies.' It's a minute-and-a-half of 'Hello, how are you?' They're making up their minds as to whether they like you."

Among the Hollywood stars who came to see Gordon's act at El Rancho Vegas was Cary Grant, although the night he chose to drop in was not exactly routine. As Van Alexander gave the downbeat for the opening number, Gordon did not bound onstage. With a puzzled look, Van started the number again. Gordon still did not appear. Van's puzzlement turned to worry. When a third try did not bring Gordon out, the look was sheer panic.

But a moment later Gordon dashed onstage. "Sorry, folks," he said, "but I've got a hot eight going in the casino, so if you'll just wait a minute longer...."

The audience burst into laughter. When he came back counting money, they exploded with applause.

"Thank you very much," Gordon said. "After the show, drinks are on me."

The applause was thunderous.

"Yep, drinks on me," he said. "*Water* for everybody!"

After the show, Cary told him, "Gordon, that hot eight bit is a wonderful opening for the act."

"It wasn't a bit," Gordon answered. "It was true."

"No kidding," Cary chuckled. "Well, my advice is, keep it in the act."

Because we knew Cary well, we were among the small circle of his friends who had kept the secret that the suave and handsome leading man was bisexual. Therefore, I found myself startled to discover that he could not take his eyes off one of the club's chorus girls, a ravishing beauty known as Yellow Bird.

"Cary," I whispered as he ogled her, "this is a side of you that I've never seen before."

"Until my psychiatrist introduced me to lysergic acid," he replied, "neither had I. It's been a real awakening."

I didn't have to ask for an explanation. The expression on my face was questioning enough.

"It's a marvelous drug," he continued excitedly. "I take it every day. It opens the mind. I see the whole world differently." He gazed longingly at Yellow Bird. "I see *women* differently! It's turned me into a rampant heterosexual."

Apparantly so. I saw him hand in hand with Yellow Bird the next day, the two of them dancing down the street.

Years later, the lysergic acid that Cary had praised to me in the early 1950s became known to the entire world of the 1960s as LSD.

As for Yellow Bird, she later caught the eyes of another admirer and became the mistress of the Latin American dictator, Trujillo.

Cary's use of LSD remained a Hollywood secret until 1968 when it was revealed during his divorce from his fourth wife, Dyan Cannon. By that time, the nation's mores had changed. What would have been a scandal in an earlier era was greeted by a yawn from the public, and the following year Cary was given a special Academy Award for his lifetime contribution to the movies.

While Gordon did not include the "hot eight" opening in his act, he did take to heart the criticisms and suggestions made by Sammy Cahn and Orson Welles. He let me put together a true nightclub act.

Of course, he remained the centerpiece, but now there were production values and bits of business that shifted the staging away from what, before, had been a solo concert. For a segment in which he sang

Scottish songs, I suggested setting up the premise with a "wee bonnie lass" coming out on stage to engage him in a bit of repartee, interrupting him as he sang "Highland Fling."

"I hear you were flirtin' with Annie Macpherson," said the girl.

Gordon replied, "I thought she was a terrible person."

She then joined Gordon in a string of Scottish ditties.

"Now who do we get for the girl?" I asked.

"Sheila MacRae," he promptly answered. Then he fixed me with teasing brown eyes. "You *can* sing?"

With a shudder, I answered, "I don't know."

"Well," he laughed, "we'll soon find out."

Going onstage for the first time since my fledgling efforts at the Millpond Playhouse before the war—not only as an actress but singing!—I was billed as Sheila Stephens. This was at the insistence of Gordon's agent. He had serious doubts about my ability to handle the demands of performing. "You're so shy," he reminded me. "What happens if you get stage fright? Suppose you freeze and ruin his act?"

He also had qualms about whether Gordon's adoring public would accept the "suitability" of working with his wife. While I thought of that attitude as rather foolish, I didn't really care about the billing. I also suspected that, very quickly, everyone would figure out who "Sheila Stephens" was. Which is exactly what happened. Thus, the short, happy show business career of "Sheila Stephens" came to an end.

Emboldened, Sheila MacRae now took a daring step. In 1959, I appeared with Gordon in a Kansas City production of *Bells Are Ringing*, which had starred Judy Holliday on Broadway in 1956. I was Ella Peterson, an employee of "Susanswerphone" who was madly in love with Jeff Moss (Gordon), a customer. The Betty Comden and Adolph Green lyrics and Jule Styne's music provided Ella (and me) with a pair of marvelous numbers, "Just in Time," a sweet duet with Gordon, and "The Party's Over," a melancholy solo by Ella when she thinks Jeff has left her.

We broke records all over and I was teamed again with Gordon in 1960 on a CBS-TV variety series for Revlon, with different performers each week. That same year, we did a revival of *Annie Get Your Gun*. Gordon was Frank Butler and I was Annie Oakley, the two of us having a perfectly wonderful time with the give-and-take of "Anything You Can Do, I Can Do Better," just one of Irving Berlin's hits that went on to become classics.

Even more delightful than the show and its amazing songs were other members of the cast—the MacRae children. Making their stage debuts were Meredith, Heather, and Garr.

When I first went on the road doing my impressions as part of Gordon's act, we were booked into a theater in Baltimore where he had appeared right after the war. As we entered the stage door and headed for our dressing room, terrible memories of the most macabre scene of my young life came flooding back to me.

The day before Thanksgiving 1947, the weather forecast called for snow, possibly a blizzard. Gordon was away, trying to make some money. He'd gotten a job singing at Baltimore's Hippodrome Theater. I was staying with my parents on Long Island—a young mother with two darling little girls, pregnant again, and ideas about being an actress long gone. Missing Gordon terribly, I moped around the house and drove everyone to distraction.

The phone rang. It was Gordie. "Hey, Sheersie, I miss you! How about coming down here and spending Thanksgiving with me? I'm so lonely. We'll have a romantic dinner."

Watching me flinging clothes into a suitcase, my father thought I had gone mad. "A blizzard is coming and you're going to take an airplane to Baltimore? You could be killed! What about the baby?"

"Gordie wants me with him. I'm going!"

Defied yet again by his hardheaded daughter, my father said, "Well, I'm driving you to the airport. You'll survive that far, anyway."

Aboard the last plane allowed to take off before they closed the airport, I gripped the arms of my seat so tightly I gave new meaning to the phrase "white-knuckle flight." Wind-driven snow stung the frozen window. The plane struggled to get into the air. Once up, it bounced and swayed, its two engines laboring against the storm. (The age of jets that would knife through clouds and break through into clear blue sky, leaving earth's tempests far below, was a decade distant.)

To make matters worse, seated next to me was a courtly man who looked for all the world like John Barrymore. There were plenty of other seats; the plane was almost empty. That he had elected to sit by the only young woman aboard led me to brace myself for an amorous advance, what we used to call a "pass." He had obviously steeled himself for the journey with lots of liquor, judging by his breath.

"You realize, of course, we could all die at any minute," he said. "You must be a fatalist."

"No, I'm *married*."

"I know being married is hell," he said, sipping scotch from a flask, "but a wedding ring is no reason to kill yourself on an airplane."

"My husband's in show business and wants me to be with him in Baltimore for the holiday."

"In this lousy weather?" he growled, half rising in indignation. "Pardon me for saying so, but your husband must be a real selfish son of a bitch."

Miraculously, what I now think back on as "the little plane that could" got us safely to our destination in the infamous Blizzard of '47. Like all cities along the coast, Baltimore was buried. Gordon, who had promised to meet me, was nowhere to be seen at the airport. Mercifully, I found a little taxi that could. "Where to, miss?" asked the driver.

"Can you take me to the Hippodrome Theater?"

"Ah, I get it," he said. "You're an actress! The show must go on, huh?"

Arriving at the theater, I plowed through knee-deep snow to the stage door. Its keeper was a little man with a cigar in the corner of his mouth and black slicked-back hair. "Auditions are cancelled, honey," he barked. "Come back Tuesday."

"No, I'm not here to audition," I said, anxiously. "I'm Mrs. Gordon MacRae."

"You'll find him over there," he said, cocking his head. "He's in a hot game with the midgets."

Midgets? The image that came to me was of the little people in *The Wizard of Oz*. Making my way along a wall spider-webbed by ropes and through a backstage maze of scenery and lights, I envisioned delightful Munchkins dancing and singing their welcome to me as they had to Judy Garland as Dorothy, with squeaky, exuberant little voices. Perched atop stools around a small table in a pool of dim, smoky light were three tiny people—two men and a woman—and Gordon. They were playing poker.

He still had on his pancake makeup and the splendidly tailored dark suit he wore only onstage. Hesitantly, I stepped into the light. "Gordie, it's me," I whispered. "I'm here."

He barely lifted his eyes from the cards in his hand. "Hey, Sheersie! Be with you in a minute."

When the losing hand was played, he introduced the midgets, George, Sammy, and Olive. Munchkins, they weren't. "So you're the little housewife, huh, sweetie?" said Olive with a raspy alcohol voice. "You got a sweet hubby." Bolting off her stool, she leapt into Gordon's lap. "Hey, Gordie," she cackled, "ever go to bed with a midget? You'd like me, Gordie. I'm a spinner. Does your wife know what a spinner is?"

"Knock it off, Olive," whined a grizzle-bearded little man named George.

"A spinner," continued Olive, "is a small person who gets on a man and twirls herself on his…"

"For Christ sake, Olive," Gordon groaned, "it ain't nice to talk like that in front of a lady."

"Well, ex-*kyooze* me," she sniffed, sliding off Gordon's knee.

My stomach churned sourly. My hands were shaking. I battled tears. "Gordie," I begged, "shouldn't we be going to dinner?"

A new hand was being dealt. Gordon gathered up his cards. "In this storm?" he said. "We'll grab a couple of sandwiches at the greasy spoon across the street. Soon as this game's over."

What could I do but wait? As hand after hand was dealt, with Gordon rarely winning, he looked at me and pleaded, "Just one more, Sheersie. Okay?" Hours passed, punctuated by the midgets talking their trade—a new act they were working out, who was appearing where, who had gotten a bid to go to Hollywood. A world beyond did not exist for them. Dear God, I thought, is *this* show business?

A decade later I was no longer a starry-eyed teenager. I had turned thirty and was the mother of four children as I returned to the scene of that ludicrous but illuminating experience, and I was about to get another firsthand lesson in being a performer that further shattered my romantic ideas about the glamour of show business.

On opening day after the second performance, I was again backstage at the Hippodrome, starting to put on my coat. Gordon looked up in amazement. "Where you going?"

"Back to the hotel," I said wearily. "I'm tired."

"You can't leave," he said, looking astonished. "We've got two more shows to do."

Now I was astonished. "You mean we have to do this four times?"

"Yep," he said, hugging me. "The contract says four a day, every day!"

Another shock awaited me. Our manager spoke the words that no American ever wants to hear: "The government's coming after you for seven years' back taxes." We owed, he said, $800,000, plus interest.

"How can that be?" I gasped.

"How it can be doesn't matter," he said. "What matters is, the money's owed. It's the Indian Land Grants."

In the long silence that followed, I began to understand. Like flashbacks in bad movies, I saw Gordon playing cards with midgets backstage at the Hippodrome, high-stakes games with Desi Arnaz at the Thunderbird, Vegas casinos, Tahoe gaming tables, the kid in Syracuse shoving his allowance into pinball machines, his mother sternly lecturing him: "It's easy come, easy go with you, Gordon. It's a fault."

Had Gordie really gambled away our money?

I had never paid a bit of attention to what we were earning and where the money was going. I put my faith in Gordon.

"Now, things aren't as bleak as they look," continued the manager. "I'm pretty sure I can work something out with the IRS. I think they'll go along with paying the money in installments. It's a lot of dough, sure, but I figure if you work for forty-eight or fifty weeks, you'll be able to satisfy the claim, keep some money for yourself, and have enough left over to give up this nutty way of life, if you want to."

The reality of what he was saying hit hard. In my life in show business, it wasn't going to be the "show" that ruled, it was going to be the "business." From now on, my existence was going to be in the hands of agents and bookers and the IRS. For months ahead, what I did was going to be planned by others.

Some other woman would have said, "Enough! The drinking was bad, but I will not be tied to a gambler!" But "some other woman" was not married to Gordon MacRae. Others might have dismissed him as utterly selfish and without conscience. I looked at him and still saw "God's Chosen Boy." I believed in my heart that he hadn't set out to do harm. "It's all right, Gordie," I told him. "Things will work out. We'll work it out *together*."

While the act was billed as "Gordon and Sheila MacRae," I never saw myself as his equal. Gordie was the magician. I was merely the magician's assistant. Truly, there was a magic in him. I immediately recognized it. When his mother told him that if he didn't become an opera singer he would become a bum, I could not believe that was so. I saw in Gordon qualities that went beyond the "All-American Boy, ain't I cute?" look. With his voice he could evoke, not the raw sexuality of a Sinatra, but something mystical. His talent for touching people through his singing was so natural that he didn't recognize it. He had no true idea of what he could do with his music. He'd always known what remarkable sounds he could make, but he didn't appreciate the effect his voice had on his listeners.

Although I never viewed myself as anything more than a small part of Gordon's act, I discovered that performing before audiences freed me from the very shyness that Gordon's agent had been so worried about. When impersonating others, I discovered, I was able to shed all my inhibitions. In my personal life, I never could have gone out in a clinging, low-cut gown. In the act, I went on as Elizabeth Taylor with a neckline that plunged almost to my navel. I could be as sultry and sexy as Lena Horne. Dressed as Cleopatra, I had almost no clothes on. As Carol Channing I was able to be dizzyingly effervescent. I was discovering I could be very sexy to someone other than Gordon.

My presence in the act also served to bring home some of the lessons which Gordon had such a hard time grasping when he was being lectured by Sammy Cahn and Orson Welles. In duets with me, a person with considerably less musical talent than his, he had to show his softer side. He was forced to share the magic I had always seen with the people out front.

An audience, I learned, is a many-eyed creature. Observing them became almost an obsession for me. Standing just offstage while Gordon was on at the Sands in Las Vegas, I studied the people. They were enthralled. He had taken them out of themselves. They had come in bearing all the burdens that beset human beings—their pain, their worries about money, fears of the future, the sheer ordeal that everyday living can be. Yet for the moments that Gordon stood before them, singing, they were lifted up. "Gordie," I said tearfully as he came offstage, "do you understand the power you have?"

He gave me what I can only call "the Gordon MacRae look." Half amazement, half puzzlement, it was a familiar expression of utter bewilderment. "Hell, yes," he said, turning away to go back for an encore. "I'm the greatest singer in the world." He was not kidding. He believed in his talent. So did I.

Singers exert a uniquely seductive power over an audience. They come to a performance with a confidence in their material that an actor has in a well-written play. Although most singers are good-looking, they don't have to be sexy or provocative; the songs are. I always found it curious that some of the greatest love ballads have been written by men who were rather plain looking: Irving Berlin, Ockie Hammerstein, Dick Rodgers, Sammy Cahn—even Cole Porter. Unfortunately, some handsome singers believe it's their voices and looks that put their audience in the palm of their hands, when it's the songs that deserve the plaudits.

A love song is a very intoxicating thing. It draws you into an eternally romantic world that doesn't exist in real life. The soap operas on radio and TV achieved the same effect, as did the so-called "women's pictures" that Hollywood made in the 1930s and 1940s. Written for housewives hoping to escape the humdrum and daily drudgery by going to matinees to lose themselves in love stories, the pictures usually starred Bette Davis or Joan Crawford and were accompanied by lush romantic scores.

Jack Warner, who produced so many of those films, knew how vital the score was. In that hard heart he was said to have, Jack appreciated that romantic music was as vital to the love stories he put on the screen as the words and images. He also understood that audiences wanted musicals as a way of escape. Of course, he also knew how expensive musicals could be. Appearing at a sound studio where the background music for one of his women's pictures was being recorded, he noted that the conductor kept stopping the orchestra to have them play a certain portion of the score again. Mindful of costs, he demanded to know why that particular section was being redone again and again. "It sounded okay to me."

"But it wasn't okay," said the conductor. "The string bass came in two bars early."

"If you say so," Jack said, scratching his head as he turned away, "but I must say, I never heard anybody leaving a theater whistling the bass part."

Gordon was one of the few singers I knew who was truly a musician. Quite aside from his ability to sight-read a score, he understood music. He knew instinctively what was right. No one had to tell him what was a good take and what wasn't. Orchestra conductors didn't have to grasp him by the hand and lead him to a proper performance. As a result, musicians respected him. Conductor Carmen Dragon thought Gordon was a genius.

Gordon worked hard at his craft. He bragged that he was the world's greatest singer, but he never really took his voice for granted. He honed it. "Breathing is the key," he told me. "You exercise the breathing. Thirty in, thirty out. And you do your E's. He, he, he. Me, me, me. Ye, ye, ye. On the E, the tongue is most relaxed."

Frank Sinatra said much the same thing. "When I vocalize," he told me, "I imagine a little ladder. Each note has to get on that ladder and go up."

Lena Horne was also a conscientious vocalizer, as was Peggy Lee. All of these singers, because of their hard work before going on stage, were able to hypnotize their audiences.

Because of his discipline and preparation, Gordon had little patience for those who were not disciplined and prepared. He liked singing with Doris Day and Kathryn Grayson. But he said that because of their range, he had to constrain his. He could go from high baritone, to baritone, to bass, and even could encompass the tenor, so he felt thwarted by demands that he forgo the melody and do the harmony.

Gordon found singing with Doris Day difficult because Doris had an aversion to rehearsing with the orchestra. In musicals, the songs were recorded and then played back during the actual filming, with the singers synchronizing their mouth movements with the sounds. It's called lip-synching. Recording of the songs was known as "laying down tracks." Curiously, for one who had been a band singer before coming to Hollywood, Doris would have a bad case of stage fright in front of an orchestra. To cope with it, she stood behind screens that concealed her from the band—the first singer to do so. Today, it's common practice.

Gordon found Jo Stafford a delight. A genuine artist, Jo knew what she was doing. "That lady," Gordon exclaimed to me after a recording session with her, "can actually *read* music like me!"

Certainly, I was no match for him. Mercifully, in our act I didn't have to be. My strength was in comedy, in my impressions. It turned out to be a winning combination.

The magnitude of the success of our act was signaled when we were booked to appear in the Empire Room of New York's Waldorf-Astoria Hotel. "Everything in the Empire Room," noted a guidebook, "is of the highest elegance—the music, the dance floor, the service, the cuisine, and the show. If you seek entertainment that is smart, viands that are savory, and ambiance that is sumptuous, you will find that combination here."

The food *was* fabulous. Whether choosing a *duck bigarade* or *filet mignon* unequaled anywhere, diners were likely to finish their meal with *Café Brulot* elaborately produced by blending hot coffee with cinnamon, clove, and orange peel—spiked with a jigger of *Courvoisier*.

Because we did our shows at 9:15 P.M. and midnight, we had a great deal of time on our hands during the day. Living at the Waldorf at the time were the Duke and Duchess of Windsor. Running into them frequently in hallways and elevators, we became friends. While Gordon and the Duke went golfing, the Duchess and I sipped tea in her suite.

For the transplanted English girl whose tony English accent had enchanted Louella Parsons, being so close to members of British royalty had the potential for being a heady experience. My dad was a fervent royalist but I was made aware that the Duke had given up being King of England to marry a twice-divorced woman. As I had not been able to forgive Gene Nelson for divorcing my friend Miriam, I could not, in my heart, forgive the Duke for casting aside the British crown for Wallis Simpson. He had done so, he had declared during his abdication address, for "the woman I love," but whenever I was in their company, I asked myself, "Does he ever say to himself, 'Was it really worth it?'" I never realized I would ask the same question of myself.

In addition to afternoons golfing with the ex-king, New York offered Gordon opportunities to spend time with many of his male friends—Mickey Mantle, Joe DiMaggio, Casey Stengel, newspaper reporter Jimmy Breslin, and Toots Shor, the legendary "saloon keeper" whose place was on West Fifty-second Street, an easy walk from the Waldorf. A mecca for the great and near-great among baseball, football, and basketball players, boxers, and other sports figures, Toots's bar could accommodate a hundred customers at a time. It was also a spot where a drinking man could find another willing to make a bet.

While Gordon was fraternizing—and drinking—I spent many afternoons catching the new Broadway shows and some left over from last season. Even if Gordon hadn't preferred to belly up to the bar at Toots Shor's, he probably wouldn't have gone to the theater with me. Usually the experience bored him or simply made him impatient with what was happening on stage. He didn't care for plays that dealt with "problems" or had people in the cast who didn't fit their roles. He would put up with such shows as long as possible, then walk out.

He had done so smack in the middle of a preview of *The Sound of*

Music. Having made up his mind that a middle-aged Mary Martin was just too old to be playing a girlish nun, he hiked after the first act, although he did concede to Ockie Hammerstein later that evening that the show did have "a couple of good songs in it" and that the musical would probably be a hit. Oscar just smiled at me and winked.

At opening night of *Cat on a Hot Tin Roof*, he turned to me and whispered, "I'm not gonna sit through this." He promptly got up and left, softly singing, "Fags and cancer, fags and cancer," to the tune of "Love and Marriage."

Faced with the prospect of having to endure scenes of drug-taking and pills in *Sweet Bird of Youth*, he crawled past a row of stunned people in the loges. When Alfred Lunt and Lynn Fontanne were playing a couple whose ages went from twenty-three to eighty-eight in *I Know My Love*, Gordon took one look at the short pants Alfred was wearing to make himself appear younger and headed for the aisle.

Departing in the midst of *Death of a Salesman*, which starred his good friend Lee J. Cobb, Gordon said to me, sotto voce, "I'll meet you at the bar at Sardi's."

Appalled, I said, "But what will I say to Lee?"

Gordie answered, "That's where I always meet him."

For me, going to the matinees while Gordon was off somewhere drinking, Broadway was a smorgasbord of first-rate choices. High on my list was a musical that had opened in September. *Take Me Along*, starring Jackie Gleason, was based on Eugene O'Neill's *Ah! Wilderness*. I'd been told that it was a tour de force for Jackie. I wasn't disappointed. Jackie was precisely the great actor I had always believed him to be and, of course, the prince of comics. I also wanted to catch Dick Van Dyke in *Bye, Bye Birdie*, a riotous send-up of rock and roll in general and Elvis Presley in particular. Then I went back to see Dick Rodgers and Ockie Hammerstein's *The Sound of Music*.

Even if it hadn't been a monster hit, I would have led the cheering. It's a theatrical custom—showfolk boosting other showfolk. It's called "peppering the audience" and goes all the way back to the beginnings of the theater. Sinatra's publicity man did it to foster the mob scene of screaming bobby-soxers who nearly tore down the Paramount Theater on Broadway when Frank was appearing there in the early 1940s. Ed Sullivan had done it to hype Elvis's first appearance on Ed's Sunday night TV show. Charles Lowe, the devoted husband of Carol Channing, always organized groups of their friends into cheering squads for Carol's shows.

"C'mon, kids," he would say enthusiastically, "let's go put Carol over!"

For the performer onstage, it's comforting to know that there's someone out there who cares. So what if it happens to be a bunch of your friends? No one wanted to have to repeat Sarah Bernhardt's awful words: "God, how I hate matinee audiences. They're either asleep or Anglo-Saxon!"

Returning to the Waldorf those afternoons, I would let my high heels sink into the plush carpets of a hotel whose very name signified grandeur. I thought, "How did I, a girl from England, get here?"

However it happened, I was happy.

Wrapped in fur, bejeweled, dripping with pearls, crossing the grand entrance to one of the most elegant hotels in the world. I swam in the moment, understanding what Evelyn Waugh intended to convey in *Brideshead Revisted* in the words of Charles Ryder, "I was drowning in honey, stingless."

Kay Thompson had written a series of wildly popular books about a little girl who lived at the Plaza Hotel. Her name was Eloise. Because I had become so closely associated with the Waldorf, my friends began calling me "Eloise of the Waldorf." Though never as mischievous as Eloise, I was just as ubiquitous, meeting all the residents.

I often encountered Noël Coward. I had met him when I was a child in England but he continued to pop in and out of my life in Hollywood, in Las Vegas, London, at many a party, during weekends at mutual friends' country homes and at the Waldorf. Gordon and I liked him very much and felt quite honored when he asked us to fill-in for him in Vegas when he had a severe case of laryngitis, a malady familiar to those who entertained in air-conditioned palaces of the resort in the heart of the Nevada desert. We called it "Vegas throat."

During his periodic swirls through New York, Noël insisted that we go to the opera with him. Sitting next to Noël Coward at the Met was always a memorable experience. As the curtain rose, he invariably drew the libretto from his pocket and followed along from the first note to the last, often singing along.

The man who ran the Waldorf-Astoria was Claude Philippe, but on weekends he prided himself on playing the host at his country home. Edith Piaf drove us to one of these informal gatherings at which

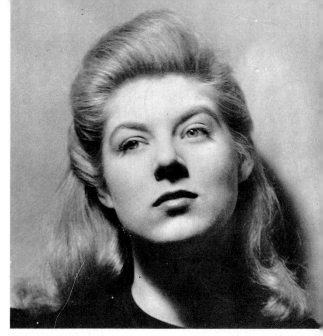

My sister Paula (left, age 5) and I (age 3) were brought to America from England by our father, Louis Albert Stephens, an automotive engineer, and our mother, Winifred Baker Stephens.

At the tender age of fourteen, I played Viola in *Twelfth Night* touring with a fifth-rate Shakespearean Company, but my debut in Shakespeare had been seven years earlier as Cobweb in *A Midsummer Night's Dream.*

Third from the right, I am joined by other fledgling actors in the Millpond Playhouse production of *The Trojan Horse,* including Jeff Chandler (second seated figure from left), future comedian Jack Carter with a balding wig and goatee (fifth from right) and twenty-year-old Albert Gordon MacRae, already claiming the title of "world's greatest singer," with slicked-back hair, crossed legs, and off-the-shoulder toga.

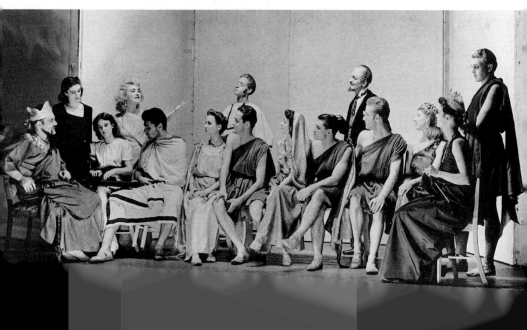

Here I am in *Helen of Troy* (second from left) at the Millpond Playhouse in Roslyn, Long Island.

On the day we became engaged (April 1, 1941), I was sixteen and a half years old. Gordon was twenty. The photo was snapped at Gordon's mother's home in Scarsdale, New York.

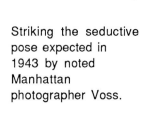

Striking the seductive pose expected in 1943 by noted Manhattan photographer Voss.

Because we did not drink or smoke, Go[rdon called us] "the Malted Milk Kids." Here's the idea[l night out at a ball] game. I was the bat girl. That's Heathe[r...]

(Above left) When Gordon and I got married, he was touring the Midwest with the Horace Heidt orchestra. Our honeymoon consisted of one afternoon, then it was back on the bus for a series of band engagements that took us from Ohio to Texas and back north to Chicago.

(Above right) U.S. Army Air Force cadet and Mrs. Gordon MacRae, Houston, Texas, Christmas, 1944. I lived with Meredith near the air base in a converted garage.

(Below) Until I could join Gordon in Texas where he first was stationed in World War II, we kept our love alive by telephone and through letters. This one from me anticipates the birth of our first child, Meredith.

[A]lthough I had dreamed of becoming an [a]ctress, in 1953 I was content to be Mrs. [G]ordon MacRae and the mother of Meredith [l]eft), Gar, and Heather.

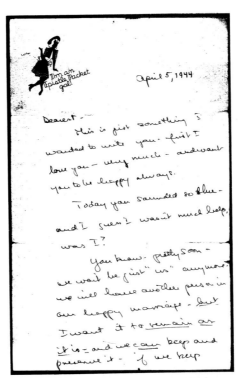

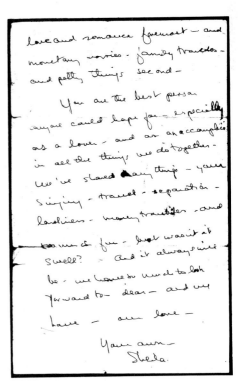

This picture of Gordon and me with his mother Helen MacRae was taken at her summer home in Spring Lake, New Jersey, in 1947, shortly after the birth of our second child, Heather.

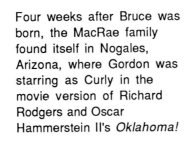

It was a boy, Robert Bruce, born April 1954. PHOTO COURTESY MOVIE WORLD

Four weeks after Bruce was born, the MacRae family found itself in Nogales, Arizona, where Gordon was starring as Curly in the movie version of Richard Rodgers and Oscar Hammerstein II's *Oklahoma!*

At the 1956 premiere of *Oklahoma!* in Oklahoma City: Gordon, Shirley Jones, Jay C. Flippen, me, Piper Laurie (not in the movie), and Gene Nelson.

In this 1958 photo, I'm in the triangular number between
Gordon (with Bruce on his lap) and my father, Louis Albert
Stephens. That's Meredith next to me. Beneath the white
saucer-style is my mother, Winifred Baker Stephens. Next
to her in the cloche bonnet is my aunt, Elsie MacDonald.
Closest to the camera are Heather (with a girlfriend) and
Gar, mugging outrageously with two of his pals.

The occasion of this gathering of Hollywood families was
Dinah Shore's popular 1950s television show. With Dinah are
her children and her actor-producer husband George
Montgomery. Movie legend Roy Rogers and his wife Dale
Evans are surrounded by their own and adopted children.

As Gordon's problems with alcohol increased, Christmases were not always so merry. Sometimes Gordon was absent. In this seasonal picture-taking, a friend had to stand in for him. The image of the smiling Gordon was later superimposed.

Merry Christmas *circa* 1960 from (clockwise from top left) Bruce, Gar, Heather, and Meredith.

Christmas 1962 with the MacRaes, (from left) Bruce, Gar, Heather, Gordon, me, Meredith. Displayed behind us are oil portraits of the children. Don't be misled by the small white tree. The one with the gifts beneath it was always the largest Gordon could find.

Claude's personal guest was Grace Kelly, then undisputed darling of the movies and reigning queen of Hollywood, known by the insiders as an actress who fell in love with her leading men. The hush-hush talk was of affairs with Bing Crosby, Bill Holden, and Ray Milland. Probably because of these liaisons, Gordon didn't like her. He could be very righteous about people having affairs, so he was not exactly thrilled about having to spend a weekend at Claude's and knowing that his host would be going to bed with Grace.

While she was a very good-looking young woman, she was not as beautiful in person as she appeared on the screen. If film stardom rested on a magical, mystical relationship between a face and a lens, she obviously had what it took. But the first time I met her with Bill and Joy Orr, she looked rather plain in a polo coat, sweater, and skirt. I liked her right away. She had lovely manners, which was always my measure of a person. I had been raised not to talk about sex, politics, and religion, and to behave myself. Clearly, Grace had been brought up the same way. Her father started out as a bricklayer. He worked hard and made his fortune in construction in Philadelphia so that his children could have a fine home on the Main Line.

Weekends at Claude's were fun and relaxing. In the daytime we walked in the woods, swam, went boating, or just relaxed in a chair with a good book. Nights were lively with conversation and wit around the dinner or card table. On those fresh-air sojourns, I had the pleasure of the company of Jean-Pierre Aumont, Oleg Cassini, Truman Capote, and, on visits from his upstate New York farm, our old friend Jimmy Cagney, who seemed to be just as happy as I was to talk to people for whom there were other interests in life than the movie business.

One of the first friends I made in Hollywood was Ann Warner, Jack's beautiful wife. I relished every occasion to have tea or lunch with her or to sit up late in one of their five homes listening to her talk about the machinations of the movie world. The place they owned in Palm Springs was a special favorite of mine.

The desert spa for the rich and famous wasn't discovered by the Hollywood crowd. The Cahuilla Indians were the first to find recuperative value in its hot springs. The Spanish named the area Agua Caliente in 1774. A century later it became a stop on the new Southern Pacific Railroad as it cut its way through Coachella Valley. A sleepy little hamlet with one store and a roadside inn, it remained a dusty byway until the 1930s, when Ralph Bellamy and Charles Farrell found it and decided that it was just the spot for people who wished to escape from the pressures of movies and play polo. The word spread and, as the 1939 *WPA Guide to California* put it, "a new highway was cut through, Los Angeles and New York promoters got to work, and the modern town sprang up almost with the speed of a movie set."

Ralph and Charlie organized the Racquet Club, to be a member of which was a mark of grace and a badge of elitism. It was at the club that I sat in the sun and watched Monty Clift doting on a tennis-playing young lover. There Lucille Ball and I consoled one another about troublesome husbands, and there Ann Warner spun tales and doled out advice for my amusement and benefit. On an afternoon in the mid-1950s, she was especially voluble about a new singer who had hit Hollywood and the country rather like a tornado. "His name is Presley," she said, wrinkling her nose as if a bad odor had wafted her way. "Elvis Presley. Elvis! Did you ever hear of such a name? But, honey, the kid is fabulous. Sex exudes from every pore. He's being managed by Colonel Tom Parker. There's a man to avoid. Truly crude. And bigoted. Every third word from his mouth is 'nigger.'"

The Warners had two lovely daughters, Joy and Barbara. Once, Jack and Ann asked us to look after fifteen-year-old Barbara while they dashed to Hollywood on business. "It's just overnight," Ann said. "Frankly, Jack wouldn't trust anyone to look after Barbara but you." Honored and flattered by Jack's confidence, I agreed to baby-sit, although there was little about Barbara that fit the description "baby." She was quite mature-looking, tall and leggy, and very precocious. Late that night when I peeked into her room to be sure everything was all right, I was flabbergasted to discover she was gone. Past midnight, Barbara walked in the front door. "Where have you been, young lady?"

"Riding a motorcycle with Marlon Brando," she answered blithely. "You're *not* upset, are you?"

In my ear I heard the whisper of sixteen-year-old Sheila Stephens: "Think of it! Marlon Brando! If you were fifteen and knew that you could go biking with Brando, wouldn't you? And before you answer no, think back to the Millpond Playhouse and your crushes, William Saroyan and Richard Brooks!"

"No, Barbara," I said, "I think he's fabulous!"

For the Hollywood establishment, Brando and his style of acting were a shock. Asked about him, Greer Garson, whose image of refinement and grace was exemplified by her portrayal of Mrs. Miniver, replied, "Actors like him are good, but on the whole I do not enjoy actors who seek to commune with their armpits."

When James Dean hit town and was greeted with much the same head-scratching and wonderment as Marlon, Jimmy reportedly observed, "You know, I think I've got a chance to really make it, because in this hand I'm holding Marlon Brando saying, 'Fuck you!' and in the other hand saying, 'Please forgive me,' is Montgomery Clift. 'Please forgive me.' 'Fuck you!' And somewhere in between is James Dean."

As the nature of acting and actors changed, starting in the 1950s, the attitude of the press and the public also changed. Once upon a time, people in the movies were put up on pedestals and idolized, protected, and nurtured in their public image by studio publicity departments. Stars—and, indeed, all celebrities—became targets of opportunity. An industry of scandal magazines and sensation-seeking newspapers bloomed. Anyone was fair game, and few who were the quarry did anything about it, suffering the slings and arrows in silence.

A bygone star whom I came to know well was Marion Davies. Her career spanned two decades, 1917 to 1937, but she did not make an easy transition to sound because of her squeaky voice and occasional stutter. These impediments notwithstanding, she starred in several talkies under the protection of her mentor and lover, newspaper titan William Randolph Hearst. Smitten by Marion when she'd been a Ziegfeld Girl in 1916, Hearst promised to make her the world's greatest movie star. Millions were spent on her films by Hearst's studio (Cosmopolitan)—so much money that the pictures couldn't possibly turn a profit. The public and Hearst's newspaper competitors, as well as movie exhibitors, resented what later would be called "the hype." The fictional newspaper mogul Charles Foster Kane's drive to make an ordinary singer into an opera star in Orson Welles's scathingly satirical *Citizen Kane* was based on the Hearst-Davies relationship.

By the time I sat down with Marion for tea, she was Mrs. Horace G. Brown. Her film career was over; her last picture, *Ever Since Eve*, had been made in 1937. When I met her, I expected to meet a "dumb blond" actress. I was wrong. Charming, smart and savvy, she brimmed with

riveting tales of the Golden Age of Hollywood when she and Gloria
Swanson reigned as the queens of the silver screen.

"Gloria and I always had to have our little fun," she said with
twinkling eyes. "One of our favorite games was to creep up on a couple
who had slipped away to..." She paused dramatically, her face wreathed
in an impish smile. "There is no delicate way to say what they were
doing," she said. "We sneaked up on them while they were *screwing*.
Then, at the—shall I say, climatic moment?—we pelted them with ice
cubes!" Covering her mouth with a gloved hand, she giggled. "We really
did act like naughty kids!"

Recalling that the radio evangelist Aimee Semple McPherson had
denounced her for having a bar in her home, Marion frowned. "It was so
unfair! Everybody had a bar. But mine was *not* a bar. It was a soda
fountain!"

On that first of several sunny afternoons as my guest, she regaled me
with stories of hobnobbing with British royalty. "So boring," she said,
"like being in a prison." Carried back in time to fabulous weekends at
Hearst's castle at San Simeon, I heard names dropped like autumn
leaves, always judgmentally, George Bernard Shaw, Benito Mussolini,
Bing Crosby, Clark Gable, Robert Montgomery, Ray Milland, everyone
who was somebody, including Hitler.

She liked Leslie Howard, although he had been "a naughty little boy."
And Gary Cooper. "What I liked about Coop," she said, "was that he
liked to eat as much as I did. He also told me that if a horse loves you,
you're a good person."

I had always been intrigued by the fact that so many of the successful
people I met, like Marion Davies, had come from modest beginnings.

Jimmy Cagney rose from the hard streets of the Lower East Side of
New York and the just-as-hard neighborhoods of the Upper East Side's
Yorkville. His little trick of jamming his elbows against his sides and
hitching up his pants, he told me, came from seeing a man who
habitually made that gesture as he hung around a New York street
corner.

Frank Sinatra had been a poor Hoboken boy. Jackie Gleason sprang
from a broken home in Brooklyn and got his "education" in pool halls.
Buddy Hackett was born in Brooklyn and apprenticed to his upholsterer
father. Jack Cassidy was from Queens, New York. Shirley Jones hailed
from small-town Pennsylvania.

Jack Benny started out poor as Benjamin Kubelski, born in Waukegan, Illinois. Like the rest of the world, I said prayers and cried after Jack died in 1974. The world lost a man it admired for his comedy. I had lost a friend who cared for me not because I was Gordon's wife but as Sheila, herself.

The Warner brothers also came up the hard way. They were three of twelve children of Polish Jews who could never possibly have dreamed that Little Jack, the youngest, one day would have his name emblazoned in big, bold letters at the start of every movie he and his brothers made. Among the most important men in the very lucrative business of movies, Jack Warner and his brothers necessarily dealt with the top bankers in America. Pictures were made in Hollywood, but the deals that provided the financing they needed were sealed in the stuffy suites of financiers in New York and Boston. One of those was Serge Semenko, president of the Bank of Boston. I met him when Jack Warner invited Gordon to join him and his son-in-law, Bill Orr, for a cruise of the Mediterranean on Semenko's 160-foot yacht.

Neither Gordon nor Bill would go without his wife. Bill was married to Jack's daughter Joy, so Serge could hardly have refused, though his attitude made it clear to me that he wanted it to be strictly stag. So Joy and I joined the excursion. Serge's wife also came along, perhaps with orders from her husband to "keep the girls occupied." I was hoping to test my newly acquired skill of scuba diving that I'd learned from the extremely patient Philippe Cousteau, Jacques's brother, but the seas were rough and chances for underwater exploring limited as we headed through the Strait of Bonifacio between Sardinia and Corsica.

Serge was a Turk who acted as if he were a pasha and his attractive American wife, Joan, a mere member of a harem. While we were dining on the second evening at sea, she rather offhandedly suggested that we put into a port the next morning and explore. Serge's face flushed with anger. "I'm the captain of this ship," he said, tugging hard at one of his wife's earrings. Wrenching away his hand, he tore off the earring. Blood spurted over the front of her dress. Flecks spattered the tablecloth. "And don't you forget it," Serge said.

Horrified, I jumped up. "Excuse me, but I simply can't stay at this table." I ran to my cabin. Restless with my outrage, I paced the large, exquisitely outfitted accommodations. Except for the rocking of the yacht, I might have been in a small French inn. The furnishings were antiques, the bed commodious. Bookcases lined one wall. Hoping that reading would calm me down, I picked a volume at random. Untitled and slender, it fell open in my hand to reveal pornographic photos of children. "God, how disgusting!" I shouted as I threw the book down. Later, I told Gordon that I wanted to get off in Naples.

"What's the matter?" he asked. "We're all having such a good time!" With a smile and a wink, he sat on the bed. "C'mon. Let's make love. We've done it in just about every other place imaginable! Now here we are on a yacht in the middle of the Mediterranean! So Semenko's a real jerk. The hell with him. What do we care about him? We've got us."

He held open his arms. "C'mon, Sheersie, let me rock you in these to the rockin' of the boat!"

In the morning, I found out that what I wanted mattered as much to our host as had his wife's opinion at dinner. "Oh no, we shan't dock for a while yet," Serge said, imperious in his blue blazer, white trousers, canvas deck shoes, and captain's cap. "You English women are all alike," he said with a sly smile. "In the bed you are either as tame as lapdogs or as vicious as an alley cat. Which are you?"

"Both," I said coldly as I walked away.

When we finally went ashore at Porto Vecchio, the quaint, ancient, sun-drenched Corsican town and inlet on the turquoise blue Tyrrhenian Sea was aglow with ochres and golds of the palette of some landscape painter from long ago. I rushed ashore in sunglasses, a loose blouse with short sleeves, and crisp white walking shorts. Almost immediately, an old woman in a long black dress shook a scolding finger under my nose. She screamed, "*Prostituta! Prostitueé.* Why you come here dressed like prostitute?" As if being told in three languages that I looked like a whore weren't bad enough, another old woman spat at my feet.

"Gordie," I said, clutching his arm, "I think I'd better go back to the boat and change clothes."

Many years after that impromptu lecture on the propriety of one's clothing, I was dressed to the nines on a blustery evening in 1966 when Sammy Davis, Jr., took a few of his friends to Count Basie's club in Harlem. It was the last of the clubs that had flourished there from the Roaring Twenties until racial animosities of the late fifties and early sixties put an end to the uptown odysseys of white fun-seekers from downtown. In addition to Sammy and me, the party included Frank Sinatra's pal Jilly Rizzo, Jack Cassidy, comedian Jack E. Leonard,

Laugh-In producer George Schlatter and his wife, Joline, newsman Lee Leonard, and Jack Carter and a stunning blonde, Brigitte Ingeborg, who were staying in the apartment of Nat King Cole.

Had Brigitte not been wearing a fur coat I would have felt embarrassed about the fabulous sable draped around my shoulders. The sable was valued at $56,000. Even though it was not insured, I left it with Brigitte's on a pile of coats on a table.

Hours later, Jack and Brigitte left the club while the rest of us lingered to enjoy the music of Grover Mitchell.

After the last set, I went to retrieve my coat. But the only coat to be found was not mine. The sable was gone, apparently stolen. The club manager was apologetic. "I'll call the police right away," he said.

"No, don't," I told him. "I really don't want the publicity." I knew what fun the newspapers would have, writing stories about a rich, white, jet set dame dripping in sable and jewels slumming in Harlem.

Sammy spoke up. "Leave this to me."

"Oh, Sammy, what can you do?" I asked in despair.

"What I can do is get on the phone to the Count, and we'll spread the word to certain 'brothers' about what happened. Once it gets out on the streets that the Count and Sammy are not very happy, you'll have your coat back. Be patient, babe. Keep the faith."

The next day I got a call from Brigitte Ingeborg. She was very upset. "Sheila, this is so embarrassing. Your coat was not stolen. I have it. I picked it up by mistake."

"So it was *your* fur that was taken," I said, relieved that I wasn't going to be out nearly $60,000.

"The coat that was stolen was the one I wore, yes," she told me, "but the coat was not mine. It belongs to Maria Cole. I borrowed it. But unknown to Maria, her name is inside."

With this turn of events, it was even more urgent that the coat be found and returned, hopefully in such a way that Maria would never know what had happened. So I called Francis Albert.

In dealing with the recovery problem, Sammy Davis and others had put out word that if the coat were given back, a "reward" would be waiting and no questions would be asked. But implicit in the offer was the likelihood that no questions would be asked.

The reward was to be several hundred dollars left in a paper bag under a table at the Count's club. I provided the cash.

Sammy phoned that night. "The coat's back," he said gleefully. "I'm bringing it over to your place."

He arrived with a brown shopping bag.

When I took out the coat, he recognized that it was not sable. " Hey, what's going on here? If this guy thinks he can get away with this scam, he is sadly mistaken."

"Hold your horses, Sammy," I said, laughing. "Let me explain what happened."

Before I finished the story, he was almost hysterical with laughter. "Sheel, babe," he said, brushing aside tears, "this is the kind of thing that could only happen to you. Now everyone thinks *you* had an affair with Nat!"

Back then, it seemed that Sammy would go on forever, and nothing pleased me more than to watch him cavorting in concert appearances with Frank Sinatra and Dean Martin shortly before his death from cancer in 1990, long after the sixties had slipped into the mists of memory and "Name the members of the Rat Pack" was part of trivia games played by Reagan-era young people for whom the sixties were but a passage in history books.

My individual identity began emerging during the 1960s when I shared the stage with Gordon at the Waldorf. Columnists wrote about *me*. Among them was Harriet Van Horne. She noted that I had turned mimickry into an art by providing a biting, satirical glimpse into the personalities I imitated.

Unaccustomed to such public attention, I worried. All the dark descriptions by my Hollywood friends of the pitfalls of fame sprang to mind.

I read the New York reviews: "…greatest team to hit New York since the Yankees"… "A show for all seasons"… "Talent for days…"

Throughout my life, wiser people than I had told me that I should not look at success any differently than failure. Now I was required to put that advice to the test.

By most people's measure, I had it all—a husband whom I adored, my children, success, money (what the IRS allowed us to hold onto), gorgeous clothes, furs, a fabulous suite in the Waldorf Towers.

What those people did not know was that while I was emerging as "Sheila of the Waldorf" and becoming such an extrovert, Gordon was withdrawing ever deeper into himself.

He spent afternoons drinking at Toots Shor's or in the Waldorf's Bull and Bear, often returning barely in time for the first show. He seemed utterly bored.

Having learned that boredom contributed to his drinking, and that talking to him about his problem was futile, I did all that I could to keep him interested in his work. The way to achieve that, I decided, was to change the act to give him new material that would excite him. For my part, I wanted to leave no doubt that the star of the show was Gordon MacRae.

I centered my thoughts on creating a truly dramatic opening in which Gordon would be free to move about the stage. He simply could not be tied to a microphone fixed to one spot.

Nor did I like the idea of his using a handheld mike that had a long, trailing, encumbering cord. What he had to use, I decided, was one of the new battery operated mikes with a built-in transmitter. That would permit him to roam freely. Terribly expensive, the mikes also required special equipment.

This meant making some structural changes in the Empire Room, including moving an antique crystal chandelier. Permission for such a drastic alteration had to come from Conrad Hilton. "That's quite impossible," declared the world's most famous hotelier.

"Ah, hell, Conrad," Gordon blustered, "what's the big deal? If you're afraid of the cost, I'll pay for it!"

Like so many before him, Conrad ultimately could not resist Gordon's charm. He allowed the changes.

The number which relied on the wireless mike was "Lonely Town," from the hit Broadway show and movie *On the Town*. The blues melody and downbeat lyrics were exactly the opposite of what audiences of the Empire Room had come to expect in a show-opener. Shattering this melancholy mood from the opposite side of the stage, I entered in a magnificent gown, singing "The Sweetest Sounds" from *No Strings*, Dick Rodgers's daring musical in which in 1962 he made his debut as both composer and lyricist.

The audiences of the Empire Room were the most sophisticated we had ever played for, mostly New Yorkers, and accustomed to and even jaded by the best. Furthermore, we could expect to see the biggest names in show business out front, "dropping in to catch the act."

When Jerry Lewis came back to our dressing room, he had tears in his eyes. "Sheila, when Gordie looks at you and you look at him as he's singing 'I've Grown Accustomed to Her Face,' I was bawling like a baby. It's just perfection. I looked at the audience and I could see what they were thinking: 'Those two people are going to be together forever.'"

Although Henry Fonda came to see me to say how much he had enjoyed the show, I soon found out he had other things on his mind. Visiting me in our suite in the Waldorf Towers, he asked, "When Gordon goes out drinking, what do you do with your time?"

I didn't know what to say. Hank was an old friend. I decided to be honest. "I cry a lot," I said.

"That's not good for you," he said, drawing closer. "Why don't we go out together?"

"Basin Street in an hour?" I said, pulling away. "Peggy Lee's my favorite."

I had always thought Hank was a very sexy man, but I had never known him to be so direct. No doubt, countless women would have been swept off their feet in such a moment, but the only man on my mind at the time was Gordon.

He stood in the doorway. "You're good at bluffing in a bridge game—but it's not working now. Meet you later."

When charming, funny Peter Sellers visited, it was obvious that he, too, wanted to get me into bed. But what interested him was making love to me when I was "transformed." He told me, "I think I most want to fuck you when you're Lena Horne. It's that look you have when you walk out."

For my impersonations of the women I referred to as "my girls," I had a glorious wardrobe—more than thirty changes of costume in each show. Comedian Don Rickles, renowned for his brash style of put-down humor, did a joke about me in his own act. "Have you ever seen the Sheila MacRae doll?" he asked. "You wind it up and it changes clothes."

When Peter Sellers opened my closets, he exclaimed, "Oh, this is fabulous, fabulous." And one of the screen's greatest comedic actors held up gowns and hats, decreeing which was funny and which was not.

Other great comics also came backstage to see us after the show. Milton Berle and Jack Carter were eager to give us advice on the act's jokes. Get rid of this one. Drop that one. Here's one that's much better! They're gonna love this one!

Another friend who raved about my impressions was Sammy Davis, Jr., a brilliant impressionist himself. He liked my work so well that when he had his own TV show a few years later he asked me to come on as a guest to do a dozen or so impressions with him. During that week of rehearsals, we had the opportunity to talk about our shared talent for taking on the characteristics of other people.

"We take the essence of the people we impersonate," Sammy said, "as well as the sounds of their voices." He was right. A singing impression was by far the easiest thing to do. Tackling someone like Jackie Kennedy was another matter.

When I told Sammy about my earliest attempts at impersonating people and related my telling the woman with the big chest how lucky she was to be able to rest her teacup on her bosom freeing her to eat cake with both hands, he howled with laughter. "You know, Sheel," he said, "I think that just proves that people like you and I are born with a good ear for doing impressions. I guess I'm a lucky guy and you're a lucky lady."

The reviews of the Empire Room show were overwhelming. "Incredible show with just Gordon and Sheila." "Sheila MacRae has perfected this to a science." "Sheila *is* Gordon MacRae's secret weapon."

Thrilled by the notices, I showed them to Gordon. "Gordie," I said, "isn't this terrific? Aren't you happy?"

"That's newspaper talk. Don't believe any of it."

Shocked, I verged on tears. "I thought you'd be pleased. If I had known you wouldn't be happy, I'd never have suggested the new show. We could have stayed with the old, saved a hundred thousand dollars. I only wanted the best for you. Gordie, please, tell me—what is it you want?"

He looked at me for a long, agonizing moment. "What I'd like," he said, "is to quit and be a golf pro."

Of course, quitting was out of the question. We had to go on working until all the debts were paid.

White House Invitations

IN THE 1960S, GORDON AND I began our odyssey on behalf of the IRS; "business" dictated that we put on the "show" for the largest possible audiences—the greater the receipts at the box office, the sooner we would pay off what we owed. That meant playing in huge outdoor theaters and under the canvas of big-top circus tents.

Filling them wasn't going to be any problem. While Gordon's standing in Hollywood had been undercut by his problem with drinking, the American public knew only the Gordon MacRae they had seen in *Oklahoma!* and *Carousel* and on television. They adored him. And why not? He was handsome. He was a fine singer. And now, here he was appearing in person, in their hometowns. On stage with him was his wife—funny, pretty, and obviously devoted to him. For audiences across the country, we personified not only the American dream of success, fame, and fortune, but the ideal American family. They flocked to the shows.

We toured first in the musical we knew best, *Bells Are Ringing*, followed by *Guys and Dolls*. This fabulous show had opened at the 46th Street Theater on November 24, 1950, and skyrocketed into Broadway legend. Adapted by Jo Swerling and Abe Burrows from a story by Damon Runyon, with lyrics and words by Frank Loesser and staging by George S. Kaufman, it was, in *Times* critic Brooks Atkinson's words, "a sassy, irreverent love poem of low-life in New York." Its colorful cast of gamblers bore such names as Sky Masterson, Nathan Detroit, Big Jule, Benny Southstreet, Harry the Horse, and Nicely-Nicely Johnson. One of the masterworks of the American musical theater, it ran for 1,200 performances and was made into a movie starring Marlon Brando as Sky and Frank Sinatra as Nathan. Vivian Blaine recreated her smash Broadway performance as "Miss Adelaide," one of the greatest comedy roles ever written for a woman.

Drawn from one of Runyon's more obscure yarns, "The Idyll of Sarah Brown," the plot of *Guys and Dolls* consists of a pair of wacky love stories. The main story is about Sky Masterson, a big-time, big-betting night owl, and Sarah Brown, who runs the Salvation Army's Save-a-Soul Mission. But it is the other romance, between Nathan Detroit and Miss Adelaide, that provides the musical with its most hilarious and touching moments.

Operator of "The Oldest Established Permanent Floating Crap Game in New York," Nathan has been engaged to Adelaide, a singer at the Hot Box nightclub, for fourteen years. It's their oft-postponed nuptials that prompt "Adelaide's Lament," a number that is both pathetic and uproarious. It begins with a sneeze and a labored dissertation on psychosomatic respiratory ailments. "Just from waitin' around for that plain little band of gold," she sniffles in explanation, "a person can develop a cold." A born-and-bred New Yorker, Adelaide pronounces "person" as "poyson" and "word" becomes "woid." "And foythugh maw," she coughs, "just for stallin' and stallin' and stallin' the wedding trip, a poyson can develop *la grippe*."

It's a real showstopper, but it's only one of three big numbers for Adelaide. With the "Hot Box Farmerettes," she belts out "A Bushel and a Peck," which shot to the top of the Hit Parade (but wasn't in the movie), and the hilarious "Sue Me." "You promise me this, you promise me that," she protests in the duet with Nathan. "All right already," moans Nathan. "Serve a paper and sue me, sue me." Of course, it turns out happily for Adelaide as Nathan finally succumbs.

When Gordon and I took *Guys and Dolls* on the road, he was Sky. I was Adelaide, a woman with whom I certainly empathized and sympathized, although Adelaide had only one problem with her man Nathan—his gambling. Struggling to cope, she was never hopeless. "Marry the man today," she sings. "And change his ways tomorrow." It's the poignant but vain dream of every woman in love with an alcoholic or compulsive gambler, or both. Of course, *she* can't change him. He must change himself.

Although *Guys and Dolls* proved to be as successful for us as *Bells Are Ringing*, we still had a long way to go—more touring, more theaters-in-the-round with their capacious seating, more tents. Facing a third season on the road, we both wanted fresh material. Someone suggested *Redhead*. This was the 1959 musical that had starred Gwen Verdon and Richard Kiley on Broadway. A most unusual story for a musical, it was very loosely based on the murderous exploits of Jack the Ripper. The music was by Albert Hague. The book was by theatrical veterans Herbert and Dorothy Fields and David Shaw and Sidney Sheldon (destined to be the master of the game when it came to writing not only *I Dream of Jeannie* but also blockbuster novels that were made into movies and TV miniseries). The redhead of the title is Essie Whimple, who works for her aunt in the Simpson Sisters' Waxworks. She meets handsome Tom Baxter, whose lady partner in a strongman act was murdered. They soon discover that Essie is also being stalked by a killer. By the time the villain is caught, Essie and Tom have fallen in love. These macabre doings had been directed and choreographed by Bob Fosse.

I was excellent at comedy and impressions, quite good as an actress, and pretty good as a singer—but a dancer I wasn't. Could I learn? Should I dare to attempt to fill Gwen Verdon's shoes?

"Hell, yes," was Gordon's answer. "Sheersie, you can do *anything!*"

Teachers of Christian Science had told me that by faith I could do anything. I had also believed throughout my life that one should live life by saying not "I can't" but "I'll try."

We broke in the show (and my dancing) in Connecticut, where we made some changes aimed at shifting the focus of the story to the star everyone was coming to see—Gordon MacRae. Reviews in Connecticut were quite good. Buoyed by them, we went on to open in Framingham, near Boston, in a tent, with Boston's most influential theater critic, Elliot Norton, out front. Retired now, he told me on the phone recently, "If you need help call."

In the timeless phrase (now a literary cliché) of Victorian author Edward Bulwer-Lytton: "It was a dark and stormy night." The rain was torrential. Ceaseless thunder shook the earth. Lightning turned the sky to daylight. For a story about murder and terror, mysterious shadows, and lurking figures, the "effects" were perfect. Everything was proceeding nicely. The audience had loved our duets, "Just for Once" and "Look Who's in Love." Late in the second act, we had a third—"I'll Try," a playful exchange between Essie and Tom in rapid-fire musical repartee much like that of the dueling lovers, Frank Butler and Annie Oakley, in *Annie Get Your Gun.*

"You're better than all the bankers and lawyers and green-grocers and princes and kings rolled into one," extols Essie in a breathlessly exuberant Cockney.

"Me?" booms Gordon. "No!"

At this dramatic moment, Mother Nature took her job as our provider of sound and lighting effects way beyond the script with the loudest clap of thunder I had ever heard, a lightning bolt that rent the tent's roof, and a gust of wind that ripped away canvas like laundered lingerie torn from a clothesline. The orchestra scrambled away in a mad dash for cover for themselves and their instruments, leaving behind their music, much of which was swirled away by the wind.

The stage was drenched, making impossible any attempt to go ahead with the last scene. As its title in the program promised, "Chase and Finale" was full of action and involved the entire cast. A challenge in normal conditions, it would be too and dangerous on a wet stage. Soaked with rain, the audience didn't know what to do. Should they leave or stay? Might the show continue? Could it continue?

Obviously, it couldn't, but I wasn't about to let people who had paid their admissions go home disappointed. "Now isn't that just the story of my life?" I said in Essie's Cockney voice. "Poor little me! Poor Essie! Everything goes against me, doesn't it? Here I am about to get my man and down comes the bloomin' rain!"

The audience roared with laughter.

"You've all heard the term 'raincheck,' I'm sure," I said, yanking off Essie's red wig and letting my long blond hair tumble loose. "Well, Gordon and I are giving you all a raincheck. We'll mend the tent and arrange to have better weather, and you'll all come back and find out who our murderer is."

When we resumed performances, Elliot Norton returned. He gave us a great review and said of me, "We've found a second Gertrude Lawrence."

From Massachusetts we went to Chicago and then to Milwaukee, where I became the only person in the history of show business to be upstaged by... well, you shall see! As all my comedian-friends advised me, "Never telegraph the punchline!" Again, we were in an outdoor theater, in the round, surrounded by a packed matinee audience. After the glowing Elliot Norton review I was feeling quite secure as I readied myself for the second act. It opened with "Look Who's in Love," sung with Gordon. It's the moment when Essie and Tom realize they're in love. During the scene, the audience was always hushed and attentive.

But this afternoon as I moved around the stage in a lavish, low-cut ball gown with a long train, the audience in each section that I passed giggled. Why? I wondered. Was there something amiss with my costume? Had something slipped? Was I revealing more than cleavage? Furtively, I glanced down. No, thank God, I thought, it isn't them! The giggling was now a low murmur of laughter. Had my wig slipped? Discreetly, I touched my red hair. It was fine, with every curl in place. I smoothed my hands over my skirt, front and back. Nothing wrong there. I knew it couldn't be my makeup. The laughing was now riotous.

I shot a glance at Gordon. He was also laughing.

Now people in the front rows were stabbing the air with the fingers and pointing behind me. Turning, I saw, at last, what had upstaged me. Sitting on the train of my gown, blithely content and unconcerned, gazing up with glistening black eyes, was a small skunk.

What to do? One wrong move and this little black-and-white show-stopper could do more to clear a theater than any storm. "Go slow, Sheersie," Gordie advised between laughs. "Slow" was the thing, I decided, moving cautiously toward a long sloping aisle and an Exit sign. Outside, I maintained my easy pace, knowing from the drag upon the train of the gown that my unwelcome costar was following along. Crossing a patch of grass, I came to the edge of a woods and waited, motionless as a figure in the show's waxworks. A moment later, cued perhaps by the rustle of the breeze in the trees or simply bored, the skunk waddled off.

Fleeing back into the theater, I dashed down the aisle and flung myself into Gordon's arms and the embrace of thunderous applause.

In January 1964, we took our nightclub act to the Bing Crosby Golf Tournament. Played against the ruggged seaside cliffs and hills of Pebble Beach, California, and one of the most glamorous sports events in the world, the Crosby tournament also served as a setting in which powerful men pursued beautiful and sometimes powerful women. The other game being played was gossip. Everyone knew about Gordon's drinking.

"How is he?" they asked.

"He's fine," I lied.

Only one person asked how *I* was. The individual was Francis Albert Sinatra.

He was attending the tournament with an entourage of buddies that had become known as "the Rat Pack." Veterans of the rough road of show business, Sammy Davis, Jr., Peter Lawford, Joey Bishop, and Dean Martin were stars in their own right by way of the movies, television, records, and clubs. Yet they'd fallen into Frank's orbit like moons around a great planet. In the dawning sixties, when being famous seemed to justify anything, they were celebrities. Francis Albert Sinatra was "chairman of the board."

Dean Martin had come to Pebble Beach for the Crosby tournament. He was reading the film adaptation of Lillian Hellman's *Toys in the Attic* and asked me what the stage play was like. "A mood piece—terrific and sad," I told him.

"Well, I'm starting the movie after my last round of golf."

In 1958 he starred in *The Young Lions*, with a pair of movie heavyweights, Marlon Brando and Montgomery Clift. Great in that film, by 1962 he rated as a number one actor.

Despite all the movie credits to his name, none of Dean's roles compared to the challenge he was facing in *Toys in the Attic*. He asked if I had heard of an actress named Wendy Hillerman "or something like that." Her name, I explained, was Wendy *Hiller*. In addition to this great British stage and film star, the cast included Gene Tierney, Geraldine Page, and Yvette Mimieux. Dean did well playing opposite these talented women, and he succeeded in many subsequent dramatic roles such as *Some Came Running*, but I think he had the most fun with the Rat-Pack films.

Gordon liked Dean because he was a golfer. Dean was also a drinker, but despite the image he cultivated as a boozer, he was not a drunk.

"Gordie spills more than I drink," he said to me jokingly—with no way of knowing how much the well-intended humor hurt me.

I liked Dean for his genuineness, though he could cross the line into bluntness, as he did when I was rehearsing for our show at the Crosby tournament. "Hey, Sheil," he shouted, "do you know what a guy with a ten-inch cock has for breakfast? Well, *I* had bacon and eggs!"

The joke wasn't meant to be mean-spirited, and Dean knew me well enough to know I wouldn't take it that way. The person who was offended was Frank Sinatra. As the band snickered, he spoke up. "Hey, watch it," he protested. "This is Mac's lady here!"

Touched by his concern, I suddenly saw Frank in a new light.

Peter Lawford was another of the Rat-Packers. Born in England, Peter had been in movies since 1931, making his debut at the age of eight. For MGM in the 1940s and 1950s he had been given breezy, romantic, playboy roles, including losing Judy Garland to Fred Astaire in *Easter Parade*. Ironically, the fame that eluded Peter in his movie career came to him as a result of marriage. His wife was Patricia Kennedy, the sister of the President. Because of Peter's connection to the Kennedys, it was inevitable that the Rat-Packers would come out strongly for JFK in the 1960 election.

I also supported Kennedy. Gordon was a Nixon man—a true, dyed-in-the-wool Republican. Naturally, our differences were thoroughly debated—but only at home. Gordon didn't believe in performers taking public stances politically. Nor did he care for any suggestion that his wife might do so.

Loyal to him first and foremost, I did not go out onto the hustings on behalf of JFK, as so many of my friends were doing. However, even if I had wanted to hit the campaign trail—and if Gordon had given me the green light—the plain, hard truth was that Gordon and I had to be out on the road on our own behalf. We still had to work out our dismal, crushing financial plight.

While the campaign trail carried Kennedy to the White House, the road Gordon and I were following led us back to New York and the Empire Room. Wanting, always, to keep my part of the act fresh and "relevant," as the people of the sixties liked to say, I introduced a new face to "my girls." In her pillbox hats and French-designer gowns and with that little, husky, breathless voice, how could I not have included Jacqueline Kennedy?

Inevitably, JFK heard about it and wanted to find out for himself if my Jackie was as riotous as he had been told. We were invited to go down to Washington for several weeks at the Shoreham Hotel.

"Good lord, Gordie," I said with a shudder. "I can't possibly do Jackie with the President sitting at the back table."

"Why the hell not?" was his response.

With an anxious, darting glance toward the President as I began doing Jackie, I saw him grinning broadly. The next morning, basking in the newspaper raves, I was lounging alone in our hotel room. Gordon had gotten up early to go golfing. The phone rang. "Mrs. MacRae," said a woman, crisply but nicely, "the President is calling."

"Sheila, I just wanted to tell you how much I enjoyed the show lahst night." No mistaking the voice, the Harvard accent. "Lahst night!" This was no joker on the phone. This was the President of the United States, John Fitzgerald Kennedy.

My hands were shaking. My throat, dry. Had I any voice at all? Would I just stand there, unable to speak? Mercifully, I found words. "I'm so pleased you liked it, Mr. President."

"Your, uh, imitation of, uh, Jackie was, uh, terrific."

"Oh, I was so afraid you'd be offended."

He laughed.

"You took the jokes about you pretty well. I was watching you. And I can't express what it means to me that you're taking time from your busy schedule to call. I just wish Gordie were here! But he's playing golf."

"That's a Republican game. Eisenhower had a putting green built out behind the Rose Garden. Jackie's going to have it torn up, part of her grand design to bring grandeur back to the White House. Nixon's a golfer, too, and just as bad at it as he is at politics, I hear." He laughed again, a satisfied little chuckle. "If Gordon is getting in eighteen holes," he said—cautiously, I thought—"he's not likely to be back in time to join you for lunch, is he?"

"No, I don't expect so."

"Too bad. A beautiful woman shouldn't have to eat lunch alone. How'd you like to come and have lunch with me at the White House? I'll send a car."

"That's very kind of you, Mr. President, but I couldn't."

"Why not?" He sounded surprised. "I'm talking about you and me. Just the two of us. Very, uh, discreet. Quite, uh, intimate."

A chill ran through me. I had flashes of memory—Henry Fonda visiting me at the Waldorf: "When Gordon goes out drinking, what do you do with your time?" A mind's-eye glimpse of Peter Sellers. The Hakim brothers and their proposition by way of Gary Cooper's wife.

Into my head sprang memories of so many other men over the years, each with come-on looks and bedroom eyes.

"You're very flattering to ask, Mr. President," I replied, "but I'd feel awful if I were to have lunch with the President of the United States and Gordon couldn't be there to share such a privilege and an honor."

In a long silence that followed I was afraid he had hung up.

"I hope you do understand," I said urgently.

"Yes, of course," he said, sounding not at all like a man who understood.

A few months later I ran into JFK's press secretary, Pierre Salinger, who then was with CBS. "Sheila," he said, chortling, "you're one of the few women I know who actually turned down an invitation to go to bed with John F. Kennedy."

That aspect of Kennedy was hushed up during his thousand days as President, with all the deftness of the Hollywood studios stifling stories about the peccadilloes of movie stars. The truth, came out only in the years after his death. A book by Judith Exner, a woman who had been a lover of Mafia boss Sam Giancana and of Frank Sinatra, revealed liaisons she had with JFK in White House bedrooms.

Hurtful to Jackie, I'm sure, and a shock to the American people, sniggering headlines blared from the front pages of supermarket tabloids about the playboy President's affair with Marilyn Monroe, arranged by Peter Lawford.

I met Marilyn years before she burst onto movie screens as the quintessential Hollywood goddess. Taking an acting class in the early 1950s given by Michael Chekhov, I noticed a pretty, curly-haired girl in a polo coat. She was very intense. "Hello," I said. "I'm Sheila."

"I'm Marilyn," she replied

Over coffee after class, she told me about herself and her dream of becoming a movie star. She had made her debut in 1948 with a bit part in *Scudda-Hoo! Scudda-Hay!* (in which all of her close-ups had been left on the cutting-room floor), followed by a leading role in a low-budget musical, *Ladies of the Chorus*. A period of unemployment followed during which she posed nude for a calendar that sold a million copies after she rocketed to stardom.

Opinions of her acting talent varied. Some people gave her the back of their hand. Constance Bennett said, "Marilyn Monroe! There's a broad with her future behind her." Producer Darryl F. Zanuck thought she was temperamental and not very fit. "Wave a script in front of her face," he said, "and she comes down with a cold." Clark Gable, who costarred with Marilyn in *The Misfits*, his last film, said, "I have never been happier when a film ended." Tony Randall thought she was absolutely talentless.

But most people who worked with her saw magic. Anne Bancroft was in one of Marilyn's early films, *Don't Bother to Knock*. "It was a remarkable experience," Anne said. "It was one of those rare times in Hollywood when I felt that give-and-take that can only happen when you are working with good actors." Thelma Ritter, who played Bette Davis's assistant in *All About Eve*, adored Marilyn. Filming *Gentlemen Prefer Blondes* with Marilyn, Jane Russell found her to be far more intelligent than people gave her credit for.

So did I. In our classes together I thought she was wonderful.

Much of the criticism of Marilyn stemmed from her inability to show up on time. Lateness was chronic. Everyone complained, but few did so to her face, except Laurence Olivier. An actor being late was something Larry was not prepared to accept. After keeping him cooling his heels on the set of *The Prince and the Showgirl*, a tardy Marilyn felt the bite of his ire. "Why can't you get here on time, for fuck's sake?" he demanded.

"Oh," Marilyn replied. "Do you have that word in England, too?"

Apparently, the result of deep psychological problems, the Monroe tardiness was not limited to the set. She was constantly late in her private life, as Gordon and I discovered during the romance between Marilyn and Joe DiMaggio.

An old friend of Gordon's, Joe asked us to look out for Marilyn on an overnight flight, to meet her for lunch and talk shop. This was well before the era of jet travel, when night flights from California offered sleeping berths. Except for a brief stop in Chicago for refueling and, as Gordon put it, "to pick up the racing sheets," we had been in the air for at least ten hours. In New York at last, we were eager to get off the plane and into town where Marilyn was to rendezvous with Joe. Before landing, Marilyn had gone into the lavatory to prepare herself to be seen in public. She was there for what seemed to be hours, oblivious to the fact that she was keeping not only Gordon and me waiting but also the airline crew who were eager to service the plane.

That same day, she was more than and hour late in arriving for lunch at Toots Shor's. She kept us waiting again and Joe DiMaggio, too.

Exasperated, Gordon grumbled, "She's such a jerk."

Although neither Gordon nor I worked with Marilyn, she did use her voice in Gordon's act. To deal with his unwillingness to learn lines and cues, I had written the act so that Gordon would be told what to do next by an offstage voice. For this purpose I recruited our friends, including Jeff Chandler, Jack Carter, Kirk Douglas, and Rock Hudson. After seeing the show at Cocoanut Grove, Sidney Skolsky, her escort, asked if she might be the voice.

Hearing her little whisper, Gordon was not happy. "Geez, I could hardly hear her," he complained. We used her only once.

Serious about her acting, Marilyn decided to study with Lee and Paula Strasberg at the Actors Studio at the same time I was observing—having been encouraged to get to know the Method by Rod Steiger. I felt it was a smart move for Marilyn, and I believe her experience with the Strasbergs permitted her to overcome the dumb-blond stereotype and emerge as the fine actress one sees in her later films.

In 1955, she returned to Hollywood to make *Bus Stop*, directed by Joshua Logan. "I treated her with respect," he said. "I found the poor thing had been treated like a tramp all her life. People yelling at her, 'Come on, Blondie, lean over, wiggle your rear.' Yet she knew everything there was to know about a camera."

When I saw *Bus Stop*, I thought she gave a poignant, fantastic performance.

Of her work in 1959's *Some Like It Hot*, director Billy Wilder said, "Making a picture with Marilyn Monroe was like going to the dentist. It was hell at the time, but after it was all over it was wonderful. The greatest thing about Marilyn Monroe is not her chest. It is her ear. She is a master of delivery. She can read comedy better than anyone else in the world."

Although never close, Marilyn and I saw each other around town from time to time, usually at parties given by mutual friends. Unlike me, she did not care much for socializing. "I've never been very good at being a member of any group," she said. "More than a group of two, that is."

The psychoanalysis of Marilyn Monroe has been treated in countless books, articles, and television programs, so no more need be said here, except to note that I felt deeply sorry for her and wished I could do something. Of course, we now realize that she was probably beyond help.

Sammy Davis, Jr., dismissed the stories that surfaced about her after her death. "A number of guys came out of the woodwork claiming all sorts of things about her," he said. "But she was no whore. She was unhappy and insecure. She was an extremely caring and sensitive person who was easily bruised."

When I learned of her death, I was not surprised, but I do not accept the explanation that she had committed suicide. I believe she accidentally overdosed on the sleeping pills and other drugs that had become her only source of escape from the terrible burden of being Marilyn Monroe.

Nor do I believe the theory that she was murdered in order to cover up her sexual relationships with President Kennedy and Robert Kennedy.

The President had had a long affair with Judith Exner but no one harmed her, even though we have learned that, bordering on panic, JFK's brother Robert took steps to protect Jack from the scandal that would have exploded if it became known that the President had been sleeping with a woman connected to "the Mob."

When the President decided to ban Frank from "Camelot," it may have hurt and disappointed Frank, but it couldn't have surprised him. Rumors and innuendo about his being "in" with mobsters, that it was sheer gangster strong-arming which had fostered his career, were nothing new to Frank. He did not deny that he knew underworld figures. "I know a lot of those guys," he said. "People say to me: 'Why did you have friends in the mob?' I say, 'I was not *friends* with them.' When the Copacabana was open, there wasn't one guy in show business who didn't meet them there. Let them buy you a drink. So I've stopped trying to explain that to people."

Everyone I know has met and spoken with certain notorious figures, because nightclubs are a common ground for all people.

Nonetheless, the millions of people who read Mario Puzo's *Godfather* or saw the movie leapt to the conclusion that Frank was the inspiration for Italian crooner Johnny Fontaine, who was bought out of his big-band contract after Don Corleone made Johnny's bandleader boss "an offer he couldn't refuse" and whose movie career was launched after a producer found a horse's head in his bed.

The Sinatra exile from the White House continued under President Lyndon B. Johnson. While Frank and the Rat-Packers had fit in quite well, for a time, with the stylish inner circle that held sway in

Washington before November 22, 1963, they were not Johnson's cup of tea. Champagne and caviar had been superseded in the White House by cans of diet root beer, chili, and slabs of Texas barbecue.

Replacement of "the New Frontier" by "the Great Society" did not mean that glamour was banished entirely from the Executive Mansion. The East Room still welcomed gala gatherings and glittering entertainments put together by Lady Bird Johnson. It didn't mean that Gordon and Sheila MacRae and their sophisticated Empire Room show were unwelcome. We were invited to perform at a "Salute to Congress" being staged by Hugh O'Brian. I was thrilled. Gordon was not. "I don't think I can put up with going down there again, Sheersie," he said, "so let's just send Hugh our regrets. Okay?"

"We can't do that, Gordie. It would be a terrible insult to Hugh, not to mention the President. This isn't some benefit that Jack Warner arranged and that you can just decide to skip. This is the President. It's an honor, a tribute to our show. To you. To me."

"Aw, hell, if you're gonna put it that way..."

For me, taking the show to Washington was not a simple task. Because of the many different impressions which I did in the act, I had lots of gowns to pack—trunks filled with them. That meant going to Washington the day before we were to appear in the East Room. Because all Gordon needed was his tux and a cowboy hat for songs from *Oklahoma!* he could wait until the day of the show to come down.

When that day arrived, Gordon didn't. He'd simply vanished. I faced two choices. Either I informed the White House that the show would have to be canceled or I found someone to go on in Gordon's place. Metropolitan Opera star Robert Merrill was also appearing in the show. Desperately, I turned to him to fill in for Gordon. "I'll be happy to," he said, "but I don't know the words." Songs from *Oklahoma!* were not in Bob's repertoire.

"Don't worry," I said. "I'll write them out and you can hide them in your hat."

Bob looked at me as if I were mad. "What hat?"

"This one," I said, thrusting Gordon's cowboy hat into his hands.

My explanation to the audience was that Gordon had been taken ill. The audience was disappointed but sympathetic. In a difficult and trying situation, Bob was wonderful, of course. The show was enthusiastically received.

Dancing followed the entertainment with music provided by the U.S. Air Force Orchestra, handsome in their dress-blues. I had heard that not only was President Johnson a good dancer but no party he gave could end until he'd glided across the floor with every woman in the hall. Presently, my turn came. "Sheila, darlin'," he said, taking me into his long arms, "you are the prettiest woman in this room." When the dance was over, he held onto my hand. "C'mon, darlin'," he said, "I'm goin' to take you on a tour of the White House."

Terribly self-conscious and feeling more than a little embarrassed by the President's abandoning wife and guests for me, I left the East Room, tugged along by his insistent hand. It was a grand tour of the first-floor public rooms and a peek into the Oval Office, then into the private elevator to the second floor's mixture of public and private chambers. Finally he pushed open a door and whispered, "This is where your President sleeps."

Never at ease in someone else's bedroom, I had real qualms about entering this one.

"Come on in," he said with a wink. "Don't be shy."

I stepped into the room—barely.

Closing the door, he asked, "How come your hubby isn't with you?"

"As I said at the beginning of the show, he was taken ill."

He crossed the room and stood by the bed. "I hear he's a drunk."

"You shouldn't listen to rumors, Mr. President."

"Hell, honey," he said, dropping onto the bed, "this town thrives on rumors."

"So I've been told," I said, forcing a smile.

"It's beyond me," he said, loosening the cummerbund of his tuxedo, "how a man could turn his back on a woman like you."

I stiffened. Nervously, I clutched my pearls. "Gordon has not turned his back on me."

"Maybe so, but he ain't here," said the President, smirking. He patted the spread. "Come away from that door and come sit by me, darlin'."

"I don't think so."

"You're woman enough for two men," he said, stretching wide his arms. "Secret Service man's guardin' the door. There's no way anybody'll disturb you and your President."

I realized that Lyndon Johnson had heard about our shaky marriage, and I was in no position to judge anyone's morals or habits, so I calmed myself down. "Mr. President, you may not believe this, but it has been interesting"—and I opened the door to find two Secret Service men with outstretched hands.

The next day in their coverage of the event, the Washington and New York newspapers wondered where the President had disappeared to for eight minutes. Now they know.

I was often teased for what Lucy Ball called "my proper English way" of looking at things, and it was true that as a result of my background and upbringing, and my strong religious beliefs, I could be downright prim at times. What was right was right, and there could be no equivocation. I heartily concurred with my eighteenth-century country-man, Edmund Burke: "The only thing necessary for the triumph of evil is for good men to do nothing." And, he ought to have said, women!

My friends Peter Lind Hayes and Mary Healy had been witnesses to my sense of outrage taking wing on a balmy evening in New York in 1956. As a husband and wife team, they'd been well known in the early days of television for witty and sophisticated shows. Unpretentious and charming, they were also theater critics, a pair of real all-around-the-town first-nighters—Peter with his owlish black horn-rimmed glasses and Mary with the effervescence of champagne.

Whenever Gordon and I came to town, we could count on Peter and Mary providing us with front row seats to the Broadway hits and a late supper at the Stork Club. As we were leaving the club on this particular evening, we ran into a brawl. Seeing five men beating up on one person, I waded in on the side of the underdog. Shouting "Stop, stop, stop!" and "Leave that man alone!" I pulled the five away one by one. Rescued, the object of the attack dashed into the street, hailed a cab, and sped off. Breathless, one of the five wheeled around and glared at me. He and the other four were Stork Club waiters. "Thanks a lot, Mrs. MacRae!" he said. "That son of a bitch you were so eager to help got away with all our tips."

During a booking at the Waikiki Hotel in Hawaii, Gordon, our children, a few friends, and I set out for an afternoon of fun in the sun on an outrigger boat. As I was about to step aboard, I saw out of the corner of my eye a man punch another, knocking him to the ground. Writhing in pain, the downed man held a hand to his bleeding nose and screamed, "Help, help!" Bounding ashore, I dashed across the sand and slammed myself against the man who had thrown the punch. He flew backward and fell. "Call the police," I shouted as I sat on his chest.

From the boat, Gordon yelled, "Sheersie, stay out of it. It's none of your business!"

"It is my business," I yelled back. "People just can't go around assaulting other people. I'm not moving until the cops come."

And that's exactly what I did. The man who'd been attacked refused to press charges. The attacker, it turned out, was his brother.

My righteous indignation was never more aroused than by the unfair attack against our friend Ring Lardner, Jr. A fine writer of screenplays, Ring had been a neighbor and a friend when Gordon and I were living on East Fifty-seventh Street. Son of the celebrated humorist, Ring had given up being a newspaperman to go to Hollywood as a publicist at the Selznick studio, then moved into script writing, winning an Oscar at one point for the Tracy-Hepburn *Woman of the Year*.

Suddenly, in 1951, his brilliant screenwriting career was cut off after he was named as one of the group of alleged Communists or Communist sympathizers who supposedly had infiltrated the movie industry and were lacing their films with Red propaganda. Refusing to cooperate with an investigation by the House of Representatives Committee on Un-American Activities (HUAC) into Communist inroads into the movies, Ring became one of "the Hollywood Ten." The other nine were Alvah Bessie, Herbert Biberman, Lester Cole, Edward Dmytryk, John Howard Lawson, Albert Maltz, Samuel Ornitz, Adrian Scott, and Dalton Trumbo.

Among those crying out against HUAC were two singers. Judy Garland begged the public, "Before every free conscience in America is subpoenaed, speak up. Say your piece. Write your congressman a letter! Airmail special." Frank Sinatra said: "Once they get the movies throttled, how long will it be before we're told what we can say and cannot say into a radio microphone? If you make a pitch on a nationwide radio network for a square deal for the underdog, will they call you a Commie?"

Americans did not swamp Congress with the message Judy implored them to send. They were heedless of Frank's warning. Engaged in a cold war with Russia and with American troops fighting a Communist invader in Korea, the United States seemed in no mood to look benignly on any Communists or their alleged accomplices. They were to be fought and defeated, not only on the battlefields of Korea but at home.

Of no mind to listen to the Judy Garlands and the Frank Sinatras, or anyone else raising an alarm, the public nodded soberly in approval of HUAC or gave silent assent to the words of Adolphe Menjou, one of the first witnesses. Looking as dapper and dignified in his double-breasted brown suit as he had appeared in so many movies, Menjou boasted to the members of the committee that he was a Red-baiter who would like to see all American Communists and their sympathizers sent to Russia. "I think a taste of Russia would cure them," he said. The House probe had stirred a horrible witch's brew of differing definitions of liberty and freedom, seasoned by resentment, recrimination, and fear.

My first taste of that deadly concoction came during lunch at the Brown Derby. Gordon and I were dining with Marty Melcher, the savvy agent and manager who was married to Doris Day. As I looked around to see who else was at the Derby, my eyes settled on a familiar figure seated alone in a corner. She was wearing dark glasses, which I thought was odd, but there was no doubt that it was Frances Chaney. She was the wife of Ring Lardner, Jr., and a fine actress who had been sweet to me back in New York when I was pregnant with my second baby, Heather. "Oh, Gordie, look," I said delightedly, "there's Frances."

"Ignore her, Sheila," Marty warned. "She's poison."

Gazing across the room, I saw that Frances had also noticed me. "Marty," I said, folding my napkin. "She's a dear friend, and I certainly am not going to *ignore* her."

As I sat beside her, Frances slowly shook her head. "You shouldn't be doing this, Sheila. Go back to your husband."

Gordon was upset. Jack Warner was furious. But it was Marty Melcher who defined that awful, wrenching period that I was having such a hard time accepting. I saw betrayal, ingratitude, cowardice, and inhumanity. "How can this happen?" I demanded. Marty answered with two words. "It's business."

Instead of being packed off to Russia, as Adolphe Menjou had suggested, the Hollywood Ten were sent to jail for contempt of Congress. Ring served a year. Ten years later, in an article in the *Saturday Evening Post*, he admitted he had been a member of the Communist Party. He had refused to admit it to the committee, he said, because he would have been compelled to name others whom he knew to be Communists. Even then, ten years later, he was unable to get work in Hollywood. He wouldn't be "rehabilitated" until the mid-sixties; and his "comeback" would not be complete until 1970, nearly twenty years after he was blacklisted, with his screenplay for *M*A*S*H*.

Another friend, Larry Parks, was ruined for life. Just five years before HUAC began its investigation, he had been taken into the hearts of movie fans for his stunning performance as Al Jolson in *The Jolson Story* and three years after that for reprising the role in *Jolson Sings Again*. His was a rising star. Then came HUAC. Subpoenaed, Larry appeared. Questioned, he admitted that he had been a member of the Communist Party. As a consequence, he found himself in a tragic no-win situation. He was both despised for having cooperated with the committee and shunned by the studios because of his Communist past. Larry and his talented wife, Betty Garrett, were neighbors of ours. I was heartbroken by what happened to them.

Incredibly, Lucille Ball was called before the committee. But the star of the most popular TV series in the nation was far beyond the power of the committee to hurt her, even if she had stood up and announced that she was "a card-carrying Commie." Of course, she wasn't. Her dying grandfather had begged her to grant his last wish and join the party. She refused.

Outspoken and fearless, as well as gifted with an eye for the ludicrous, she would have laughed if she had attended a Communist meeting. She saw how ridiculous the Marxists were. The adept manner in which she had created *I Love Lucy* and turned it into a gold mine for herself, Desi, and CBS left no doubt that Lucille Ball had a genuine zest for capitalism. She also thought it silly that anyone could believe that a movie could subvert the country.

Lucy was also a realist. Witnessing so many fine careers being smeared and smashed, she didn't want to see it happening to Gordon as a result of anything his wife might do. "I know you are very upset about your friends and that you want to help them," she said to me, "but you have to put Gordon first."

She and Desi had a ranch out in the San Fernando Valley, so we were often there, usually engaged in Lucy's favorite pastime of game playing. One evening, a game more to the taste of our husbands, poker, was underway when someone knocked on the door. It was Larry Parks. He wanted to talk to Lucy.

As she rose to go to the door, Desi caught her by the arm. "No, Lucy, dunt," he said in the accent that America's TV audience found so charming. "You mussint. I know he's your fren but if it gets aroun' that you're talkin' to him it can on'y hurt you and your career."

I was shocked. Torn between loyalty to a friend in trouble and my friendship with Lucy, I remained seated, with anguish and anger that such things could happen in America.

Another actor whose career HUAC destroyed was John Garfield, the ruggedly handsome star of so many Warner films. Never accused of being a Communist but merely suspected of being a sympathizer, he had refused to name those he knew or suspected were Communists. Blacklisted, he never worked in films again. When he died of a heart attack in 1952, his friends insisted that it was the blacklist that brought it on. Yet he had been able to find some humor in his plight.

"I wanted to join the Communist Party, I really did. I tried. Hell, I'm a joiner," said the star of *Air Force*, *Destination Tokyo*, and *Pride of the Marines*. "They thought I was too dumb. I couldn't be trusted."

Sterling Hayden also found something to joke about. "I," he said proudly, "was the only person to buy a yacht and join the Communist Party in the same week."

The blacklisting extended beyond Hollywood to radio, television, and the theater. Broadway actress Anne Revere had been called to testify, refused, and was punished, yet she kept her sense of humor. "What a season this has been," she lamented. "I did a flop play with Otto Preminger, my apartment was robbed, and then I was subpoenaed." After refusing to cooperate with the committee, the only work she could get was doing a one-woman show, readings for women's groups and colleges and stock.

Early in the Red Scare, Barbara Stanwyck had gotten a call from Hedda Hopper concerning Missy's husband, Robert Taylor. "I hear Bob is going to play a Communist in *The Conspirator*," said Hedda. "I think that's disgraceful."

Missy replied, "Who do you want to see in the role, Hedda? Joe Stalin? Get off my ass, Hedda."

Although he did play a Communist agent in the picture, Bob was never accused of being a Communist offscreen. Had he been, it would have been interesting to see if one of motion pictures' giant stars, whose appearance in a film guaranteed box office success, would have been banned from working.

"The terrible thing about being blacklisted as an actress," said Kim Hunter, "was that even though, intellectually, you knew what was happening, you still always wondered whether you weren't being hired because you weren't any good."

Jack Warner and his brothers participated in the blacklist. They were especially sensitive—embarrassed, actually—that one of the films cited as being blatant Red propaganda was *Mission to Moscow*, a Warner Bros. picture. Jack's answer was that the story of Ambassador Joseph Davies's controversial pro-Russian wartime visit to Moscow to meet with Josef Stalin on behalf of President Franklin D. Roosevelt had been forced on Warners by FDR.

Jack's anxieties about Communism in Hollywood went back many years. In 1945 he'd stood on a rooftop of his studio and observed a violent outburst at the Warner Bros. gate involving pickets during a jurisdictional battle between competing union, one of which had Communist support. Grim-faced and fearful, he muttered, "The revolution has come to Hollywood."

As to the charges that the studios kept lists of acceptable and unacceptable people, Jack is said to have cracked, "They'll never find a blacklist at Warner Brothers. Everything is done on the phone here."

To demonstrate to moviegoers that they had nothing to fear from Warners, Jack ordered the publicity department to stage a patriotic demonstration by the people who worked at the studio. A platform was set up and television and press coverage was arranged. Jack's idea was that his stars would mount the stage and profess their loyalty.

Gordon had no problem doing so. "I didn't wear the uniform of the U.S. Air Corps during the war so that everything this country stands for can be torn down by a bunch of Commies," he declared.

I had spirited debates on the issue with him, and our friends who held the opinion that in the United States of America no one ought to be punished for political beliefs spoke out.

Warner Bros. and the other studios unleashed a torrent of strident anti-Communist pictures. *Big Jim McLain* starred John Wayne as a two-fisted investigator for HUAC. It's a film that is unlikely to find its way into today's home video market as part of a collection of Duke Wayne classics. Robert Walker, fond in my memory as a fledgling actor who didn't get a part at the Millpond Playhouse, had the title role in *My Son John*. It was the story of the anguish of parents who discover that their boy has been flirting with Communism.

Frank Lovejoy had the title role in a prime example of these anti-Communist films, 1951's documentary-style story of Herbert Philbrick, titled *I Was a Communist for the FBI*. Philbrick's story then was made into a TV series, *I Led Three Lives*. Starring Richard Carlson as Philbrick, it ran for three years (1953–56). Virginia Stefan, who played Mrs. Philbrick, said the show received many letters from viewers. "It's hard to believe," she said, "but people actually write us and ask us to investigate Communists in their neighborhood." Dutifully, the show's producers passed the letters on to the FBI.

Among the Hollywood celebrities who had cooperated with HUAC's investigation was Ronald Reagan, then the president of the Screen Actors Guild and sincerely worried about a possible Communist takeover of the union. It was at this time, he said later—quite often, in fact—that he began considering a career shift from acting into politics. After spending an evening with Ronnie, talking about SAG business in particular and politics in general, Charlton Heston returned home to his wife with nothing but praise for the head of the guild. "Honey," he said, "we've got a real president." Recalling the incident, Chuck laughed. "Little did I know how prophetic I was."

During the disgraceful era of the blacklist, Gordon MacRae went unscathed. There were no demons or Red devils lurking in his shining past to suddenly surface and tarnish the image of "God's Chosen Boy." The shadows that would gather to envelop him were several years away. First, there would be shining triumph in *Oklahoma!* and *Carousel*. Then the eclipse.

"There are three times in life," Robert Mitchum once said to me, "when it's useless trying to hold a man to anything he says—when he's running for office, when he's in love, and when he's drunk." I'd laughed at Bob's cynicism, but as I journeyed around the country with Gordon to work off our tax debts in the "jet set," "Rat Pack,"

Rehearsing our first musical together, *Bells Are Ringing.*

My dear friend Lucille Ball suggested to Gordon that I join his nightclub act. After seeing us, *Life* magazine wrote "Sheila has made it one of the classiest in nightclubs. Gordon's voice is lush, Sheila's comic gifts are sharp and spirited." Gordon pays a backstage visit during my first solo appearance, in *Born Yesterday.*

In 1960, everybody got in the act as Meredith, Heather, Gar, and Bruce went on the road with Gordon and me in *Annie Get Your Gun.* "A family fling by the MacRaes," wrote *Life.* "A burst of show-business togetherness." LIFE PHOTO BY ALLAN GRANT

When preparing for *Annie Get Your Gun,* we took ourselves and our piano outdoors to practice the show's more rambunctious numbers.

This publicity picture for our appearances at the chic Empire Room of the Waldorf-Astoria in New York seems to bear out *Life*'s description of the MacRaes as "clean-cut family types." What *Life* and Empire Room audiences did not know was that Gordon was an alcoholic and that Sheila was struggling to help him and to keep their family from being destroyed

My impression of Dinah Shore's enthusiasm results in a slap in the face for Gordon and Perry Como. PHOTO COURTESY CBS-TV

Clockwise from top left: I do my impressions of good friend Carol Channing, Zsa Zsa Gabor that I did on the *Ed Sullivan Show* the night the Beatles were introduced, Keely Smith (with Gordie as Louis Prima), and sex-kittenish Ann-Margret. BOTTOM RIGHT PHOTO COURTESY CBS-TV, OTHERS LIFE PHOTOS BY A. RICKERBY

At the 1965 wedding of one of my best friends since Gordon and I first went to Hollywood, Miriam Nelson to Jack Meyers.

In 1963, we played to a packed London Palladium (top photo), in our 1960s image as jet-setters. Our travels took us to spots from the Mediterranean to the Caribbean, where we loved to go scuba diving (bottom photo).

In this picture of Gordon and me with Don Adams and his wife, Cindy, at the Diplomat in 1964, the effects of years of drinking are beginning to show in Gordon's face.

Among Gordon's "drinking buddies" was Jackie Gleason, shown here with Gordon, who is imitating a character on Jackie's TV shows, the "happy drunk" named Crazy Guggenham, played by Frank Fontaine. While Jackie was a legendary drinker, he did not have the serious problems with alcohol that plagued Gordon and ruined his career.

A pet project of mine, SHARE (Share Happily and Reap Endlessly) consisted of Hollywood wives and presented an annual fund-raising show on behalf of needy children. In a Western mood are (from left) Joanie Ehrenberg, Jeannie Martin, Gloria Cahn, Mrs. Alan (Vera) Gordon, and me.

e of my dearest
nds and a great help
ne during Gordon's
king bouts was
rge Cowan. She and
husband, Irving,
ed the Diplomat
el in Miami.

Gordon and I looked on during a SHARE party with a "Wild West" motif (top) as Frank Sinatra appeared to have cast a spell upon Gary Cooper (bottom). PHOTO COURTESY GLOBE PHOTOS

ven though our marriage was in serious
ouble, I tried to keep up appearances
at we were the perfect show business
ouple for this candid shot at the 1965
pening of Eddie Fisher's show at
ollywood's Cocoanut Grove. PHOTO
OURTESY GLOBE PHOTOS

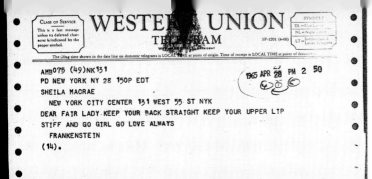

Frank Sinatra and I went to great extremes to keep our romance from becoming public, as in this telegram he sent to me when I was appearing in a New York revival of *Guys and Dolls*.

In a showstopping scene in a 1965 revival of *Guys and Dolls,* Miss Adelaide and the Hot Box nightclub's chorus wowed a star-studded audience with "A Bushel and a Peck." Alan King starred as the marriage-shy Nathan Detroit and I as the lovesick Adelaide who wanted to get him to the altar. PHOTOS COURTESY MISS ALEX JEFFRY

These are publicity pictures. On the left, me in costume for *Guys and Dolls*, 1965. Yours truly in the nautical outfit was shot in Sutton Place home in 1966.

If I look surprised again it's because Frank Sinatra had just caught me off guard by introducing me as "the prettiest girl in New York" to photographers covering 1966's *Paris Match* ball at the Village Gate. Even though Gordon and I were separated, I feared that when the picture appeared in the newspapers he might kill himself. PHOTO COURTESY NEW YORK POST

As Gordon and I guested on *The Sammy Davis, Jr., Show* on NBC-TV in March 1966, Sammy was one of the few show business people who knew that Gordon and I had been separated for five months. PHOTO COURTESY NBC/GLOBE PICTURES

For the 1966 nightclub act devised for me by Bob Fosse, this see-through costume for a number called "A British Bird" was considered daring even for Las Vegas. During preparations for the act, my professional relationship with Fosse (left) turned into a romance. RIGHT PHOTO COURTESY NEW YORK POST; LEFT PHOTO COURTESY GLOBE PHOTOS

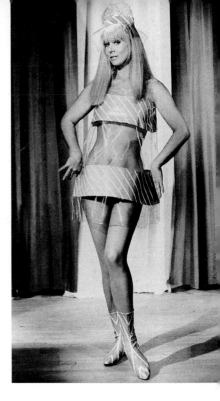

Independent for the first time in my life, I faced the challenge of establishing my own career. Bob Fosse created a lavish nightclub act for me with fabulous gowns and costumes. We had a brief, passionate affair. Bob liked this picture so much that he insisted that I promise not to release "Fosse's favorite photo." I kept that pledge as long as he lived.

This snapshot was made in Juarez in April 1967, minutes after I signed papers divorcing Gordon. I cried all the way back to New York.

"Swinging Sixties," "Camelot" of the Kennedy years, and "the Great Society" and Vietnam years of LBJ, I saw, almost daily, that Bob had been right about putting your faith in the words of a man who's had too much to drink.

SEVEN

The Day the Carousel Stopped

IN ALL THOSE outdoor theaters and tents, on television, in clubs across the country, and especially at the Empire Room I had changed, metamorphosed, as a caterpillar becomes a butterfly.

I was no longer the person Jack Warner had adored because I was not actress. I had left behind the girl Louella Parsons had approved of because I was pretty and could dance at parties. Gone was the shy, shrinking violet who had so little self-identity that she always felt she had to reintroduce herself to people she had seen again and again. "Hello, I'm Mrs. Gordon MacRae," I used to say to people who knew me very well.

I did it so often with Jack Benny that he finally had had enough of it.

Arriving at a party at Danny Kaye's house, I was met at the door by Jack. "Hello, Mr. Benny," I said. "I'm Mrs. Gordon MacRae."

Jack paused—that famous, expectant moment with the blank eyes and the limp hand against the cheek.

"I know already! I *know* who you are."

The voice rose in pitch, just as on the radio in countless duels with Rochester, Phil Harris, Dennis Day, or Mary Livingstone. "Why do you keep telling me you're Mrs. Gordon MacRae? Do you think I don't remember? Well, I *do* remember, so *cut it out*. Gordon MacRae! Big deal! Who do you think he is, God? I say *fuck* this 'I'm Mrs. Gordon MacRae' crap. And if you keep it up, well, fuck you, too." Then he kissed me on the cheek. "Hello, Sheila, my beautiful darling."

Working with Gordon, I had emerged from a shell. We were not Mr. and Mrs. Gordon MacRae anymore. Posters in front of theaters and clubs, the ads in newspapers, and marquees billed us as "Gordon and Sheila MacRae."

But accepting myself as the individual others recognized as "Sheila of the Waldorf" and a new Gertude Lawrence who had raised mimickry to an art was not easy. When and how had this happened? Had I, somewhere out there on the road in one of those storm-whipped tents and skunk-invaded theaters in the round, left my former self behind? Or had I discovered the *real* me?

In trying to answer these questions, I realized that all during my life I had sought escape from reality by resorting to disguises.

Because I had been shy, I would put on an attitude. By finding another character, I discovered I was able to cope with unpleasantness. There was security in being someone else.

As a child, I found comfort with an alias. In taking that ability to transform myself to the stage, I realized that I had become what I'd always been—an actress.

I was never happier than when I was someone else. I now had an identity of my own. I was, at last, myself. I wasn't simply Mrs. Gordon MacRae. I was Sheila MacRae—actress!

While I recognized that I had found out who I was, one aspect of me could not change. There had to be that part of me that always was and always would be Gordie's wife.

I still felt a deep need to help him and protect him from himself and, I hoped, assist him in exorcising the twin demons of alcohol and gambling.

I had been very slow to see, as his mother had when he was a boy, that Gordon's gambling was a fault. I was blind to it. It's a cliché, but love *is* blind.

Betting seemed so much fun to him and we were making lots of money. So what if he lost a little? When he found a reason to make a bet, I perceived nothing troublesome. That he bet on the most trivial things did not concern me.

When we played golf and he said, "Bet you can't make it onto the green in par," I didn't worry why he couldn't just enjoy the sport for itself.

I didn't even get upset when he'd lost the $17,000 to Desi Arnaz on the turn of a card. I blithely dismissed Lucy's warnings.

Only when the tax man came round knocking on our door did I see that his betting wasn't just for the fun of it, that the compulsion was as deeply ingrained as his drinking.

In one very important way, the gambling grew worse. When he drank, he endangered himself. When he gambled, he put all of us in peril because when he lost, it wasn't only *his* money, it was his family's.

A blessed aspect of human nature is the ability of people to find something to make the most dire circumstances bearable. With the funeral comes the wake when the grieving reach out to console one another with memories of the dear departed, almost always by recalling the happy times, the funny things, and the tales that supplant tears with smiles and laughter. We send flowers and cards to the ill. A farmer's barn is blown down by a storm, and neighbors come round to raise a new one and then have a barn dance to celebrate.

Jerry Lewis made people laugh during his annual telethon so they would give money to help the victims of muscular dystrophy. Danny Thomas entertained on behalf of children in need of medical care. Mark Twain said that humans are the only animal that blushes...and needs to. We're also the only animal that laughs. If we couldn't and didn't, our lives would be unendurable. Laughter is God's gift. In coping with Gordon's gambling, I often laughed to keep from crying.

We were appearing in Las Vegas. Our show was over for the night. Gordon had headed for the casinos. Exhausted, I had gone straight to bed. Deep in sleep, I was jarred awake by the phone ringing. It was Gordon. "Sheersie, you gotta come get me," he begged.

"Gordie," I said, half asleep. "Where are you?"

"Jean, Nevada. It's out in the middle of nowhere. I used my last dime for this call. If we get cut off and you have to call me, it's one short ring, two long. I'm stuck here with no way to get back. You have to come and get me."

I was entitled to be angry. He had lost eight thousand dollars. In the taxi I hired to drive me miles into the Nevada desert to fetch my penniless husband in a town so small that it didn't have dial telephones, I had a right to cry. But as the cab drew up to the place where Gordon was waiting, I began laughing. "Good lord, Gordie," I said as he climbed into the taxi, "if Louella Parsons could see us now!"

When Gordon was winning, I tried to wean away some of the money so that if his luck turned, as it always did, he wouldn't be completely wiped out. One night in Las Vegas, he had been on a roll. Chips worth many thousand of dollars were stacked before him. Scooping a handful, I said, "Let me cash these in. I'll keep it with me in our room." The chips came to five thousand dollars. Pleased with myself, I went to bed. My sleep was short, shattered by Gordon rummaging through every drawer. "Just ask me, Gordie," I sighed, "and I'll tell you where the money is, but I do wish you wouldn't. You're just going to lose it all."

"I'm not going to lose, Sheersie," he said, excitedly. "I'm on a streak."

Ten minutes later, he was back. "Jesus, Sheersie," he groaned, "I don't know what happened. I put down the five thousand and I won. 'That's it,' I said. 'I'm done.' I was gonna leave. Then I heard this voice. 'Put this on fourteen.' I should have listened to you, Sheersie. I shouldn't've taken the five grand. Of course, you shouldn't have given it to me."

I thought I might be able to attain some understanding of gambling's hold on Gordon if I were to learn about it. Experts who ran the casino tables were pleased to educate me in the rudiments and the rules. More instructive, however, were the people I observed at the gaming tables and the slot machines. I saw two kinds. Most played for the fun of it. They would come to the games having set limits. They made up their minds about what they could afford to lose. When they lost, they quit. The others were driven. Win or lose, they stayed. Being there was, for them, all. They had to gamble, as an alcoholic has to drink.

The drinking that had wrecked Gordon's movie career now threatened his work on television. We had become regular guest panelists on game shows, including *What's My Line? I've Got a Secret*, and the popular daytime one, *Password*, produced by the team of Mark Goodson and Bill Todman, with the affable Allen Ludden as host.

Because it was a daily show, a whole week's worth of programs was taped at once—five shows a day. On each show a celebrity guest for that week was teamed with a contestant whose goal was to identify a word based on clues given by the celebrity. They then switched sides and the contestant gave clues to the celebrity. It was a race against the clock. Gordon could be very good at it.

But the inevitable day came when he showed up drunk. Although his condition wasn't apparent to the others on the show prior to the first taping, the heat of very bright TV lights exacerbated his condition. He did well giving clues to his partner. They chalked up a lot of points. Then they switched roles. Ironically, the word to be identified was "inebriate."

The contestant said, "Drunkard."

Gordon answered, "Jackie Gleason."

The studio audience howled.

Gordon turned in puzzlement to the audience. "What the hell are you laughing at?"

From the control room boomed the decidedly unamused voice of producer Bill Todman. "Cut! Let's take it from the top."

Unfortunately, everything was downhill after that. By the second taping, Gordon could barely hold up his head or keep his eyes open. He was belligerent and loud, and when he wasn't, he slurred the clues. It was a disaster, publicly and privately. He was dropped from the show, and when word of what had happened reached other TV producers, he was banned from their shows.

How could he have done such a thing? Perhaps it was the old boredom surfacing. These were shows on which he wasn't singing. They had dulling sameness—five shows back to back. A drink or two in advance, he surely must have figured, would gear him up for it, and it wouldn't hurt his performance. Of course, it did.

Performing on television requires exactness. All depends on the placement of the cameras: movements, being precisely at a spot indicated and marked on the floor, saying the words as they appear in the scripts of everyone involved in the show. Spur-of-the-moment changes spell trouble for all actors. A lot of them could be frustrated and even angry with Gordon when he did these things, but no one ever complained, that is, until, onstage with Carol Lawrence, Gordon didn't deliver the exact cue line she was expecting. She filed a complaint with Actors Equity, the performers' union. It was, I believed, unnecessary and demeaning.

While being banned from television was a blow, he still had our nightclub act. We could still knock 'em dead on the road, whether it was under a tent in the suburbs of Chicago or in the plush elegance of a hotel nightclub in Miami Beach.

We scored a huge success at the Deauville. Returning to our suite after our final show, I was hoping that I'd find Gordon as thrilled as I was. Because he worked so hard in the act and was worn out, he often went directly to our rooms immediately after the show, while I frequently lingered with friends who had come to see us. Entering the bedroom, I expected to find him asleep. To my horror, he was sprawled on the floor, a liquor bottle beside him.

Picking up the phone, I called our secretary, Peter Terhune, to help me get Gordon onto the bed. As we did so, we found his skin clammy and his breathing so shallow that it could barely be detected. Neither Peter nor I had ever seen him in such a condition.

Undressing Gordon, I felt a hard object in his jacket pocket. Fishing it out, I found a half-empty bottle of pills. "Oh, my God!" I gasped. "He's tried to kill himself. We've got to bring him around. Peter, help me get him on his feet."

"Call the hotel doctor, Sheila," Peter begged.

"No! I don't want this getting into the newspapers. Can't you see it, Peter? 'Gordon MacRae in drug overdose.'" Peter grimaced, "You could have a problem. Pump his stomach!"

At that moment Gordon opened his eyes. He smiled sweetly. "Hi," he said.

For the next hour or more, Peter and I struggled to keep him awake, holding him under cold water in the shower, supporting him as we walked him around the room, talking to him, trying to get him to speak—everything we could think of to stir him out of his stupor.

Slowly, color returned to his face. His flesh was warm to the touch again. He breathed normally. "I think we can put him to bed now, Peter," I said. "I think he's going to be okay."

Satisfied that Gordon was now in a state of normal sleep, I sat with him for hours. Content that he was not going to die, I lay beside him and was soon asleep myself.

When I awoke in the morning, I found him gone.

Panicked, I called Peter.

"Relax," he said. "Look out the window."

Basking in the sun, Gordon sat on the patio below, blithely eating breakfast.

When I joined him, angrier than I had ever been with him, he kissed me. "Peter told me what happened," he said. "Thanks for saving my life. What would I do without you, Sheersie?"

I peered into that face, that smile, those winning brown eyes. How could I leave this sweet, troubled man?

I wanted to help, not hurt, so I carried on, ever hopeful, always scared. Waking up each day, I was afraid of picking up the morning newspapers and reading that some gossip columnist had published a story of Gordon being drunk.

Worse, I dreaded the thought that he might be the focus of an article in a current magazine that specialized in digging up dirt on celebrities, especially movie stars.

A scurrilous precursor to the scandalmongering supermarket tabloids of the 1980s and 1990s, *Confidential* had burst upon America's newsstands in the fifties. Although much of the content was based on the most spurious hearsay, secondhand evidence, and blatant speculation and innuendo, the magazine had terrorized Hollywood.

Setting the tone for later scandal sheets, *Confidential* traded in sex, taking to heart Alfred Hitchcock's words: "All love scenes on the set are continued in the dressing room after the day's shooting is done. Without exception."

What *Confidential* wanted was to get the goods, not in the gossipy and even romantic style of Louella Parsons or Hedda Hopper, but in the cruelest and most damaging tones.

"It isn't what they say about you," Errol Flynn had said. "It's what they whisper."

Probably no star was subjected to as much scrutiny of her private life as Elizabeth Taylor. "They have called me a scarlet woman for so long," she said, "I'm almost purple."

In *Confidential*'s heyday, those who feared the magazine most were Hollywood's bachelors. They lived in terror that *Confidential* would print that they were homosexuals. "Every month, when *Confidential* came out," recalled actor George Nader, "our stomachs turned." Actor Robert Arthur, a homosexual who was noted for supporting roles as a clean-cut juvenile, was so afraid of exposure that he dated young women and nearly got married.

Publicity agents worked to depict teenage heartthrob Tab Hunter as falling in love with beautiful women. Eager to disspell any doubts about the gender of Tab's romantic interests, a fan magazine promised that he was "ready to bring some girl a wonderful love, a love that must—and will—come soon."

To keep the secret of Sal Mineo's homosexuality, the Warner publicity department had put out stories complete with photographs of James Dean's *Rebel Without a Cause* costar dating starlets.

Stories about Dean having homosexual proclivities had been gossiped about as soon as he arrived in Hollywood. It was said that he had had a number of homosexual roommates in New York. Some people insinuated that he had gotten some of his early parts through sexual liaisons. Lest there be speculation in the press about Jimmy's sexuality, the Warner publicity machine went to great lengths to trumpet a "romance" between him and Terry Moore and other starlets.

I believe he was in love with Pier Angeli and was heartbroken when she married Vic Damone. A promising young star of the 1950s, Pier died in 1971 at the age of thirty-nine of an overdose of barbituates.

In the hope of concealing Rock Hudson's homosexuality and diverting snoopers who might be looking for a sensational scoop for the next issue of *Confidential*, his studio did arrange a wedding for its handsome leading man, succeeding in covering up Rock's gay life until he lay dying of AIDS in 1985.

Next to sexual peccadilloes in the back-alley appraisal of *Confidential's* editors was drinking among stars. With Gordon so vulnerable, I breathed a sigh of relief whenever a new copy came out without a Gordon MacRae story. I suppose it was inevitable. It happened when we were appearing in Las Vegas. I was getting ready to go onstage and chatting with friends. The phone rang. A friend was calling from New York. I expected to hear loving wishes for a successful show. "Sheila, I've got bad news," she said. "You should hear it from one who loves you before you find out from someone else. There's going to be a story about Gordie in *Confidential*."

"About his drinking?" I asked grimly. "What does it say?"

"No, Sheila, it's not just his drinking. It's about Gordie being with a prostitute."

I fainted. For days, I could not walk or eat. I was vomiting constantly.

Everyone pleaded with me to get immediate medical attention, but their voices were a blur to me. All I could hear was the voice on the phone—distant, disembodied, as if from another world. I picked up my Bible and told Gordo I was ready to go on.

Gordon appeared just before showtime. Drunk. Rising from my chair and crossing the dressing room, I confronted him. "You're dead, Gordie," I said, not in anger, but in despair. "You are *dead*. The husband I had is dead!"

Blinking watery brown eyes and with a bemused half-smile, he muttered, "What the hell's that mean?"

What had I meant? How could I have been so emphatic, so smugly certain, so didactic? Who was I to judge his soul? How dare I? These are proper questions. Yet they did not occur to me at the time. I spoke out of years of religious teaching that had instilled in me the conviction of the righteous. I spoke with the confidence of what some wag once defined as "a Christian holding four aces." In my view, I'd honored the Ten Commandments. I'd been devout, praying many times a day. I could be forgiving of his drunkenness. In my role as the wife of an alcoholic, I was well rehearsed. But this was different. This was sexual infidelity. This was—sin.

"Don't you understand?" I pleaded. "Because of what you've done, you won't go to Heaven with me."

As always, Gordon was abject and remorseful. Apologies and promises to mend his errant ways that I had heard before spilled again from his mouth. He knew all the words that had proved so winning so often, but suddenly, for the first time in my life, that golden voice sounded off-key.

In the following weeks, I couldn't concentrate. My hands trembled. I wept often. I prayed incessantly. Friends were convinced I was having a nervous breakdown. Finally, I turned to one of the great Christian Science practitioners, Martin Broones. "Sheila, you can't expect to bring about the Kingdom of Heaven by yourself," he explained patiently. "You have the wrong idea about living your faith. You should be concerned with taking care of yourself. Concentrate on your own thinking and leave everyone else's alone."

To his credit, Gordon did try to deal with his drinking by turning to Alcoholics Anonymous, and when he was sober I would rejoice in having the old Gordon back in my arms. Appreciating the work of AA, we helped to promote their activities by entertaining at large meetings and conventions in Toronto and San Francisco. It was a time when celebrities did not openly admit to being alcoholics, so we were warmly welcomed. Being among people who had the same problem as Gordon, I looked upon these occasions as an opportunity for me to learn.

James French, an old friend, attended one of these gatherings in San Francisco. He was a very successful lawyer and one of Gordon's favorite golfing partners. As an alcoholic for eight years, he had sunk to the depths, ruining his practice and his standing in the legal profession. Through AA, he came back, but he harbored no illusions that he was cured. "There is no cure," he told me. "An alcoholic will always be an alcoholic. That's why he must always be on guard. The simplest thing can set loose the demon."

That very day, he said, he tottered perilously at the brink. "I was in a cab going down Nob Hill toward Fisherman's Wharf to have lunch with a client. When we came to a red light the cab stopped. The window was down. I heard faint music from a jukebox. I looked out the window to see where it was coming from. There was a bar on the corner. A little breeze came up from the bay. And as it wafted through the window, I caught the slightest whiff of the aroma of beer from that little bar. At that moment, I desperately wanted some of that beer. 'Hey, driver,' I yelled. 'Get me the hell out of here!' The guy looked at me as if I was nuts. 'The light's red!' he shouted, 'I don't give a damn about the lousy light. If you get a ticket, I'll pay for it. Just *go*.'

"Thank God he did, Sheila, because I was that close..." He held up a hand, the thumb and forefinger almost touching. "*That* close to falling off the wagon. The smell of that beer! I could almost taste it. Can you believe it? Well, it's the truth."

I felt that a veil had been lifted. "Now I see," I said. "That explains it. Something like that must be what happened to Gordie that time on the FDR Drive."

Jimmy's eyes narrowed with concern. "Tell me about it."

"It was a while ago, maybe a year. I don't know. We were on our way back from a weekend with Peter Lind Hayes and Mary Healy in Pelham. We were returning to the Waldorf. That evening we were going to see Lucy Ball's opening in *Wildcat*. We were in a limousine. Gordie'd been sober for such a long time, six or seven weeks. I was so proud of him, so happy. He was relaxed and looking out the window at boats on the East River. It was a gorgeous day. One of those spring days that you get only in New York.

"Suddenly, Gordie gave this little upward jerk. His face was red. His eyes were wide open. His face looked swollen. He was sweating. He appeared to be having trouble breathing and was pulling at the top button of his shirt. I was afraid he was having a heart attack. 'Gordie, what's wrong?' I said. He snapped back. 'Leave me alone.' The moment we arrived at the hotel, he bounded out of the car. 'No, Gordie, don't go,' I shouted. 'It's Lucy's opening night. Please, Gordie, don't.' But I knew he was gone and wouldn't be back to take me to the opening. Later, I called down to the Bull and Bear and asked if he was there. He was, of course, drinking boilermakers. I went down to the bar. 'What am I going to tell Lucy?' I asked. He said, 'Tell her I'm drunk.'"

Drawing me into a consoling embrace, Jimmy French whispered, "It happens, Sheila. It happens."

When I called Lucy to tell her I wouldn't be coming to her opening— and why—she was furious, but not with Gordon. She was angry at me. Why did I put up with it? Why did I stand for it? "You're coming to the show! I'll send Cy Howard to bring you."

"No, no," I cried, "if people see me by myself, they'll say, 'Well, looks like Gordon MacRae's drunk again.'"

"You worry too much about what people think about him," she said. "You have to start thinking of yourself. You're important. You have a responsibility to yourself."

Lovingly intended from the heart, Lucy's advice could not take into consideration what she didn't know. She believed that I was acting solely out of devotion to Gordon. When I went on with a show alone because Gordon was either too drunk to perform or was simply not there, Lucy believed I did so entirely out of my loyalty to him or, perhaps, that I truly believed in the adage "the show must go on." While I felt a responsibility to give an audience what they'd paid for, I also knew that if there were no show, there'd be no pay. Having children to take care of and facing a bill for back taxes, I could not afford the luxury of thinking of myself.

Nothing was more wrenching to me than to have to step before an audience and tell those happy, glowing, expectant people that Gordon MacRae wouldn't be appearing. The sharp intake of breath, the sighs, the ohs and ahs, the groans of being let down, and the expressions of disappointment on their faces broke my heart. How could I substitute for Gordon MacRae? How could there be magic without the wizard? Who ever heard of a love duet sung by one? They'd come to see Gordon and Sheila MacRae, those happy people who shared not only a stage but their lives.

Occasionally I was able to tell an audience that another star was taking Gordon's place. Out of love for Gordon and me, wonderfully generous and caring friends with successful careers would step onto the stage and gladly share their talents with me: Jack Carter, Bob Goulet, Steve Lawrence, Alan King, Sammy Davis, Jr. Although they were all wonderful performers, they could not substitute for Gordon. It was not our act.

Because I was afraid that Gordon would become bored with the act and resume drinking, I always fussed with it, looking for fresh ideas and suggesting new material. Something new, I hoped, would rivet Gordon's attention and keep him from straying. My wish, too, was to provide a different experience for the stalwart fans who came back year after year to see us. I didn't accept the commonly held opinion that if you had a good show you could do it forever. With that in mind, I suggested that I make my first appearance in the act by flying across the stage in Las Vegas.

Gordon was dumbfounded. "You mean like Mary Martin in *Peter Pan?* Jesus, I still can't get over that middle-aged dame pretending she was a little boy! Now you want to come zipping across a stage hanging from a wire? Sheersie, you are something!"

"Gordie, listen," I pleaded. "It will be terrific."

"Yeah? Well, go ahead," he said in a dubious tone that had been so charming when he was Curly talking to Laurey in *Oklahoma!* "I'm listenin'."

"Your song is 'She's Not Thinking of Me' from *Gigi.*"

"Go on."

"Right at the end, as you're going for a big finish, I fly in all decked out in a fabulous gown dripping with jewels."

"Jewels? Where do we get jewels?"

"We borrow them from Tiffany's or Cartier or Harry Winston. They'll love the publicity!"

It was a gimmick, of course, but it worked. *Life* magazine sent a

photographer to record the phenomenon of jet-setter Sheila MacRae
rehearsing a flying act that was far more complex than Mary Martin's.
She simply dangled from a wire. My soaring entrance was to include
turns and twists and hanging upside down. As Peter Pan, Mary wore a
shoulder and back harness. I was fitted with a girdle-like rig that
supported me with two wires fastened at the hips, allowing almost total
freedom and mobility. Weeks were needed to perfect the movements.

The opening night audience in Las Vegas was packed with stars:
Lucy and Desi, Gary Cooper, Bogie, Orson Welles and Rita Hayworth,
Jeff Chandler, Cary Grant, and vitually the entire Warner roster. When I
zoomed in, they stood and cheered. As I circled above Gordon, they
roared. Gleefully I thought, "Wait till I fly right out over *their* heads!"

The high point of the stunt, it was to be a sweeping loop far out past
the front of the stage. Because there was a very narrow clearance passing
overhead lights—an inch at most—I and the team of men who were
controlling the wires had rehearsed it many times. Supremely confident,
I felt the pull of the wires that would swing me forward. Up I went,
racing toward the crowd.

Then, *crash*; I slammed into the bottom edge of a rack of lights. The
audience groaned in horror. The wire on my left snapped loose. Held
only by the one on the right, I spun like a yo-yo. The borrowed jewels
scattered everywhere, followed by scampering security guards. Result
for me: three cracked ribs, a broken foot, and a season of jokes at my
expense by every comedian: "There goes Sheila flying over the Desert
Inn."

"That's my girl," Gordon said when he was satisfied that I had
survived. "Thank God, we didn't try that stunt at the Waldorf!"

Our appearances at the Waldorf were not always perfection. Twice
they nearly were disasters. Doing our complicated twice-a-night act
flawlessly would have been a miracle.

My part was especially intricate, requiring rapid changes of costumes.
In one hour, I made eleven changes from my skin outward. Unfortunately, the Empire Room did not afford me a lot of room backstage. It
was, after all, a restaurant with entertainment, not a full-fledged theater.

Prior to me, no performer had ever had to change clothing as part of
the act. The room in which I had to make all these quick changes was
quite small—a cubicle, really, behind the bandstand. To get out of one
costume into another as fast as the act required, I had to choreograph

every movement. Twisting this arm there, the other that way, legs positioned just so, I looked like a whirling dervish.

The hanging of costumes needed detailed planning. For this task, I enlisted the guidance of Pierre David, who had been on General Dwight Eisenhower's staff during the Second World War. A clever man, he came up with a design that arranged the costumes on a series of pipes that could be raised and lowered as needed with pulleys. An ingenious system, it worked marvelously, but—remember, in a good story there must always be a "but"—one night everything went wrong.

I was changing for one of the most popular numbers of the act, "Together" from *Gypsy*. I had to quickly get out of a gown and into—in this order—a black tuxedo jacket, black fishnet stockings and black panties. At one point as I shed the gown, I was stark naked.

Slipping into the jacket and fastening the last button, I heard an ominous creaking sound from right overhead, then a grinding noise and a terrific banging as one of the pipes, loaded with costumes, ripped loose from its moorings and fell. It grazed Pierre and nearly bowled me over just as the band struck up the lead-in to "Together," my signal to go on-stage.

Clad only in the short jacket and shoes, I dashed out. Covered by the music, Gordon whispered, "You almost missed your cue."

Carefully placed hands and hastily improvised changes in my movements somehow got us through the number. Going on with the rest of the act with my entire wardrobe in a hopelessly tangled heap backstage was impossible, so, at the end of the song, I stepped forward. "Ladies and gentleman, there's been a slight accident," I said. The audience gasped. "Nobody was hurt," I said, "but the problem is, this coat is all I've got on."

Taking a quick step behind me, Gordon made an exaggerated show of examining me and bellowed, "Say, folks, she's right!"

Promising to do our best to straighten out the mess, we invited the crowd to come back in an hour. They did, and in the hallowed tradition of show business, the show went on.

A second mishap was due to the popularity of the act. To make room for two extra tables to seat a group of football players from the Buffalo Bills, a workman removed a pair of steps from the stage into the audience. Unfortunately, I used them in the act to go down among the audience while doing my impressions. Not knowing the steps were gone,

I walked into thin air, landed in the laps of the players, and broke my foot.

When we played the Empire Room, we lived in the Waldorf Towers. Rising above the main portion of the hotel, the Towers consist of suites, many of them leased by countries for the use of their ambassadors to the nearby United Nations and by visiting dignitaries such as heads of state and, of course, the President of the United States whenever he was in town.

Of all the suites we occupied in the Towers, my favorite was 39E— thirty-ninth floor, east side. It was decorated in turquoise and gold with rich, antique Oriental carpets and elegant, old-fashioned bathrooms that were larger than some New York City apartments. Bright and airy, the suite had eighteenth-century paintings of the English countryside and elegant figures riding to the hounds. A particular favorite of mine was a proper English gentleman who looked exactly like Spencer Tracy. Windows faced the East River and were filled in the morning with pink dawns. At night, the city was spangled with lights like diamonds spilled onto black velvet.

Gazing out at that spectacular view, I felt frightened and lonely. I had no taste for the bon vivant. I stayed to myself much of the time. If I wanted company I sought out another resident of the Towers, Jean MacArthur, the widow of General Douglas MacArthur. After his dismissal as commander of American and United Nations forces in Korea and an attempt in 1952 to win the Republican nomination for President, the MacArthurs had taken up permanent residence in the Waldorf Towers. When he died in 1964, she continued to live there quietly and with great charm and dignity. I felt that Jean, a woman who had been left alone by her husband often, though for far different reasons, knew that I was reaching out to her from the depths of loneliness and fear.

Another person I sought out was Carol Channing. She and her husband, Charles Lowe, lived on the floor below. Her father was a well-known Christian Science lecturer, and Carol was a follower of the religion. Born and raised in Seattle, she dropped out of Bennington College at the age of twenty to go into show business. Her first hit was as Lorelei Lee in Anita Loos's *Gentlemen Prefer Blondes*. Lorelei's big number, "Diamonds Are a Girl's Best Friend," became so identified with Carol that it became her trademark, as "Love in Bloom" was for Jack Benny and "Thanks for the Memory" was for Bob Hope.

Saucer-eyed, wide-mouthed, and platinum blond, Carol spoke and sang with a distinctive raspy voice that was ideal for mimicking. Imitating her, I chose not to do her most famous song from *Gentlemen* but another number from that show. I did "I'm Just a Little Girl From Little Rock" because I felt it caught the core of her innocence.

Carol's success was due in great measure to Charles. A savvy producer who had worked with George Burns, Charles met Carol and decided that her talent was being wasted. In his eyes, her career had no focus. He also found a lot amiss in her personal affairs. She had just been divorced and was eating too much. What Carol needed, Charles felt, was an image that would be distinctive to her, that would say to the world, "I'm Carol Channing and there's nobody else like me."

Taking charge, Charles became Henry Higgins to Carol's Eliza Doolittle. He saw to it that when she went out in public she dressed like a star. To deal with allergies from which Carol suffered when she dyed her hair, he persuaded her to wear wigs. He advised her on the roles she chose to play, culminating in Carol's triumph as the matchmaking Dolly Levi in *Hello, Dolly!*

On a sunny afternoon in Carol's suite, I told her, "I just wish all these problems with Gordon would go away."

Carol reached out and gently touched me. "Oh, be careful what you wish, Sheila," she said. "A wish is a prayer."

Like all my friends who loved me and Gordon, Carol wanted us to stay together.

Lucy Ball came to visit me in 39E with harder advice. Having divorced Desi, she spoke not only as a sympathetic friend who understood what I was going through but also as a woman who had mastered the business of show business. "You, Sheila, my darling," she scolded, "aren't paying enough attention to your own career."

It was bitter medicine—much too difficult to swallow. But not long after, I awoke in 39E to discover that Gordon had vanished again. By now I'd given up trying to find him on my own. I simply sat and waited.

Presently, the police phoned. "Do you know Albert Gordon Mac-Rae?" asked a growly voice.

"I'm his wife," I answered, feeling a surge of fear.

"We've got him down here. He's drunk. We'll bring him home if that's what you want."

"Yes, please," I begged.

They delivered him to the suite by way of a service elevator and helped me get him into bed—quiet, polite, nonjudgmental. Leaving him to sleep it off, I needed peace and quiet and being alone. I descended from our suite in the Towers and crossed the street to the magnificent Episcopal church that graces the corner opposite the hotel. I stayed for nearly four hours, weeping and praying.

When I returned to 39E, I found Gordon had gone again. In absolute despair, I fell to my knees in tears. The phone rang again. "Dear God," I gasped, "now what?"

"Sheila?" It was a man's voice, a friend who'd come to our opening night party, JP, as we all knew him.

"He's not here," I sighed. "I don't know where he is."

"He's over at the New York Athletic Club."

"Thank you," I said in utter despair.

"Don't hang up, Sheila," JP said urgently. "It's *you* I want to talk to." He paused a long time. I could hear his breathing on the line. I knew he was gathering his thoughts and expected to hear well-intentioned but useless advice—get him a psychiatrist, put him in a hospital, have you heard of Alcoholics Anonymous? "Thank you for your concern," I was prepared to say. "I've heard it all, tried it all!"

"Sheila, this is probably the worst timing," he said quietly, but I have to tell you now or I never will...I love you, Sheila."

He knew all of our friends and we had met casually. But he was a married man—albeit rumor had him separating on many occasions.

Scared and startled by this intimate phone call, I hung up. However, that night my dreams were filled with his face.

To cope with my private agonies, I read and wrote a lot of poetry about one's heart being broken in search of an understanding of how Gordon had broken mine. Poetry had always been part of me, and some of it was published in magazines: *Harper's, Redbook, TV Guide, Good Housekeeping*.

To mark the completion of our appearance at the Empire Room, Buddy Hackett giddily announced that he was going to throw a grand party for us at his splendid, spacious home in Fort Lee, New Jersey. The biggest names in show business were on the guest list, friends of ours, new and old, steadfast believers in the myth that Gordon and Sheila MacRae would go on forever.

Gordon got drunk and refused to attend.

Humiliated, I had to tell Buddy that Gordon wasn't coming. I could see to what lengths Buddy had gone. The food was lavish. Cakes had been prepared with touching and funny decorations. One had the words of a song we did in our act: "Who do you love, I hope?" Another had a heart with a cupid's arrow and the words "Gordon and Sheila." There were many hearts and flowers and red Valentine motifs. A large tent had been set up in the yard. An orchestra was hired for a show Buddy had had written just for us with jokes and skits and a medley of the songs from our act and the musicals we'd toured the country in. I knew what a party like this had to have cost—$20,000 at least.

"The hell Gordo isn't coming," Buddy declared, "I'll find him and bring him to this damn party if I have to drag him over the George Washington Bridge by the scruff of the neck."

Gamely, he went into the city to scour the places where Gordon was likely to be—Toots Shor's, the bar of the St. Regis, the Oak Room of the Plaza, the all-male, non-Jewish bastion of the New York Athletic Club, and God knows what other haunts of men who drank.

It was a futile search.

Two hours later, so wounded that tears dimmed his usually laughing eyes, Buddy said, "I'm mad at him, Sheila, but I still love him." He took a deep breath. "So to hell with him. you're here. We're all here. We'll have the party without him. Okay, Stan Freeman, play what we wrote."

When Steve Lawrence and Eydie Gorme began the medley of our songs, I fled in tears to the bathroom, physically ill.

Long after all this, Bob Newhart said to me, "We knew that day it was over."

On that awful day I also knew. It marked the moment when I understood that I didn't love Gordon anymore.

I had read Dr. Theodore Reik's explanation of how and why people fall in love—and why they fall out of love. In love, first, there was a dissatisfaction with one's self. Second, a failure to live up to one's ideal. Third, a desire to possess the qualities one finds lacking in oneself but sees in another person. This was precisely what happened to Gordon and me. He was everything I had wanted to be. He was devil-may-care. I was quite grave. He was optimistic, I wasn't. He would burst into a room. I ducked in.

Since I was a teenager I had always been thrilled to be Mrs. Gordon MacRae—the shy girl who gladly abandoned her own youthful aspirations to be an actress to be Gordon's wife and the mother of his children. Always, I had clung to him. Now I was remembering so many bad times—he had been of no help to me during the birth of our last baby because he was on a binge. I recalled with horror our younger daughter, sweet little Heather, saying to me, "Mommy, Daddy's drunk." How long could I go on putting up with his disappearances, the lost weekends, having to ask friends to step in and cover for him in the show, dreadful phone calls in the dead of night from bartenders begging me to come and get Gordon, embarrassed voices of policemen telephoning to tell me that they had him in custody?

Falling out of love, said Dr. Reik, is the falling in love process reversed. The result is pity.

There were times when I couldn't bear to look at him. He wasn't my Gordie anymore. The one I knew had vanished somewhere along the way. The Gordon MacRae I listened to adoringly now hit faulty notes. That gilded voice was gone. He was a Gordon MacRae whose eyes would be half-crossed from drink. His face was puffy and red—a drunkard's face.

The physical effects of his drinking also took their toll on him as a lover. Not only was he not interested in sex: more and more he became impotent. The splendid, unrestrained, lusty man with whom I had unashamedly enjoyed making love was now out of reach. I knew that after many years of marriage and having borne children, many women faced with such a situation were known to breathe a sigh of relief and blithely go on with their lives without sex. I wasn't like that and couldn't be. I simply could not resign myself to living without sexual intimacy. From the very beginning of our sexual relationship, we had been a pair of wantons. I couldn't get enough of him.

Though Gordon joked about it, I had been consumed by sexual passion. Making love was a daily experience, often several times a day. As drinking and gambling became addictions for him, sex became my obsession. After having engaged in exquisite sex with him, I, too, was an addict.

Though sexual addiction would not be openly acknowledged, studied, and classified by psychiatrists and psychologists as a type of addictive-compulsive behavior for many years, there is no doubt in my mind that I was as much a slave to sex as Gordon was bound to drinking and gambling. Had his drinking not affected his virility, had he been able to continue to be my lover, I might have found the strength to carry on. I might have been able to endure the anguish of the constant debts, the gambling losses, and the hotels confiscating our salary to pay them off. I might have gone on putting up with his disappearances and the unprofessional behavior. But I'd lost *him*. It was just too much.

It was time to go. For my own sake, I had to make my own life in a new kind of world. I had to think of me. Lucy was right, as always. Jack Benny was right. I couldn't go on as Mrs. Gordon MacRae. The time had come to start paying attention to the things that *Sheila* needed.

EIGHT

13 Sutton Place

I LEFT GORDON on September 24, 1965.

Alone in the Waldorf Towers, I stared out the windows of 39E at a city that seemed to have lost its magic. I felt godless. The idol I had worshipped all my life was gone. Would anyone ever take his place? Should anyone?

Because I did not want to be alone I brought Bruce to live with me. But it was not a completely selfish decision. I wanted him to have the benefit of the best schooling New York had to offer. I chose a boys' boarding school in Riverdale that let him come down to spend time with me on weekends.

During the week, I tried to get on with life without Gordon, but I felt as though I were a circus tightrope walker. I imagined people all around and below me, staring up and waiting for me to fall, for me to get my comeuppance for leaving Gordon.

The phone rang.

"So you finally did it! Hooray for you."

I had not heard JP's voice since that awful day when he had phoned to tell me that if I wanted to find my husband he was at the New York Athletic Club.

"I'm coming over to see you," he said. "I hear that you finally left Gordo."

"No, no, you can't. I want you to…but—"

"I'll be there in fifteen minutes."

He arrived from a business trip to London. After a shower, he borrowed one of my silk robes. I had to laugh. "What's funny?" he asked.

You, I thought. You with your arms and legs sticking out of that too-tight robe! "Nothing's funny," I said.

He gazed out the eastern window. "That's Welfare Island over there."

"I know. Are you trying to make conversation?"

"This afternoon I made a million-dollar deal. A dream come true, right? A guy who when he was a kid didn't have a pot to piss in makes a million-dollar deal. The kid grew up and grabbed the American Dream. Well, I'll tell you, darling, no matter how much of the big dream you latch onto, you can't get away from where you came from and what you were. I can stand here now and look at Welfare Island and say to myself 'You made it, kid' but that doesn't erase the days I spent with my father going over to Welfare Island. They had a hospital there for poor people like us. My father had bad legs. I wanted to say, 'Pop, here's the dough. Get the best doctors that money can buy.' How come I couldn't have made a million-dollar deal back then?"

"Don't ask that. Life is always surprises."

He turned away from the window. "I see right through you. I always have. I know all about you behind that smile!"

I smirked. "Is that so?"

"I know exactly what makes you tick. I've researched everything about you since you were a teenager. That's why I'm so sure I'm the man for you. It's why I love you."

My heart skipped a beat.

"Wait a minute, Sheila," said the actress in me. "This scene is going too fast. Don't let him set the pace. Don't let yourself be upstaged." This was not Hank Fonda or Peter Sellers looking for a quick one. This was serious. "I'll need time," I said.

"I've waited too long already. I'm tired of being the man in the wings." He crossed the room and kissed me. "This time," he said, letting me go, "I have no intention of letting you slip away. I'm taking a suite in the Waldorf. Don't worry! It won't be here in the Towers. I'll get one on the lower floors."

"Please don't," I said. "It will be too dangerous. For both of us."

He grinned. "Come on. You want it as much as I do. You like living on the edge."

Confused and tormented, I had to get away. I had to think. That weekend, I whisked Bruce away from the city to the home of friends in the country. He had a wonderful time but, distracted and distant, I was not a very good guest. No doubt believing I had Gordon on my mind, our hosts were gracious and considerate as I sunned myself on the patio or languished by the swimming pool.

"Poor little you," said Sheila of the Waldorf, mocking me in glaring late-spring sunlight. "You weren't expecting this, were you? All that stuff about divorce, about how wrong it was for married people to call the whole thing off? Well, it's happened to you. Now here's JP saying he loves you and has loved you for years. He's swept you off your feet. But that wasn't in the scenario! Nowhere in the script did it say that you'd fall for someone else. But you have fallen. Hard. Admit it. You want him."

The phone rang the minute I returned to 39E. Instinctively, I knew it was JP.

"Were you having me watched?" I joked.

"I called every hour," he said. "Shall I come over?"

"Yes."

He found me sunburned and wearing a white silk shirt.

"I want to see you," he said, unbuttoning it.

His wristwatch snagged a sun blister on my arm, ripping it open.

"Sorry, hon. I'll be more careful," he said, easing back to look at me. "Beautiful! Now the rest of it. Everything. I want to see every inch of you."

With shaking hands, I finished undressing with my back to him, and when I turned round I clutched my black fitted Hermès alligator handbag low in front of me.

"Jesus, you're a shy one," he said, reaching for the bag.

I slipped over the edge from natural shyness into panic. "No, don't," I pleaded. "I don't have things. I'm not on pills, I..."

Smiling, he sank to his knees, pushed away the bag, and began kissing me. Melting, I slid to the floor with him, and suddenly we were all sensuous kisses and tongues and bitings. "Yes, yes," I sighed. "Yes, come into me, darling, please." Our bodies took over, rising and falling, wanting one another again and again. I craved his unleashed sexuality. Presently, he rolled away from me laughing.

"How many times can we do it in one afternoon?" he groaned, lighting a cigarette. Then he became so quiet that I worried that I hadn't pleased him. Worse, I was afraid I'd been tricked. At last, he stirred.

"We've got to think this through," he said, pouring a drink. "You know this town, how it thrives on gossip. I don't want what we've found together cheapened by the newspapers. And I'm sure that you don't want everybody saying that you threw over Gordon for another guy. We both know it's not true and I don't want to get blamed. Until you've put that marriage behind you once and for all, until you're separated. I don't want to get the reputation as the son of a bitch who broke up the marriage between God's Golden Couple, Gordon and Sheila MacRae."

When the public that adored Gordon MacRae learned that I had left him, I was denounced. Hated. How could I do such a thing to that sweet man? I could have answered, but I kept the truth to myself. Those who knew the facts castigated me for not speaking up. Barbara Walters pleaded with me to tell all. "You've got to defend yourself," she told me. But I couldn't. I didn't want to make things worse for Gordon. It was a separation, not a divorce.

The phone rang at two AM. Sleepily, I asked, "Yes? Who is ...?"

JP laughed, "I'm in the suite ten floors down...Come on! C'mon, lady!"

As I dressed quickly and raced down the backstairs from the Towers, my heart stuck in my throat. What if he doesn't love me? What if he's changed his mind?

I tapped on the door softly...he pulled me inside quickly...suddenly we were on the floor...

As he tugged at my blouse, I said, "Wait, darling, listen...I was thinking maybe you're an angel sent to me to take away my problems." He was kissing my belly. "Angel," he laughed.

"No, no, I'm an unlikely angel...they don't exist...I've never met one...anyway you won't find one here...not this place...not this city."

He was on top of me.

"Don't you believe in angels?" he asked.

"I don't believe you have a high I.Q. when you talk like this..."

We rolled over.

"Answer me...what do you believe?"

"I believe in me...and this..."

We laughed between kissing, touching, and lovemaking that seemed to go on forever.

Afterward, back in 39E, I wrote this poem for him:

I do not count the turns of the earth
Nor how much sorrow; how much mirth
Nor the stretch of hours that push feet
To work and back on this tall street.
Beads of minutes we use, I thread
On a pendulum that instead
Of counting segments just records
Such kisses as are my rewards.
I do not need the clocks of man
Reminding me how short the span
Between your footfall at the door;
The burning when you leave once more.
Spilling sands in the hourglass still
Every grain I wait immobile,
Fixed and centered, transcending space.
I feel the shadows etch my face,
Erasing the city, bedding down
All the rest in this sleeping town.

Away from New York City, JP and I could be less guarded, especially if we were part of a crowd. We often were. Popular and gregarious, he drew people to him and liked to surround himself with wealthy and famous folk. On the sunny beach of the Diplomat Hotel in Miami Beach, he lounged in white tennis shorts and colorful sweater, lording it like a pasha over producer Irving Cowan and his wife, Marge, Bob Goulet, and Buddy Hackett.

As he regaled them with funny stories from his limitless trove, I slipped away for a swim, plunging into the surf and the entangling, stinging arms of a jellyfish. Screeching in pain, I dashed from the water and flung myself down. Rolling around, I rubbed sand on the ugly red welts of my arms, legs, stomach, and breasts, but when I stood and peered through the glare at JP, pain and humiliation were blotted out by a surging desire to possess him, to wrap him in my arms as the jellyfish's tentacles had enveloped me. Every pore, every muscle, every sinew of me wanted him. I rushed to him. "JP, come with me," I begged, pulling him toward the cabana where there was a shower. "Help me wash off."

Brushing aside my sand-crusted hand, he looked disgusted. "God, all that dirt!"

Laughing, I pinched his arm. "Sand isn't dirt."

"It is if you're Jewish," he answered, grinning ear to ear.

As his audience laughed at the joke, I caught a slight tilt of his head and a tightness around his mouth. Despite his easy quip, I felt sure that he wanted me as passionately as I yearned for him. Confident and expectant, I waited naked in the shower. It seemed like hours before he opened the door of the cabana. "Get in here, darling, now," I said, reaching for him.

"Sheila, why'd you do that? Grabbing me like that with all our friends around? What will they think?"

I stepped out of the shower. "They're already thinking it," I said, shaking a sliver of soap under his nose and pressing my breasts against him.

"Sheila," he whispered, "you're soaking me. This is a brand-new tennis sweater."

"Buy another," I said, sliding against him.

"Two hundred fucking dollars!"

"You're a rich man."

He cupped my breasts. "And you're a wanton woman." A hand slid down to my buttocks. The other slithered between my legs to wriggle a finger into me, then darted away to twist the bar of soap from my hand. "No, no," I moaned as he thrust it into me. "It's you I want inside me."

"Hush," he whispered. "They'll hear."

"Let them."

I pressed my breasts hard against the dripping walls of the shower as wave after wave of lust shook me.

As the voices and laughter of his friends filtered through the slatted shutters of the door, I thrilled to the thought of making love to JP when his admirers were so close. I thought of lines by F. Scott Fitzgerald: "Gold-hatted, high-stepping lover, if you love her, dance for her, too!" A moment later, I saw a flare of pink light upon my closed eyelids and heard the door slam—then his voice outside, telling another joke.

As much as I loved suite 39E, as thrilled as I was to throw open its door to my secret lover-prince, I couldn't return to it without seeing it as the place where my life had been shaken to its foundations. Within those walls I had watched helplessly as Gordon disintegrated. In 39E, I observed the heartbreaking self-destruction of one of the great voices and the decline and fall of my first love. I longed for a place that was not haunted by memories of Gordon and fears of being caught with my new but demanding lover.

The secrecy of our relationship created terrible strains on us, but especially on JP. He bridled at not being able to be open, and blamed me because I was resisting his demands that I file for divorce. He also viewed my reluctance to divorce with suspicion. He accused me of seeing other men, of having affairs with Sammy Davis, Jr., Irving Cowan, my agent, and Hillard (Hilly) Elkins, producer of a play I signed to appear in. In anticipation of going to London I told Hilly that I wanted out of my contract. My excuse was that I couldn't go on the road with the show because I had to stay close to Bruce. My real reason was my desire—my need—to be with JP. Hilly was furious.

Whoever said that true love never runs smooth knew a thing or two. As lovers do in such situations, we decided that we would sit down and work it all out. We set a date and made a plan. The meeting couldn't look like a lovers' rendezvous. It had to appear to be a chance encounter. Place? We chose the Bull and Bear restaurant in the Waldorf. I would be there ostensibly for a meeting with someone else. JP would just saunter in. We'd strike up a conversation, like old show biz friends, walk out casually, and then retreat to 39E via the freight elevator for our heart-to-heart. We also intended to discuss his plans to go to London and how I would join him there. Secretly, of course. The date we set for our meeting was November 9. It turned out to be an unforgettable night.

When everything went dark in the Great Northeast Blackout of 1965, I was stuck in the elevator. Like nearly everyone else caught in the blackout at the height of the cold war, I first feared that the Russians had finally done it. My second thought was that I should get out of the hotel. By then I was quite familiar with the layout of the Towers. Because I was "Sheila of the Waldorf," I had explored every nook and cranny of the place, so I was an ideal "blackout warden." Down the stairs I went, floor to floor, fetching residents from their suites and leading them as if I were their guardian angel to the safety of the darkened, traffic-choked, horn-blaring yet gay, carnival-like street.

Having done my duty, I rushed to the Bull and Bear. The always intimate atmosphere was even more so that night as candles glowed. JP wasn't there! Not surprising! I pictured him stranded somewhere in the blacked-out city. Miraculously, one of the telephones was working. Some sort of special hookup they had. There was a long line of users, each limited to two or three calls. I called Bruce at the Riverdale Country School. "I'm fine, Mom," he said jovially. "We're having a party!" He wasn't alone. The whole city was having a wonderful time. His brother and sisters in California were also okay and were quite amused by what they were hearing on the news. With my last call I tried to locate JP.

The surest way to do that, I figured, was to call Jilly's, one of his hangouts.

JP was not there. "He's probably at Toots Shor's," Jilly said.

I never did reach him. It was not until three days later that he appeared at 39E. "I've just been to my shrink," he said as he came in. He had on a handsome gray suit and a no-nonsense look. "Sit down," he said, pointing demandingly at the couch. "We've got to do something about this ridiculous situation between us. You've got to get a lawyer and get the divorce."

"I can't," I cried. "I'm afraid of what Gordon might do."

Anger sparked in his gray eyes. "Look, I'm going to put you to a test. I'm going to see how much you love me. I'm going to give you three months. Three months!"

"What does *that* mean?"

"It means I'm not going to see you for three months. And I don't want you to see anyone else."

"But I'm not seeing anyone."

"That's a lie."

"I'm not, truly. I see friends. That's all. I don't see anyone but you."

"Oh, great," he said, throwing up his hands. "I really need that guilt! It's bad enough that I'm the villain who's coming between you and God's Golden Boy!"

"I thought we were going to London together."

"No. We're not doing anything until you get this settled."

Devastated, I fled to California and then to Florida. From time to time we would run into one another at parties. Invariably he whispered to me that I should leave. "Why should I be the one to leave?" I answered. "You leave." He was implacable. He'd given me three months and he meant it.

He did allow me to telephone, and I did, so often that he said to me, "You know, I think I like phone sex better than the real thing."

Now more than ever, I had to get out of 39E. In my search for a new home, I learned that the very thing I was seeking was for sale on Sutton Place. Overlooking the East River and the intricate steel laciness of the graceful 59th Street Bridge, it had its own little garden in the back and all the seclusion I needed. The number in brass on the big red front door was 13. Superstition be damned, I thought, I shall make 13 my lucky number. Turning the brass doorknob, I breathed in the slightly stale, unoccupied air of what I was determined to make my love nest and headquarters in a fresh, brave new world for me and my love.

Immediately, I felt drawn into it. Exploring my new home, I thought that it had the air of a snug ship on high seas, isolated and unique, suffocating and placating at the same time. To this house would come people who, like me, were elite outcasts in the city: actresses, actors, artists, producers, financiers. To this narrow, four-story gray hideaway with its red door and brass knob would come my children, my many friends, and *him*. "I will marry this house," I vowed as I wandered from room to room. "And I shall never leave it."

Miriam Hopkins, the actress, owned it. "I'll be very happy if this house becomes yours," she said, peering at me across a gilded teacup from her antique chair surrounded by her chinoiserie walls.

Famed for playing both well-bred ladies and floozies when she was a seductive blonde for Paramount, Sam Goldwyn, and Warners, she was in her sixties now. After a Broadway acting career in the 1920s, her first movie was *Fast and Loose* in 1930. An important star throughout the Depression years, she saw her career fade in the late forties and be reduced to small character parts after that. Her most recent films had been *The Children's Hour* and *Fanny Hill* in 1962.

While at Warners, she costarred a couple of times with Bette Davis and shared billing with her in one of the legendary feuds of Hollywood (a publicity bonanza for both).

"I truly felt sorry for Miriam," Bette said. "She was such a capable actress. It could have been a pleasure to work with her, but she made it such an ordeal by her tricks and mistrust of everybody."

Bette took great pleasure in recounting a showdown with Miriam on the set of *Old Acquaintance* in 1943. "When Miriam tried to upstage me by wandering around the set not listening to my character's big speech of reproval," Bette recalled, "I stopped the action and said to her: 'By God, Miriam, if I have to get on top of the piano, you're going to look me in the eye!' The rafters were filled with spectators from all over the lot. They were hoping to see me slap her. It was in the script, and I must admit I was pleased by the prospect."

An interviewer once asked Bette what in life annoyed her most. She replied, "Unused fireplaces, pink sweet peas, badly made beds, and Miriam Hopkins."

"Was it ever fun in Hollywood when you were there, way back when?" I asked this once-upon-a-time movie queen.

Miriam sat silent for a long time, then, with a shrug of her shoulders and a shake of the head, said, "There is no Hollywood anymore. It's just a post office and a phone no one ever answers."

Her attention returned to the house. She spoke lovingly of it. "I've lived in a lot of places," she said, "but this was my favorite." She accounted for her property: many other houses, apartments, parcels of real estate she owned here, there, and everywhere—not boastfully but, I surmised, to let me know that there could be life outside of marriage. She named those who had resided at 13 Sutton Place before me: Doris Stein, Dinah Shore, Judy Garland. "That fool. She pasted telegrams on the walls!"

"I will cherish your house, Miss Hopkins," I promised.

Black-suited, and wearing pearls and diamonds, she set aside the teacup, rose, and touched my hand sympathetically. "Allow me to give you some advice," she said, obviously sensing that I was teetering on the brink. "You're alone for the first time in many years. You'll be seeing men. Beware! It's vicious out there."

Moving-in day was hazy and fragmented. I was by myself in my snug cocoon. I arranged and rearranged, changing the flowers, the furniture, and me. Most of all, me. I put on layer after layer of clothing: gilt and not gilt, plain and buttoned, ribboned, laced, black, white, gold, rainbows. I dressed and redressed, like Solomon's mistress.

I thought about the sundering and ripping apart that I saw going on all around me. Gordon and me, Marge and Gower Champion, Joy and Bill Orr, Tony and Janet Curtis, Sammy and Mai Davis, Doris Day and Marty Melcher.

I had literally run into Marty in the lobby of the Waldorf Towers. The mornings and nights when he had quieted Dodo's shrieking nightmares by singing hymns were behind him now. He had cajoled, scolded, and guided her—and used her. "Angie Dickinson loves me," he said to me at the Waldorf. "She wants to jump on my bones."

I'd expected Marty and Doris to break up sooner or later. But when Gower Champion arrived at No. 13, I was surprised that Marge was not with him. I had always adored them. Like Gordon and me, they were husband-and-wife performers whom no one could imagine parting company. Now we had something else in common. "I hear you're divorcing Gordon," Gower said.

"Not yet."

"The worst thing when two people go their separate ways is that the breakup puts their mutual friends in a tough spot," he said rather sadly. "The friends are forced to take sides. What I like about you, Sheila, is that you refuse to. But if you did choose, I think you'd side with the guys."

"Why do you suppose that?"

"Because you always seem to get along better with men than women."

"Do I?"

"Don't you?"

Reflecting, I thought of my women friends—Lucy Ball, Joy Orr, Miriam Nelson, Shirley Jones—and the men friends; so many more. Why? Was it because the movies were the business of men? Or was it that all women instinctually distrusted other women? Or might it be a natural trait of *actresses*? Were we all, deep at heart, Bette Davis, Miriam Hopkins, and Joan Crawford? Had Jack Warner, in warning me never to be an actress, been shrewdly perceptive? Was he afraid that if I became an actress I would change?

I certainly had. But was it for better or worse? Might the metamorphosis of Mrs. Gordon MacRae into Sheila MacRae have contributed to the decline and fall of Gordon MacRae? Was I as much to blame for our ruination as Gordie? I looked at Gower with an expression as quizzical as his. What a dangerous thing a stream of consciousness is, I thought, to sweep me along like a fallen leaf in a torrent of floodwater from whether I was friendlier to men than women to finding blame in myself for breaking up with Gordon. "Gower, I really don't want to talk about any of this. Okay?"

When he had gone, I sat disconsolately in my fortress-home and pondered the wreckage of lives I found all around me.

Even Shirley Jones and Jack Cassidy were separated. He was in New York, footloose, at odds with himself, searching for someone. Coming to stay, he stood at a window. Smoking and brushing away the ashes, he turned his cunning blue eyes to me. Beacons, they searched out my secrets. "We were meant to be happy, Shelayhley," he said. He had a thesaurus of nicknames for me. "Why aren't we?"

"But I am," I said.

He snorted a laugh. "Who the hell are you kidding? This new man in your life is a bastard. He'll fry you for his dinner, you dope." His eyes crinkled devilishly. "If it's sex you want, I'm the best lay in town."

In 1966, I gave in to the pleadings of Jackie Gleason to play Alice Kramden in a series of TV musicals of *The Honeymooners.* I had hesitated because it meant leaving New York for Miami Beach. But when the deal was made, I couldn't help but let out a yell of delight in my Sutton Place garden. PHOTO COURTESY NEW YORK TIMES

Jackie Gleason hated this outfit, featured in a *TV Guide* story on my becoming Mrs. Kramden. He thought the dress was too chic for Alice. When I dyed my hair red on Jackie's orders, I insisted that he let me play Alice as a woman with a mind and soul. PHOTO COURTESY TV GUIDE

Gordon surprised me by showing up at a "good luck" party given for me by my friends Marge and Irv Cowan as I began the role of Alice on *The Honeymooners.* Left to right are Gordon, Marge, Arthur Godfrey, Lucille Ball and husband Gary Morton, me, Mrs. Godfrey, and Irv.

A script run-through for *The Honeymooners* with (from left) Art, director Frank Bunetta, writer Ed Deverno, Jackie, me, and with their backs to the camera, producer Ron Wayne and Jane Kean. PHOTO COURTESY CBS-TV

Rehearsing with me for *The Honeymooners* are Jane Kean as Trixie Norton, Art Carney as Ed, and Jackie Gleason as Ralph Kramden. Jackie was notorious for not wanting to rehearse. He thought it took the edge off the live performance. PHOTO COURTESY CBS-TV

Between seasons of *The Honeymooners*, I played the summer theater circuit. In July 1968, I took out this ad in *Variety* to let everyone know that I was looking forward to a new season as Alice.

During the summer of 1967, CBS replaced the vacationing "Honeymooners" with *Away We Go*, featuring singer Buddy Greco, comic George Carlin, and the Buddy Rich band. (Top left) Buddy is Napoleon. I am Josephine. (Top right) As Barbra Streisand, I accept an "award" while Buddy seems more interested in my legs. (Bottom right) Buddy, George and I also teamed in song (Buddy on the left, George, right). The shows also gave me a chance to kick up my heels (bottom left) and toss around the furniture. PHOTOS COURTESY CBS-TV

In 1968, neither Jackie nor I ever figured Larry King (left photo) would become the big media name that he is today. In the right photo, the young beauty on Jackie's left is his long time love, Honey Merrill.

NBC's *Personality*, starring Larry Blyden, provided the opportunity for the game show debuts of Meredith (left) and Heather (right).

In 1967, I married Ron Wayne, a producer on the Gleason show. Because I was still worried about how Gordon might react to my finding another romance, the wedding was held quietly in the garden in my home in New York. Here, Meredith feeds me wedding cake at the reception while Ron, Heather, and Gar look on.

The Honeymooners and their upstairs neighbors: Jackie, Art, Jane, and me in costume on the set. PHOTO COURTESY CBS-TV

Mrs. Ronald Wayne, 1972.

After Jackie Gleason decided he did not want to continue with *The Honeymooners* after four seasons, I toured the country in the romantic comedy *Luv.* My director and costar was talented actor, Jack Heller.

In 1976, I played the not so dumb blond Billie Dawn in a road company revival of *Born Yesterday.*

Sheila Mac Rae

The year is 1980.

As Dolly Levi in *Hello, Dolly!* in San Diego. Our opulent production was hailed as "one of the most beautiful 'Dollys' ever staged."

One of the two most overwhelming men I met in my life, Albert Finney
PHOTO COURTESY ALAN DAVIDSON/ALPHA/ GLOBE

This publicity shot was taken in 1984 in Canada as I toured in the play *First Person Singular* with debonair English actor Patrick Macnee.

The family gathers for Bruce and Mari's wedding in 1985. I'm on the left next to Gar. Then come Mari and Bruce, Heather, Gordon, Meredith and husband Greg Mullavey, with daughter Allison in front, and Gar's wife, Paula. (Right photo) William Gordon MacRae (Gar) with his children, three-year-old Caitlin and three-week-old Michael, at the affair.

One of my favorite pictures, this was taken in the garden of
my house at No. 13 Sutton Place on the day I married Ron
Wayne. Although I had had romances with other men,
marrying again marked the final break with Gordon and the
true beginning of the rest of my life.

I laughed aloud. Jack could always make me laugh. He was much funnier than all the professional comedians we both knew. I liked being with him and going out with him when I couldn't go out with JP. Jack and I had been doing the town so often that the gossip columns were hinting at something serious between us. There wasn't. He was my friend. So was Shirley. Sean, their son, was my godchild.

Part of their difficulties was Jack's identity problem. He was tired of their being called Mr. and Mrs. Shirley Jones. It happened to lots of men whose wives were more famous than they. Jim Aubrey, before he became the head of CBS, was always being introduced as Phyllis Thaxter's husband. Before Marty Melcher won a reputation as an agent, he dwelt in the shadow of Doris Day. Having spent years as "Gordon MacRae's wife," I sympathized. Jack had also been self-conscious about the talk that the only reason he had married Shirley was because she was a movie star. What else led them to part I did not care to know about. I asked neither and grieved for both.

At the moment, Jack was in the midst of a torrid affair with Dani Greco. She was temporarily a resident in my house, occupying rooms on the top floor, because she, too, was separated. Buddy Greco, her singer husband, was known far and wide for his hot Latin temper, hot talent on stage, and hot way with women. How Buddy could want another woman was a puzzlement. Dani was much prettier than any film star I'd known, except for Ava Gardner. In the seventies, she'd been married to David Janssen and stuntman-turned-director Hal Needham, and was said to have had steamy love affairs with Howard Hughes and J. Paul Getty. Now she was with Jack, more in mutual admiration and fun than anything else.

Immediately after breaking up with Shirley, Jack had been involved with Yvonne Craig, sharing digs with her in a rented house in Hidden Hills. If ever there was a disastrous union, I had thought at the time, it was Jack and Yvonne. I held out as little hope for him and Yvonne as Jack held for me and JP.

"He's going to be nothing but trouble for you," Jack kept insisting. He scoffed at the secrecy that JP and I tried to keep. "Who the hell is *he*? Is he God? If a mere mortal such as I looks upon his face, it's death? The two of you can't carry on this charade forever."

Jack was right. It *was* a charade. To stave off reality, I was creating an illusion. Just as I had dressed up and mimed others as a child in order to escape unpleasant situations, I was pulling out of the bag every trick I could think of to be with JP, yet avoid being unmasked in my relationship with him and hurting Gordon. But I wanted to be with him.

When the doorbell rang and I knew it was him, I raced down the stairs and pulled him in, my thoughts zooming ahead to the moment when we would embrace in the small room on the second floor, our favorite for making love. Abandoned. Wantonly.

My desire to possess him was especially acute when he was out of town preparing to bring a new show into New York. I begged to be allowed to go to Boston. "No," he said. "I'll come down there."

"You can't. Perry will be here." My houseman, Robert Perry, had butlered in this same house for Judy Garland, Dinah Shore, Mrs. Guggenheim, and Miriam Hopkins. "If Perry answers the door and finds you..."

"Call that African queen and tell him to stay up in Harlem."

"I can't do that! It's not his regular night off. He'll be suspicious."

"Do you want him to see you with your panties around your neck and honey spread all over you? That's what's going to happen. I'll be there as soon as possible."

"It's been snowing all day and night."

"The hell with the weather!"

When I answered the door, snow dusted his shoulders. "So you gave Perry the night off after all," he said, thumping ice from his shoes.

I had on one of my most alluring robes. Stroking it, he said, "I don't know who'd look better in this. You. Or Perry."

He led me to the stairs. "I fought my way through a blizzard for this, you know."

Moments later, we lay exhausted in each other's arms. "That was quick," I sighed.

JP sat up. "How about fixing me an omelet? I'm starving."

A few minutes later, he was hugging me as I stirred the eggs in a bowl. "Ready in a second," I said.

"Which shall I devour first? You or the eggs?"

"Very funny, " I said, reaching for a skillet.

"You know, you've got this place decorated like a French whorehouse. I can't stand that rug upstairs. Everytime we fuck on it, I spend an hour picking lint off my ass. And that damned ugly Picasso on the wall. Who gave that to you? Jack Warner? What did you have to do to get him to part with it?"

I spun round. Furious, I swung the skillet. Glancing off the side of his head, the pan rang hollowly, like a gong.

Stunned, he staggered forward and sagged against me. "Jesus, what are you doing?"

"That painting's a loan from a friend."

"I should have such friends."

I swung the pan again.

"Okay," he said, grabbing my wrist. "Well, you are human, huh?"

Appalled by what I had done, I sank to the floor in tears. "You made me do it! I never hit anyone in my life!"

"So it's a first! Why don't you write a poem about it?" He kissed me. "The hell with the omelet. Let's go upstairs and try for two in a row."

When his show moved to Philadelphia for further tryouts, I was determined to see him. He was adamant. "I've got enough *tsuris* with this damned production. That's Jewish. It means trouble. It's spelled S-H-E-I-L-A."

More determined than ever, I turned to what I did best, impersonation. From my treasure trove of disguises, I took a black wig, nondescript glasses, and a dress that fit the persona of an attractive but demure woman from a conservative home in a Main Line suburb.

Unrecognized, I took a train to Philadelphia and a taxi to JP's hotel. I called him on a lobby phone.

"Where are you?" he demanded, half angry, half surprised.

"I am in the lobby."

"You'd better not be."

"Well, I am."

"I don't believe this! I told you not to come!"

"I had to see you."

Anger turned to resignation. "Use the freight elevator."

Confident in my disguise, I took the main elevator.

When he opened his door, he stared in disbelief. "You know, Sheila, you're a chameleon! You're always playing some damn part! Sometimes I think you don't have a brain in your head!"

"That is a mistaken assumption a lot of people have made."

"Are you sure nobody saw you?"

"Everyone saw me," I said, removing the wig. "But no one saw what they thought they saw."

Presently, I found out that despite our efforts at secrecy, what was going on between us was widely known. The first person to make this clear to me was Steve McQueen. He had become one of Hollywood's brightest new stars and was riding the crest of his success as the supercool POW who had vaulted a barbed-wire fence on a motorcycle in *The Great Escape.*

I thought Steve was a very attractive man, he was a few years younger than I, and I was taken by surprise when he sent flowers to me at the Waldorf. Even more fascinating was the note he enclosed: "Spring is here, why doesn't my heart go dancing?"

When he called, I suggested that if he wanted to go dancing we could go to Arthur, one of the trendy nightspots. "Let's go somewhere more intimate," he said.

I reminded him that I was married. He replied, "I hear the man you're seeing is also married."

Shocked that he seemed to know about me and JP, I denied I was seeing anyone. But a worse jolt was yet to come when the quiet of my Sutton Place shelter was shattered by the ringing of the telephone. On the line was Dorothy Kilgallen, the "Voice of Broadway," who actually was better known to Americans for her appearances on television panel shows such as *What's My Line?* than for her newspaper gossip column. "I know about the affair you're having," she stated coldly, "and I'm going to blast you."

What a hypocrite, I thought. Here was this married woman whom everyone knew was having an affair with the singer Johnny Ray, and she was damning *me.*

"That's different," she replied. "I'm not news. You are. And so is the man you've been sleeping with."

Horrified, I phoned JP. He was brusque. "We're not supposed to be talking to each other for three months!"

"Kilgallen is onto us," I blurted.

"Yeah, the bitch has been calling here trying to get hold of me. My manager's practically having a heart attack. It'll all blow over once you've gotten your divorce. How's it going? The three months are almost up."

It was not going as smoothly as I wished. I had called the many lawyers I knew in New York, Washington, and Hollywood—Mickey Rudin, Jack Katz, Robert Shulman—only to be turned down. They were all friends and wanted no part in my divorcing Gordon. One lawyer said, "Why don't you two try to work things out? The guy's in love with you, Sheila. He keeps asking me, 'Why did she leave me?'"

Others told me similar stories. Gordon was in a terrible state. Stories about me and other men were ripping him apart. He was drinking harder than ever. He looked bad and sounded worse. Each was a quick dagger-stab into my heart, but I could not go back to him. That was settled. The golden idol had toppled. There was to be no raising it up. Could I make the final break with him and get a divorce? Not now. Not when he was so precarious. Could I *ever* divorce him? I simply didn't know. Certainly, I couldn't do it in the time JP had decreed.

The three months of his ultimatum would be up on February 12. I called on the tenth. When he picked up the phone, I blurted, "Don't ask me for an answer." I told him of my experience with the lawyers. "I talked with Gordon," I said. "He says he'll kill himself if I get a separation."

"And you believe that?"

"Yes, I believe it."

"So you still love him and don't love me."

"A person always loves the first love."

"Darling," he said icily, "you're making a big mistake."

"Perhaps," I cried. "God knows it's not the first."

"So this is good-bye." His voice was flint.

"Good-bye? Can't we be friends? Darling, please—please."

"You know what Edmund Kean said on his deathbed: 'Dying is easy; comedy is hard.' Loving you is easy, Sheila. Being friends may be a little harder."

It's been said that when God (or Fate or Luck) closes one door, another opens.

Not long after I told JP there would be no divorce, Perry came into my favorite room, the little blue space that I called my den and JP hated so much. "Excuse me, Mrs. MacRae," he said quietly. "There's a man at the door asking to see you."

"Who is it?"

"He looks like a banker in a homburg hat and Chesterfield coat," he said with a twinkle. "He *says* he's Frank Sinatra."

NINE

Mr. Francis Albert Sinatra

The Way Back

for F.A.S.

They are avenues, these things,
These gilded silks, these pieces,
These buttons on a dead coat.
They are perhaps avenues.
That one for the last time,
That one when you burst
In my mouth like a honeyed stick.
And that one and that one...
Avenues.
Dress, me love. I am Solomon's daughter.
A seventh sister of a seventh sister,
A sweet-lipped jasmine doll, a carnal friend.

But we who are strangers now
Were strangers then,
When hot liquid gold
Laid us under the then cornerless sky,
Descending shafts of air colored our bodies,
Disgorging deathless, breathless phrases
Of I want—need—love you.
Now we are strangers
Who meet in the far reaches of dreaming.

ROBERT PERRY KNEW Frank Sinatra very well. He had butlered for Frank, too. "Mr. Frankenstein," said Perry, using one of Frank's favorite nicknames, "told me that if you were in bed I wasn't to get you up, but to tell you it's five PM! He said, 'Tell *Mrs. Witch* to call me.'"

I flew out of bed, into a robe, and down the stairs. Tipping back his hat, Frank smiled. "Well, look at you. Do you greet all your guests in sexy lingerie?"

"Have you nothing to do, Francis, but roam the streets knocking on ladies' doors?"

"Are you going to invite me in for a drink? Or won't that stuffy English upbringing of yours permit you to uncork your liquor before six o'clock?"

"In your case," I said, dipping into an exaggerated curtsy, "the bar is open."

The conversation was about old times. Of course, I felt as if I had always known Frank Sinatra. Like every girl in America, I was crazy about the crooner who made bobby-soxers swoon in the aisles of the Paramount Theater, a very clever stunt arranged by Paramount publicity men. But I was interested in more than "The Voice" and his skinny good looks. I was amazed at the way he drenched himself in the songs, acting them!

In Hollywood, he and I had laughed across many a tabletop at dinner parties, and I had been front-and-center at so many of his shows in which the Frank I had always called Francis transformed himself into the Chairman of the Board. Onstage he was never less than the self-confident, bravura entertainer, perhaps the best of all time. Few stars had reached a point in their careers where they were defined simply by their last name: Chaplin, Valentino, Garbo, Caruso, Crosby, Sinatra.

Offstage and private, I saw Francis: quiet, sensitive, and often lonely. I recalled him coming to our house in the wee hours of a wet 1950's night in California, tapping on our door, apologizing for disturbing me, and telling us that he'd just cut a new record.

"I've got it here," he said, shyly holding up the acetate disc. "I know it's late, but could you give it a listen and tell me what you think of it?" The song was "It Never Entered My Mind."

I thought it was great, of course. Name a Sinatra performance that wasn't.

He was our neighbor when we lived at Taluca Lake, and he was a friend of mine, nothing more. To him I was Mac's lady. Otherwise, I should have fallen under his spell, just like every woman in America. Frank was the perfect gentleman and always asking about my children; first one, then two, then three, then four.

Now, at 13 Sutton Place, he asked, "How are the kids?" He wasn't inquiring as to their health, of course, but how Meredith, Heather, Garr, and Bruce were handling their parents' separation.

"They're doing fine. Every one is all right," I lied. They were not taking it well. Like all children whose parents part, they looked for fault in themselves. "What's wrong with me?" a child asks. "Don't Daddy and Mommy love me anymore?"

"They're great kids," Frank said. "And how 'bout you?"

"I'm sleeping days and out at night!"

"I hear there's someone special right now."

I detected an undertow of interest. "You know him."

"I hear you've gone from the frying pan into the fire," he said.

He sipped his drink. "Well, you know what I always say. 'Whatever gets you through the night.'" He put down his glass. "Speaking of getting through the night, what do you have on tap for this evening? Harry Kurnitz and I are getting together for dinner."

A former reporter, Harry was a novelist, playwright, and screenwriter, and one of my favorite people to play bridge with.

"How'd you like to join Harry and me? Or do you have...other plans?" Frank asked.

My intention was to remain at home in the hope that JP might call. It seemed as though I'd been spending all my time waiting for the phone to ring. Should I spend one more night playing the fool? Harry was a brilliant author, wit, and raconteur. Francis was, well, *Frank Sinatra!*

"At some point in the evening," Frank continued, "we're going to call Spencer Tracy. Today's his birthday. We're going to ring him up and wish him the best. I'm sure Spence would rather hear it from you."

"If it's Spencer Tracy's birthday," I said, "anything I was planning can damn well wait." To hell with waiting by the phone!

"Great," Frank exclaimed. "I'll pick you up at eight. That is, if Perry lets me in."

The dinner was delicious and fun. The call to Spencer Tracy was approached with trepidation and awe. I was as nervous as a schoolgirl told to report to the principal. I blurted out "Happy Birthday, Spence" and then totally inane blatherings about the movies of his that I adored.

"Sheila, my dear," said the movies' greatest actor, "I see that you ignored my advice instead of doing something really worthwhile. Kiss Francis for me."

Late that night, Frank escorted me to my red door. "This was nice," he said. "We should do it again sometime. The people at *Paris Match* have invited me to a big shindig. 'Bring somebody,' they said. How about if I bring you?"

"Sounds fine to me."

He grinned. "Good, because I already told them I'd be escorting the most beautiful lady in town. They asked who. I said, 'Sheila MacRae.' But that's a month from now. What about tomorrow night? Shall I call for you?"

"I'd like that," I said.

We kissed.

Perry opened the door, wordlessly. Going in, I asked, "Were there any calls?" I meant, "Any calls from JP?"

He replied with a favorite name for me. "No, Mrs. Mackie."

Barely upstairs, I heard the phone ring.

"It's the man who just said good night," called Perry.

"Hey, Sheel," Frank said excitedly. "I just found out Jack Benny's in town for a benefit, so a bunch of us are getting together with him late tonight at Jilly's. Then we're going up to my place for more festivities. Ava's also in town." He paused. "It'll be a crowd. Is that okay?"

"But *what* a crowd," I laughed. "I'll get a taxi and meet you."

"Great!"

Just west of Broadway on 52nd Street, Jilly's was a piano bar that would have been called a "joint" had it not become a hangout for Frank,

Tony Bennett, Judy Garland, and other top singers who were quite likely to feel the urge to get up and perform. The owner-host, Jilly Rizzo, was a longtime pal of the Chairman of the Board and saw to it that nobody sat at "Frank's table" as long as Frank was in town, not even Jack Benny.

Frank was the only person I knew who could order Jack around. "Tell the Ritz Brothers story," Frank demanded.

"Well, if you insist," Jack said coyly.

"I *do,* I *do,*" Frank said, feigning the impatient style that had made Jack famous.

"You all know the Ritz Brothers," Jack began. A comedy trio in vaudeville and movies, Al, Jim, and Harry were invited by Jack to an intimate party at his home in honor of Stewart Granger and his wife, Jean Simmons.

"I was worried," Jack continued. "You know how unpredictably zany the Ritz Brothers are! I was afraid they might do something to embarrass Jean. I told them, 'She's a very proper young lady and Stewart is a proper gentleman. So I expect the three of you to be on your best behavior!'"

"Jack!" Harry cried. "Would we do anything to embarrass you?"

"Yeah," Al said. "We know how to treat a lady."

"Of course we do," Jim asserted.

"On the evening of the party, the Grangers were late," Jack continued. "I was nervous. When they arrived. I rushed to greet them. 'What happened? I was worried!'"

"You wouldn't believe the shitty time we've had," Stewart said. "The goddamned car broke down right in the middle of the fuckin' freeway."

Smiling wanly as a fluttery hand rose to a jaw gone slack, Jack muttered, "Really?"

"It just pissed me off," Jean snapped, elbowing past Jack in the direction of the bar. "What I need is a fucking stiff shot of booze."

The Ritz Brothers rushed forward. "Hey, ain't you Jean Simmons?" Harry asked.

"Yes," Jean said, disdainfully.

"We've been waiting for you to show up," Al said.

"Yeah. We got somethin' for you, Jim said.

Whereupon, they spun around, dropped their pants, bent over, patted their bare behinds, and bellowed, "Kiss these, your royal highness!"

"Naturally," Jack said as his captivated audience at Jilly's roared with delight, "it was a setup! *She* planned the whole thing!"

To a thunderclap of applause, Jack sat beside me. "I was glad to see you laughing. I know you've been going through some rough times. But no long faces tonight, okay?"

"I'll try," I said.

"If you find yourself slipping into a blue funk, talk to Frank. He's a good listener."

Around midnight, we adjourned to the splendor of Frank's new penthouse. Created for him by combining two large apartments, it afforded a stunning panorama of the city. The guests were a panoply of major stars. It's rare when entertainers can get together because their work usually takes them far apart. So this sparkling autumn night was unique, like a gathering of eagles on a very high cliff with an East 72nd Street address.

Ava Gardner arrived late. For six years, from 1951 to 1957, she and Frank had been husband and wife. Now she took a seat beside Joe E. Lewis, holding the comedian's hand and taking in the room with her glorious green eyes framed by black-rimmed glasses as our host tended to his guests. "Hey, Francis, relax!" shouted Joe in his graveled, alcoholic voice. "You've got the job."

I was delighted to see that Frank and Ava could still be friends and for them, and maybe me, there could be life after divorce. I sat beside her. Presently, the conversation drifted to the subject of fans. Ava recalled seeing Bette Davis in a hotel in Madrid. "I went up to her and said, 'Miss Davis, I'm Ava Gardner and I'm a great fan of yours.' And you know, she behaved exactly as I wanted her to behave. She said, 'Of course you are,' and swept on."

Frank brought Ava a drink. "The ones who hang around stage doors and ask for autographs—they're fans," he said. "The ones who follow you all over the place—they're friends." My quote from Bennett Cerf.

By now, Frank Sinatra was far beyond the faked sensation of squealing bobby-soxers at the stage door. Since I had first met him backstage at the Paramount, as dreamy-eyed and swoony as my teenaged sisters outside, he had crossed the Rubicon into show business mythology.

The bony boy-crooner of the zoot-suit era was now in dapper middle age with a list of illustrious film credits to prove he was more than a heartthrob singer. On a shelf in his house stood the Oscar he had earned as Maggio in *From Here to Eternity*. Word was that Ava paid for his screen test that won him the role. He had been paid a paltry, low salary of $8,000 to play the part. In 1955, he had been nominated for an Academy Award for playing a drug addict in *The Man With the Golden Arm.* The next year, he made *High Society,* costarring with Bing Crosby and Grace Kelly, playing comedy to the hilt.

In 1957, he portrayed Joe E. Lewis in *The Joker Is Wild* with the same gritty reality and brash iconoclasm that Joe E. still possessed. At the party, he ordered Frank to stop fussing over his guests "like a nervous probationary waiter."

Several films in which Frank played tough guys and the ugly, persistent rumors that he was connected to "the Mob" created in the minds of some people who were neither fans nor friends of Frank Sinatra the impression that he had a chip on his shoulder in real life. From time to time someone figured he ought to knock it off. I had seen it happen. We were attending a party at the home of photographer Douglas Duncan in Palm Springs. Rather than the small gatherings I was accustomed to going to, this was a very large affair with many unfamiliar faces. Frank was there with Dean Martin.

Of course, Frank was the center of attention. Paying very special attention to him was a flirty young woman whose jealous boyfriend was not amused. Whatever sordid images may have been simmering up in his brain boiled over. Clutching Frank's collar in the ball of a fist, he yelled, "Keep away from my woman."

"Take it easy, pal," Frank said, calmly adjusting his jacket.

The man jabbed a finger into Frank's chest. "You think you're a big deal, don'tcha? Well, you're nothin' but a dago wop."

"Hey, fella, settle down," Frank implored.

Lurching to the bar, the man grabbed a whiskey bottle. Smashing it, he lunged toward Frank.

Dean Martin, who had once been a saloon bouncer, thwarted the attack, grasping the hand that was holding the jagged glass. "I don't know who the hell you are," he said, "but nobody gets away with calling my friend Frank a dago wop except another dago wop like me."

Wrenching the bottle from the man's hand, Dean twisted his arm behind his back. "Had a little too much to drink?" he asked, shoving the man toward the door. "Well, why don't you just go home and sleep it off?"

If there was anyone "more equal" than the other members of the Rat Pack—excepting Frank, of course—it was Dean. Probably this was because Dean and Frank had so much in common, being Italians and singers who had successfully crossed over into movies, whereas Joey Bishop was a Jewish comedian, Peter Lawford was the suave and sophisticated Englishman with Kennedy family connections, and Sammy Davis, Jr., was a product of Harlem and the humiliations of life on the road as an entertainer in a segregated America.

In an Oscar-winning and, at the time (1945), controversial short film for RKO titled *The House I Live In,* Frank had made a strong appeal for racial and religious tolerance. "All races, all religions; that's America to me," he sang. "And the right to speak my mind out; that's America to me." Its message was one in which Frank deeply believed, as he had proved in the stand he took during the HUAC period and was demonstrating in his public friendship with Sammy in the raging battles of the 1960s, when celebrities were told that they risked their careers if they came out for equal rights.

I first became conscious of the plight of blacks in the United States soon after my father transplanted us here from England. We lived first in New Orleans, where my grandfather had settled, and I had the children of our black cook as playmates. From them I learned how to imitate their speech. Indeed, it was an early display of my ability to impersonate people, even if it did shock my grandfather to hear me talking like our cook's children. But when he told me that because we were in the South I couldn't invite my black friends to my birthday party, my mother insisted.

Another reason for my having an early appreciation of racial prejudice was an aunt. She had confronted considerable resentment and some ostracism in England because she had married "a man of color." That he was the son of the Maharaja Rattan Chakravati, and therefore Indian royalty, made no difference to race- and class-conscious bigots.

Some of Gordon's friends repeatedly warned him not to get involved in the civil rights movement. Our neighbor, Gene Autry, was especially dire in his view of the negative effects Gordon could expect from audiences that were turning out in great numbers to see him in person.

"They're paying to see Gordon MacRae and to listen to you sing love songs," Gene said. "They don't want to be reminded of what's going on in the country right now. They want to escape. That's your job, your cause. If you become associated in their minds with politics, they'll be turned off. Look what happened to Paul Robeson. Once the public associated him with Communists, he was washed up, no matter how well he could sing 'Old Man River.'"

Other friends pressured us to come out strongly behind the civil rights movement, especially when a giant protest march was being organized for Selma, Alabama, where a previous one had been brutally suppressed. In the lead in soliciting support from celebrities were Harry Belafonte and Marlon Brando.

"Sheila, I'm trying to raise money to hire an airplane," Marlon explained to me on the telephone. "It's to take a bunch of kids down to Selma. Will you help?"

"I'll not only help," I said, "I'll go along."

Gordon was flabbergasted. "The hell you will," he said.

As in the HUAC period, my closest friends were against my taking a public stand. "It could be bad for Gordie," Lucy said. "I don't think your going to Selma is a good idea," Bob Newhart told me.

"Well, I'm going," I told them. And I did. Once again I was a lady in disguise. Flying down alone and wearing a wig and dark glasses so as not to be recognized as Mrs. Gordon MacRae and possibly embarrassing Gordon, I marched far behind those who had linked arms with the Rev. Martin Luther King, Jr. I was simply another face in the crowd, one more body in the incredible show of solidarity that was a turning point of the struggle. Three years later, following the assassination of Dr. King, I was separated from Gordon and free to be myself, taking part in a memorial for Dr. King in New York arranged by Harry Belafonte, Barbra Streisand, and Sammy Davis, Jr.

Sammy and I were kindred spirits because we were both impressionists. Impersonations were woven into his song-and-dance act, and he had a penchant, as did I, for blending into his surrounding and taking on the style and tone of the people and places around him. He was—and so was I, as JP would later point out to me—like a chameleon. This was never more obvious than when Gordon and I ran into Sammy in London as he exited his hotel on his way to the theater. He was wearing a black bowler and spats and carrying a walking stick, and his voice had taken on the cadences of the English.

"What I love about the theater in London," he said in a Mayfair accent, "is its texture. It's the very essence of London."

Gordon guffawed. "What is this bullshit? Sammy, you never did legit theater in your life!"

What Sammy was doing seemed perfectly fine to me. I didn't think, as Gordon did, that he was putting on an act. He was simply fitting in. I'd done so countless times. All actors did it. Except Gordon! With

Albert Gordon MacRae there was never artifice, which, perhaps, is why he enjoyed the company of men who weren't actors.

In the early years of Sammy's struggle, he had a mentor in Hollywood who was also a very close and old friend of mine, Jeff Chandler. With chiseled cheekbones and curly prematurely gray hair, this rugged he-man often found himself cast in Westerns. Twice he played the Indian chief Cochise, and he was nominated for an Oscar for the role in *Broken Arrow*. Born Ira Grossel, in Brooklyn, he'd been a dear friend of mine since we had met in acting classes in New York. The last thing I imagined him becoming was a star in Westerns.

Alas, his brilliant career ended much too soon. He died in 1961 of blood poisoning following surgery. He was forty-two. "Too damned young to go," Sammy said. "How come so many of the good people die young?"

We had all seemed ageless then, immortal, especially Frank. With each passing year he got better, miraculously transforming himself from "The Voice" to "Chairman of the Board" and carving a niche in American theatrical history that no performer is likely to come close to matching.

Frank was direct and honest in a way that neither Gordon nor JP had been. I'd never known a man as considerate of me. I knew he was having troubles with his family and that the business of being Frank Sinatra imposed enormous burdens on him, yet he never brought those concerns into our relationship. When he was with me, he was able to bury all his cares in a separate part of him like the chambered Nautilus. He wasn't Frank Sinatra. He was Francis.

I felt that my soul was connected to Frank as it had been to Gordon in the earliest years of our marriage when he was in the air force. There was with Frank that same inexplicable link. No matter how far away he was, I sensed him nearby. Then, quite suddenly, on a day when Frank was on the West Coast and I was wrapped again in the comfort of my bedroom on Sutton Place, I awoke with a start. It was as if someone had spoken my name. I'd been dreaming. Oh, dreaming a horrible vision of Frank aboard his Lear jet as it skidded off the runway, I shuddered with the same cold dread that had gripped me when I'd had a vision of Gordon's plane in trouble during the war. Terrified, I grabbed the phone. It was seven in the morning in New York. In California, it was four o'clock. "Hey, Sheila," Frank said, "what's so important that you're calling at this ungodly hour?"

"Thank heaven you're safe," I exclaimed.

"Hey, I'm in bed. How safe can I be? Now tell me what this is all bout."

"I had a bad dream. You were on your plane. There was an accident. Are you going anywhere, Francis?"

"Yeah. Dean and I have to zip down to San Diego today."

"Oh, Francis, no." I told him what I had dreamt. "Don't go." I pleaded.

"Gotta go, sweetheart. Dino and I have business down there."

"Well, please don't fly."

He laughed. "Darling, I'm certainly not going to waste the whole damned day on the San Diego Freeway. Don't worry. Go back to bed."

Sleep was impossible. The day dragged by.

At five that evening, the phone rang.

"Guess what, Mrs. Witch?" Frank said. "That dream of yours? It came true! There was a landing gear problem as we were taxiing for a takeoff. The jet did this crazy little jig and wound up stuck in the grass. Nobody hurt." He paused. "That damned dream proves what I always suspected about you."

Hearing his voice, I felt my anxieties melt. I laughed.

"What's so funny?" he asked.

"When I hear your voice my teeth buzz!"

"Wadda ya mean, yuh teeth?" he said, imitating the "deze and doze" accents he had heard on the streets when he was growing up in New Jersey. "Wha'd about dat place down dere?"

I laughed. "Next time, *listen* to the witch."

"The plane's got to be fixed, so I won't be able to send it to collect you. You'll have to fly commercial."

"Where am I going?"

"Why, you're coming out here. Gotta see you! We'll go to Minna Wallis's for dinner. There'll be a lot of old friends there including Hal, her brother. Then to Palm Springs. Jimmy Van Heusen says not to show up without you. And he promises that this time you won't have to worry about no bikes and blood all over the floor!"

The songwriter was a great friend of Frank's and had been close to Gordon and me. Having gotten Gordon started in radio, he was thrilled when the protégé he had discovered in Syracuse wound up in Hollywood with him.

A native Syracusan himself, Jimmy, whose real name was Edward

Chester Babcock, had started his show business career at the age of fifteen as a piano player in a music publishing house in his hometown. Studying both piano and voice at Syracuse University, he also worked at a local radio station as an announcer, just the job Gordon's mother had had in mind for her son.

Had either Gordon or Jimmy stayed with it, the course of American musical history would have been different; no *Oklahoma!* and *Carousel* for Gordon, no timeless hits written by Jimmy Van Heusen and Sammy Cahn and recorded by Frank Sinatra: "Young at Heart," "The Tender Trap," "The Second Time Around," "My Kind of Town," "The September of My Years," "Love and Marriage," "All the Way," "High Hopes," "Only the Lonely," and my favorite, "But Beautiful," which Jimmy had written with Johnny Burke.

A bachelor with a keen eye for women, Jimmy named his house in Palm Springs "Casa de Lobos." Despite the inherent warning, or because of it, beautiful women flocked to it, guided by a pair of palm trees towering over the forbidding desert. With their eyes on those beckoning fronds, Jimmy's Hollywood friends also wended their way to the house of wolves. He enjoyed having company and was always a generous and solicitous host.

Not long after Gordon and I arrived in Hollywood, and long before we could afford a Palm Springs address of our own, Jimmy invited us down for a weekend. Barely settled in, Gordon got a phone call from the studio. "I've got to go back," he announced. His new picture was in the postproduction stage. "There's a problem with the sound. I've got to do some looping. Come on, Sheila, pack your things."

"Why should your wife be stuck in town," Jimmy said, "just because you have work to do?"

Knowing there was no arguing with Jimmy when he'd made up his mind about something, Gordon agreed that I could stay.

The centerpiece of Jimmy's friendly oasis was an immense swimming pool. Heading for it in a modest one-piece bathing suit, I heard Jimmy groan. "What is *that* you have on? No, no, it just won't do. You'll get a real tan in a bikini! C'mon, we'll hop in my jeep and go into town and get you one."

"Jimmy, I don't think Gordie would approve."

"You leave Gordo to me!"

"But I didn't bring any money."

"We'll put it on my account."

Along with an array of skimpy suits, the owner of the shop presented me with a selection of short, lacy, black and pink see-through short nighties. "Oh no, I'm not interested in these," I said, blushing.

"Don't be bashful," she said. "All of Mr. Van Heusen's girls take them."

On the way back to Casa de Lobos, Jimmy swung the jeep off the main road. "Let's drop by and see if the dago's at home," he said. Lounging by his pool in a silk robe that accentuated his thinness, Frank appeared as a silhouette against the glare coming off the smooth water. "Get dressed," Jimmy commanded. "You're coming with us to my place. A bevy of chicks is coming over for dinner. I need you to cook the spaghetti sauce."

The party took place at poolside, the quiet of the desert night punctuated by girlish giggles. Amidst this frivolity and feeling totally out of place, I slipped away to call Gordon. "Hell, don't worry about it," he said.

"I miss you, and I got a sunburn."

"Just relax and enjoy yourself."

After Frank left the party, I went to my room. Anticipating the peace and quiet and the clean air and tranquility of a weekend in the desert, I had brought a couple of novels. Reading proved impossible. There was just too much noise. "Whatever are they doing?" I wondered as the night crept toward dawn.

Quiet settled, at last, but around three in the morning I still was wide awake and wishing that Gordon were beside me. As the sun came up, I realized I was hungry. Creeping from my room, I made my way in the dim light toward the kitchen. Stepping into the living room, I was stepping on debris. The room was a mess. Furniture was shifted and overturned. Ash trays overflowed. The air was thick with the smell of stale cigarette smoke. There seemed to be a hundred half-filled liquor glasses. Pillows were strewn everywhere. Pictures hung askew. My horrified eyes fell on a badly misshaped bicycle. A trail of bloodstains led to the door. "My God," I thought, "somebody's been killed!"

I raced to Jimmy's bedroom. I knocked several times on the door. Unanswered, I turned the knob and pushed open the door. In the half-light I saw a form upon the bed. It was Jimmy, sound asleep and naked. Taking a step into the room to call him, I felt something squishy beneath my feet. Looking down, I gasped at what I was standing on. A doormat, it was made of rubber breasts of all sizes and shapes with their pink nipples jutting up. "Oh my God," I groaned. "Gordon will love it!"

Jimmy awoke with a start. "What is it, hon?" he asked, still half asleep.

"There's . . . there's . . . blood!"

"Oh, that," he said, settling back. "One of Brenda Allen's girls fell off a bike."

"Brenda Allen?" I recognized the name of Hollywood's most notorious madam. "*She* was here?"

"Yeah. The girl's fine. Don't worry about it."

Gordon returned that evening to howl with laughter as Jimmy told him everything. "You've got a terrific wife, Gordie," said Jimmy, joining in the laughter, "but she may be too sensitive for this town."

Jimmy finally married late in life. He died in 1990, leaving a reputation as a legendary lover and a legacy of music that will be listened to for as long as young lovers play the recordings of Frank Sinatra.

After nearly three decades of singing, Frank often talked about retiring. "I'm going to get out of this business of being Frank Sinatra," he said to me one night as he stood in front of the fireplace in his sprawling, brownish house in Palm Springs. "I may leave the country. I certainly ought to get out of this state, now that Reagan's governor."

He had not forgotten or forgiven Ronald Reagan's cooperation with the House Un-American Activities Committee.

"Maybe I'll just chuck everything and become a hermit!" He gave it a try in 1971. Happily for his fans, he quickly abandoned the idea and went on to become a bigger star than ever.

Although he lived in California, Frank loved returning to his roots in New York, ever mindful of his beginnings in Hoboken, New Jersey, just across the river. Lying beside him in the Sutton Place cocoon that he had come around to share with me one cold gray afternoon, I thought about what a movie his life story would make—skinny kid starts out singing with "The Hoboken Four," gets a big break on Major Bowes' Amateur Hour, lands jobs singing with Harry James and Tommy Dorsey, creates a sensation at the Paramount on Broadway as bobby-soxers swoon in the aisles right on cue from their prompters, is known as "The Voice," goes on to take Hollywood by storm, hits a slump, makes a smashing comeback and rockets into superstardom in every aspect of show business, and becomes an American icon that nothing could tarnish or topple.

Now, here I was lying beside him in his New York penthouse and experiencing emotions that I had known with Gordon. In making love with Gordon, I felt I was a mortal favored by a god. That Gordon loved me had been overwhelming. Now it felt the same with Frank.

I was humming.

"What?" Frank asked.

"Gordie used to sing to me in bed."

"You'll like this better," he said, turning to me, bending down, kissing me. "You okay, baby?" He lifted his head and fixed me with those famous blue eyes. "Old blue eyes," they called him. Gazing into those eyes, I realized I was falling in love with him.

"Picking you up at seven," he said on the phone later. "We're having dinner at Côte Basque with Bennett and Phyllis Cerf." Most people knew Bennett as the owlish panelist on *What's My Line?*, not as the publisher of Random House books.

Arlene Francis, superb actress and Bennett's cohort on *What's My Line?*, and her husband, Martin Gabel, a distinguished actor, joined us at dinner. Seated between Gabel and Bennett, I was, at last, able to ignore Lucy Ball's advice about not talking of poetry. Of course, if you were in the company of the Cerfs, the Gabels, and Francis Albert Sinatra, any topic was fair game.

As long as I was with other people when I was out in public with Frank, I was at ease. In the midst of a crowd, I felt safe from criticism and any suspicion that there was something going on between us. Because I was so sensitive about being apart from Gordon but not divorced, I was nervous about being seen in public with Frank under circumstances that might be construed as a Frank-and-Sheila love affair. That concern was demonstrated at its most extreme one day when we were at Frank's house in Palm Springs. It was a gorgeous day, and he was eager to go out. "Are we going to sit around here all day?" he asked pleadingly. "C'mon. Let's get in some golf."

Thinking that a game of golf with a friend could be easily explained, I agreed, but the moment we left the house and walked out onto the course, I saw Lucy's husband, Gary Morton. Gripped with panic, I dashed back into the house. Desperate not to be recognized, I braided my hair and put on a large bandana and black sunglasses. To complete the disguise, I adopted a German accent.

Gary was fooled.

Frank was astonished. "You know," he said, shaking his head, "you're bizarre." Later, he said, "You're ashamed to be seen alone with me."

"It's not you," I cried. "It's just that you're single and I'm not."

Nowhere did Frank attract more attention than in Las Vegas. "I'll be leaving town next week. Playing the Sands," he announced one day.

"I shall miss you terribly," I said.

"Hell, babe, you're coming with me!"

Because I knew he would be surrounded by many friends, I felt that I could be among them without causing tongues to wag, so I accepted the invitation with confidence that I would not read in newspapers that I was betraying Gordon for an affair with Sinatra.

We shared the "Star Bungalow" at the Sands. It had two huge bedrooms and a couple of smaller ones for the use of some of his "retinue," as some newspapers termed Frank's pals, the Rat Pack.

Dean Martin was staying nearby, experiencing another of his separations from Jeannie. Keeping him company was the actress Rosemary Forsyth. A dazzling five-foot-eight twenty-year-old with blue eyes, long hair, and a gorgeous body, she had come to Hollywood from a modeling career and TV. She'd been in *Shenandoah* and *The War Lord* and was signed for *Texas Across the River* with Dean and Joey Bishop, a charter member of the Rat Pack.

Rosalind Russell and her husband, Freddie Brisson, were also in our group, as were Laurence Harvey, Mike Romanoff, his pretty young wife, Gloria, and Gary and Lucy.

Peter Lorre was also there, that lovably charming bogeyman of so many wonderful movies. Because he was involved in a messy divorce, he had not wanted to register under his own name, so Frank had him listed on the books as Piper Laurie. There was also an arrangement to pay a young girl $700 to keep Peter company for the weekend.

Opening night, Frank was in high spirits. I was in a highly nervous state. Wearing a white beaded dress, I was to be seated in front. Being with Frank so publicly, I feared that Gordon's fans might say hurtful things to me. I was painfully aware that my mother and sister, Paula, weren't happy with me seeing Frank. They wanted me to go back to Gordon. I understood their feelings. Divorce was anathema in our family, all Church of England. Paula was particularly upset because her children had told her that they were teased in school about their aunt's separation from Gordon MacRae. There'd been a photo in the *New York Times* of me with Frank, and although Gordon was half a world away, appearing in Australia, I was afraid someone would make sure he saw the picture.

After the first show, we were all to have dinner with Frank. Going into the dining room, he took my hand and led me aside. "You should know that Mac called from Australia." My heart sank. "It's okay," Frank said. "He just phoned to wish me luck."

After the second show, I raced to the bungalow to wait for Frank. In bed, I delighted in watching the meticulous way he had of putting away cuff links and hanging up his clothes. He was so totally sure of himself, so confidently masculine that he could scent his handkerchiefs with Jungle Gardenia. He came to bed in a loose-fitting robe. He was silent for a long while. At last he stirred. "When's the last time you saw *him?*"

"Three weeks ago," I said.

"JP hasn't called?"

"How could he? You had my phone number changed, don't you remember?"

"Oh, yeah."

"Robert Perry wants to know if you can also get his number changed. He says his bookies are driving him crazy."

"I'll see what I can do about it. No promises. The bookies probably have more influence than I do at the phone company. You know, I'm in this too deep already. Well, let's not get answers tonight."

"Good," I sighed, happy to be lost in Francis's world of tender, comforting sensuality and out of JP's domain of demands and ultimatums.

Hours later, drowsy and languid, I was lying with my head on Francis's chest when the door burst open. With a roar, he lurched up and flung the sheet over me. "Get out!" he yelled toward the startled figure silhouetted in the doorway. "I'm not alone!"

"Sorry," Frank Sinatra, Jr., gasped, sheepishly ducking out and closing the door. He'd come to the bungalow quite innocently, hoping to have breakfast with his dad.

"He ought to know better," Frank growled. "He's not a kid anymore. He should knock before entering."

"It's all right, Francis," I said, rather more amused than embarrassed.

"No, it is not all right!" he snapped. "I would never do that to him, or anyone else."

He fell silent, and I thought he'd gone back to sleep, but then he reached for my hand. "Sheila, you've got to tell me what you're feeling," he said, kissing my fingertips.

"I—I don't know, Francis," I said, bursting into tears.

"What's the problem?" he demanded.

Lawyers were a problem, I answered. The lawyers I knew were Gordie's friends and didn't want to help me get a divorce! "No one will take the case."

"I've got lawyers," he said.

"It's no good," I cried. "Gordon won't consent to a divorce anyway."

He fixed me with those dazzling blue eyes. "Hell, you can zip down to Tijuana. In a Mexican divorce, Mac will have no say."

Now that Gary Morton would be seeing me with Frank, I did not have to hide, and Lucy told me, "Francis is good for you, he's so smart." Many other friends felt the same way. However, there was another voice that demanded to be heard, that small, quiet, but nagging voice that is separate from heart and head and speaks up on the topic of what is best at this moment, regarding me and JP. What it whispered and then shouted was: "Run away! This is not for you now."

Francis and I saw each other on both coasts. He made plans for us to go to Mexico as house guests of Merly Perly (Merle Oberon), a lady we both knew. I didn't tell him I had no records for a passport. Neither my sister, Paula, nor I. But the plans changed and I ran to Margy Cowan's yacht.

I did not rush down to Mexico to divorce Gordon.

A few weeks later, Frank showed up at Sutton Place. With him was Jack Entratta, the Las Vegas showman. "I belong here in this house," I said.

"I'll buy this house. What are you going to do?"

"Frank, listen to the lady," Jack said. "She's saying nothing."

Francis Albert Sinatra stared out at the river. "I want to be married."

One day later in Las Vegas, he married Mia Farrow, a much-heralded and talked-about surprise of which Ava Gardner quipped, "I always knew Frank would end up in bed with a boy."

TEN

Jackie Gleason and the Last Alice Kramden

IN AN ARTICLE IN *TV Guide* in 1967 I was quoted as saying, "Frank Sinatra and Alice Kramden saved my sanity." By that time Francis Albert Sinatra and JP were both out of my life and Gordon was still a part of the personal drama I was writing ... but like a ghost: Banquo at the banquet.

While trying to uncomplicate my life, I drowned myself in work by plunging into a revival of *Guys and Dolls,* playing Miss Adelaide, as I'd done many times in road-show versions starring Gordon. Now I had the great fun of bringing Adelaide to the stage again.

The production was a New York City Center revival with Alan King as Nathan, Anita Gillette as Sarah, roly-poly Stubby Kaye reprising his Broadway triumph as Nicely-Nicely Johnson ("Sit down, you're rockin' the boat!"), and Jerry Orbach as Sky. It was a splendid show, one of the best I'd ever seen put together, and there was serious interest on the part of Frank Loesser in keeping the production going in a different theater.

Unfortunately, Alan and I had other commitments, so the project never materialized.

Had it become a reality, I would not have been able to seize an opportunity that breezed into my dressing room in the rotund form of Jackie Gleason. "Sheel, you were great," he blared. "Just fabulous." He was quite familiar with my impressions and comedic abilities from my appearances on his television shows, but this was the first time he had seen me act. "Are you serious about this acting stuff?" he asked.

"Yes, I am." If Jack Warner could hear me now, I thought. "I started out to be an actress."

"Well, you sure are good at it."

Praise from Jackie meant a great deal to me because, like almost everyone else, I was a tremendous fan of his. Not only was he one of the greatest comedians, as his riotous performances on his television shows had demonstrated, but he was a superb actor. He had created many fabulous characters: the pathetic Poor Soul, the outrageous lush Reggie van Gleason, garrulous Joe the bartender, and the bellowing, conniving, "hoping to strike it rich" dreamer and bus driver Ralph Kramden of *The Honeymooners*. He truly was "the Great One."

One of the pioneers of television, he made his debut on the small screen in 1949 in the first version of *The Life of Riley*. The following season he starred in a variety show on the Dumont network, *Cavalcade of Stars,* when he introduced most of his indelible comedic characters to a growing television audience and added new phrases to the language: "How sweet it is!" "And away we go!" and "A little traveling music, please!"

An integral part of these shows was *The Honeymooners* sketch, featuring the exploits of Ralph, the hapless Brooklyn bus driver who schemed and plotted to find a quick way to get rich and to extricate himself and his patient wife, Alice, from their two-room cold-water flat in Bensonhurst just downstairs from their best friends, the equally long-suffering Trixie Norton and her sewer-worker spouse, the scatterbrained Ed. These roles had made stars of Art Carney as Norton, Joyce Randolph as Trixie, and Audrey Meadows as Alice. The phenomenally successful quartet eventually starred in a series of half-hour productions in Jackie's 1955–56 season, and, preserved on film and released in TV syndication, *The Honeymooners* attained television immortality, retaining its popularity and freshness decades later.

Some of Jackie's TV shows were spotty in their success. After *The Honeymooners,* he had a live half-hour series on Fridays that featured Buddy Hackett. It was yanked from the screen in midseason. In 1961 he was host of a game show, *You're in the Picture.* It was so bad that Jackie canceled it himself after its debut and went on the air to apologize to the audience for "that bomb," Gordo and I at his side!

Nobody knew the ups and downs of show business better than Jackie. He'd been at it since the age of thirteen after winning an amateur-night contest. He was in vaudeville and carnivals and had worked in nightclubs and on Broadway. In 1940, Hollywood beckoned when Warner Bros. signed him for small character roles. What the movies failed to discover in Jackie Gleason, television found in abundance, an amazingly versatile comedic talent and acting ability which, ironically, took him back to Hollywood in the 1960s for major roles in film dramas as a pool shark in *The Hustler,* a prizefight manager in *Requiem for a Heavyweight,* and an army sergeant in *Soldier in the Rain.*

"When I first went to Hollywood, I made two hundred dollars a week," Jackie recalled, "and I had more fun there than I did in my entire life. It's a whole different climate now. Segregated as hell. There are five-hundred-dollar-a-week actors, and they hang out together. Then there are the thousand-dollar ones, the two-thousand, the five-thousand. And they all hang out with their own. It's so boring. It stinks."

I first met Jackie in 1954 when I was pregnant with Bruce. He was doing his popular Saturday night variety show at the CBS Theater at Broadway and 54th Street, since renamed in honor of Ed Sullivan, whose shows also came from there. Jackie liked the studio because it was only a few blocks from the hotel where he had his offices at 58th Street and Sixth Avenue. Then called the Park Sheraton, the hotel had a notorious moment in 1957 when gangland boss Albert Anastasia was assassinated in a hail of bullets while having a haircut in the barber shop, a scene somewhat replicated in *The Godfather.*

If Jackie especially liked a male guest on the show, he invited him to his extravagant home in Peekskill, a manly, woodsy, and remote spot up the Hudson from New York. Accordingly, when Gordon was booked onto the show, he was asked to go up. Telling me about it on the phone, Gordon became very excited. "Guess what?" he said. "Jackie is going to let you join us."

The tone of it put me off. "Let" me join them? "Who is this guy

Gleason?" I said to myself. Is he a royal personage? Then I understood what was happening. Jackie had intended a compliment. He was allowing me into his all-male bastion.

"Jackie's sending a limo to pick you up," Gordon continued, "and then you'll pick us up at Toots Shor's."

I waited in the car outside for an hour, knowing exactly what was going on inside, the "guys" crowded at the bar, each with another story to tell and then one to top that, lots of yarns about "broads" while Toots kept the liquor flowing. When, at last, Gordon and Jackie piled into the back of the limousine, Jackie leaned toward me and said, "Gordon tells me that you're a great believer in spiritual stuff and that you used it to save his life once. Something about the Ninety-first Psalm? He wasn't too clear about it, so I want to hear it from you. Tell me everything."

Embarrassed and shocked that Gordon had revealed the episode to a man I knew only from television, I had a feeling of being trapped and that the only way out was to tell the story. Jackie listened with rapt attention. "That's amazing," he said. "When we get to my house, I'm going to show you my ectoplasm."

"Your *ectoplasm?*"

"You'll see," he said, patting my hand as my father had done so often when counseling patience and faith.

The house in Peekskill was a surprise. It was round! Not a straight wall in it. "No corners," Jackie explained. "No place for spirits to lodge in!"

From a shelf in his den, he took down a bronze box with a thick glass lid. Inside lay a glutinous substance that looked like aspic or white Jell-O. He looked at me with the quizzical expression of a child. "If I thought you'd laugh or think I was nuts, I wouldn't be showing you this, Sheel, but that stuff is ectoplasm. A spiritualist captured it for me."

He showed me his library of books on spiritualism, the occult, and UFOs. "I'm kind of a nut on the subject," he bellowed, laughing. "Hey, maybe 'nut' isn't the right word, eh? Think of the fun the columnists and the writers for *TV Guide* would have if they got a load of all this, hunh?" Beneath the laughter was a plea: "I've let you in on my little secret, Sheel. I trust you to keep it to yourself."

Having experienced acute embarrassment after Gordon told fan magazines about my experience with an apparition in the house that Gordon and I were considering buying shortly after we went to

Hollywood, I appreciated Jackie's anxiety in having confided in me. "I shall tell no one," I vowed, a promise I kept so long as Jackie lived.

Our friendship was sealed that day in Peekskill, though I never could watch Jackie on television and not see a more complicated, deeper soul than the roustabout comedian which he flaunted so brilliantly on the air.

In the fall of 1962, he was back on television with a new show. *Jackie Gleason and His American Scene Magazine* was crammed with comedy sketches and musical numbers. Gordon and I again had such fun being guest stars. In 1966, he moved this highly rated show from New York to Miami Beach, where he could play golf year-round.

What I did not know on the evening when Jackie "dropped by" backstage at City Center to heap praise on my performance as Adelaide was that he was planning to revive *The Honeymooners* as an hour-long show with singing and dancing. He would drop the "magazine" from the title and simply call it *The Jackie Gleason Show.* That he had ideas about putting me on the show was not mentioned during his dressing room visit. I learned this later when the phone shook me out of a deep sleep at 13 Sutton Place. Right away I recognized Jackie's voice. He was in his cups. "Lissen, Sheel, I wanna talk to you about somethin'. Don't worry. I'm not gonna ask you out. This is business. I want you to play Alice."

"Alice?" I asked, too sleepy to comprehend. "Alice who?"

"Alice *who?*" he barked incredulously. "Alice Kramden, that's who! I'm bringing back *The Honeymooners.* Only this time it'll be different. This time it's gonna have music and songs. With your singing voice and sense of comedy, and being such a good actress, you'll be perfect as Alice. Will you do it? "

"Well, Jackie," I said hesitantly, "I can't live in Florida. I have a house here. My son is in school here. I'm going to make my life here in New York."

After a long pause, he sounded quite disappointed. "Listen. If you change your mind, will ya call me?"

In the morning when I awoke, I first thought I had dreamed everything. When I realized I hadn't, I wondered if I had made a terrible mistake. What had he seen in me similar to Alice Kramden?

My next thought was to call Sammy Davis, Jr. He was always wise in matters concerning show business. And he was a genuine expert on TV, a real buff. There was nothing he didn't know about it. He would know everything about the role of Alice, I expected, and I was right. He gave me her entire history.

"The first gal in the part was Pert Kelton," he said on the phone from California. A veteran comedic actress on stage and in films, the Irish Pert had played Alice for one year. The quieter Audrey Meadows had brought a no-nonsense independence to her Alice for four seasons. Beauty queen Sue Ane Langdon had played Alice once. "It's obvious that Jackie thinks you'd be perfect if he's going to be doing musicals," Sammy said. "Incidentally, so do I."

I thought of reasons why I should turn down the part. "Sheila, Sheila," my agent, Bobby Brenner, warned. "You can't play Alice Kramden. You've got a totally wrong image. You're a jet-setter. You're too classy to play a Brooklyn housewife in a cold-water walk-up!"

I replied, "I'm an actress."

"Yeah, yeah, I know. Actors can be anything," said Bobby. "But I didn't put you on the list. Forget all that Stanislavsky stuff."

I phoned Jackie in Miami Beach. "What are you doin' up this early?" he joked.

"I've been thinking about Alice Kramden. I could do *one* show playing Alice for you."

"What do you mean *one*? Look, let's talk it over. Come down to Florida. A car will pick you up at the airport and bring you out to the Doral Country Club or the track."

The track was Hialeah. Again, I waited, picturing him out on the golf course and totally absorbed in a game, just like Gordon. "Sorry to keep you, Sheel," he said, as blasé as Gordon had ever been. "I beat the pants off the guy!" We talked during lunch in the clubhouse. "So, tell me what you think of *The Honeymooners*."

"Ralph and Alice are not the honeymooners. It's really Ralph and Norton. They're the real honeymooners." I said. "It's really an innocent *ménàge à trois*. The Alice keeps changing, but you and Art go on forever."

Rearing back and dragging on his cigarette, he cocked his head and grinned. "You're pretty sharp, lady. Of course it's a triangle." He ground out the cigarette and lifted a tumbler of scotch. "So what do you say? Will you be my new Alice? And you got great legs!"

I gazed out the window at the beautiful club grounds. I'd played in Florida hotels often—the Deauville, the Diplomat, and others—and enjoyed myself, but after a few weeks I found myself growing tired of Florida. "I just don't think I could live down here long term."

Suddenly, a quizzical light flashed in his eyes. "I'm thinking of a number between one and twenty-five. What is it?"

My answer popped out. "Seven!"

"Right! Seven. I'm planning seven *Honeymooners!* See? You picked right up on it. That number seven wasn't just in my mind, it was in yours! It's a destiny number for both of us. It means that you're gonna be my new Alice! It's fate."

Was it? Might I be destined to become Alice Kramden? I gave no answer. "I have to think about this."

"Sure. Meantime, I'll talk to your agent. Just in case the answer is yes, which I'm sure it will be. Seven, Sheel! It's our destiny number."

Lucy Ball had no doubt what my answer should be. "Look, hon, you've got to think this through clearly. So, you don't like the idea of living in Florida! That's no reason for making a business decision. From a money standpoint, this is good for you. You're out on your own now. It's not Gordon and Sheila MacRae anymore. It's you, hon. Sheila MacRae, up in one, solo spotlight. The exposure will be good for your career. It will establish you. It will make you a wage earner. You do have four kids to think about, hon."

When Milton Berle invited me to lunch at the Friars Club, I took the opportunity to ask his advice. "Are you kidding?" he said. "Take the job. But if you don't, let me know. I'll dig out one of my drag outfits and do it myself!"

Sammy Davis was as convinced as ever that I should do it. "It's a star role, babe. You deserve it."

I called Frank for his opinion. "My advice is, don't."

"Why not?"

"For one thing, Jackie's got the same problem Mac has, with the booze, though not as bad as Mac. Second, you're a perfectionist. You rehearse and rehearse and rehearse. Jackie's notorious for not rehearsing."

"Sammy Davis says I should do it, and he's my manager!"

"Sammy's your manager? Oh, you're in big trouble. Talk about the blind leading the blind! But look, witch, if you do decide to do it, let my lawyer, Jack Katz, handle the deal. That way, that pretty behind of yours will be protected."

Hesitant and undecided, I was the Hamlet of Sutton Place. Then came an offer that seemed to provide a logical way for me to turn down Jackie for sound business reasons. Producer Frank Perry asked me to be in a movie he was going to be shooting that summer in Connecticut. Based on a John Cheever story that I'd read in *The New Yorker,* it was titled *The Swimmer.* Burt Lancaster was to play the title role of a gorgeous, sexy swimmer, who, in the short space of the film, reviews his life and romances by swimming in various pools. I agreed to be in the picture. Then the rains came, the rainiest July in recent memory. As shooting was delayed again and again, pressures from friends and my agent to forget the film and go with Gleason mounted.

In the meantime, Jack Katz was discussing terms which I'd set that I expected to be unacceptable to Jackie. The main one concerned my qualms about being away from my children, especially Bruce, who was in boarding school in New York. If I were to take on the role of Alice, I was insisting, I must be permitted to have Bruce come down to Miami Beach over the weekends. Because the show was to be live on Saturday nights, I expected Jackie to reject anything that would mean having a kid underfoot.

He didn't. "Fine with me," he said.

Still reluctant, I hoped that something would come up to provide me with an excuse not to take the offer. Two things that changed my life: I had a terrible argument with JP—it was over. And Sammy Davis, who had decided to go into full-time management. "If you don't want to do the Gleason show," he said, "put together a nightclub act. I can book you into Las Vegas. And I asked Bob Fosse to help you get it together."

The prospect of working with the brilliant choreographer and director proved appealing. When we met to talk about it, he was bubbling with ideas about the numbers, staging, and costumes. Most of it was avant-garde, even for the 1960s. "Everybody will expect you to have good-looking guys backing you up," he said. "No! You'll have four great-looking gals. See-through costumes!"

Sammy expressed surprise that I would even consider sharing the stage with women. "Most women stars wouldn't do it," he said.

Frank Sinatra was against the idea. "Just get up there and do your stuff," he said. "Why do you need anybody else?"

"I can't just get up there and sing," I replied with a laugh. "I am not Frank Sinatra!"

From the beginning of our work on the act, Bob and I felt more than a mutual professional interest in one another. The physical attraction was electric. But Bob was aware of what was happening in my personal life. He knew that I was separated from Gordon. He also had heard that I had been involved with JP and with Frank. "Are you serious about anyone?" he asked. "If you are, anything between us could turn into a mess."

One night, at three AM, he grinned: "I figured out why you don't make dates until late. You're waiting for someone to call. If he's not coming over, then you do the town! Better get free!"

Free! The word, the idea, resounded in my head. I was a woman of forty-one years and mother of four children in their teens and twenties, yet with Bob I felt as giddy as a schoolgirl. The adolescence that I had never known exploded forth in rampant sexuality that Bob more than equaled.

He loved making love. A superbly conditioned dancer, he came to bed with a tireless, exquisitely satisfying willingess and energy. But he knew that JP was still an unresolved part of my life.

The nightclub act which he created was fabulous. The girls. The see-through costumes. Wonderful showcasing of my impressions. Very clever, very entertaining voiceovers, Dean, Sammy, and Frank set up the premise of other girls taking part in the show and led up to their making their entrance.

During three weeks at Las Vegas, I played to a packed room. But on our closing night, my secretary, Peter Terhune, drew me aside. "Sheila, there's bad news," he said. "There's no money."

"What do you mean?" I gasped. "How can that be?"

It was an old, familiar story. Gordon owed the club for his losses in the casino. Because I was still his wife, they claimed the right to apply my money to his debts. The income that I had counted on for myself and for paying costs of putting together the act was not there. Rather than coming out ahead financially, I was just about wiped out.

Dispirited and angry, I returned to New York and accepted Jackie Gleason's offer, and had a secret meeting with JP.

The announcement that I was to be the fourth Alice Kramden created an unexpected splash. Naïvely, I had underestimated Jackie Gleason's value as a news story. Nor had I given much thought to the likelihood that being associated with him would attract attention from the press. And I had had no idea how much interest the public would have in the person who was to be the new Alice, replacing Audrey Meadows, whom fans of the show had grown to love.

"I don't want to be a carbon copy of Audrey," I told Jackie and his producers, Jack Philbin and Ron Wayne. "Please don't ask me to look at her tapes. If I saw them, it would be too easy for me just to do an impression of her. I've got to be my own Alice Kramden. Different tone of voice, different hairstyle."

Jackie also had strong feelings about my Alice's hair. She was a redhead, but Jackie didn't want me to wear a wig, so I had to dye my hair. But if Jackie had ideas about Alice, so did I. My Alice had to be not just a woman whom circumstances had placed in a drab two-room flat with a fire escape for a view. She was not in that dreary walk-up in Brooklyn because she had to be. She was there because she wanted to be. She stayed because she loved her husband, just as I had stayed with Gordon. I wanted the audience to see that between Ralph and Alice there was a sensual and sexual relationship, as there'd been between Gordon and me. She was also to be a woman with a touch of the poet in her and flower pots on the fire escape.

Though Jackie was notorious for not rehearsing, he rehearsed hard prior to our first show. Eventually, though, he reverted to form and rehearsed only when he absolutely had to. Not wanting to go over things again and again was not caused by laziness. He just believed that rehearsing took the edge off the final performance. He was able to get away with few rehearsals because he had an incredible ability to memorize whole scripts at one reading.

In control of every aspect of the show, Jackie knew exactly what shots he wanted from the cameras, what songs he wished to use, how the orchestra should sound (if he'd had the time he could have directed the musicians), and what Jane Kean and I, as Trixie and Alice, should wear in every scene.

He also had strong ideas about the atmosphere in the studio. It had to be *cold*. He made sure that the engineers of the Miami Beach Auditorium, where the show originated, kept the temperature at fifty degrees. He believed that people performed better when the air was chilly, though musicians griped, jokingly, that "it's so cold in here the brass sticks to our lips!"—but I relished that!

Old hand that he was, Jackie knew, as did Helen Hayes, Katharine

Hepburn, and the Lunts, that a chilled audience was an alert audience. "If that's true, Jackie," I said, blowing on my hands to warm them, "how come we're doing this show in Florida and not Alaska?"

"Ho, ho, ho," he said. "Already you're talking like Alice! Keep it up, Sheel, and... *boom!*" His fist shot out and up as it had in so many *Honeymooners* shows. "Pow! Straight to the moon!"

Because the new Honeymooners were to be singing as well as acting, there had to be a great deal of practicing the songs. The music for each show was written by Lyn Duddy and Jerry Bresler. They had worked with Jackie a long time, knew Art quite well, and had written material for Gordon and me. Much of what they wrote for us required harmony, though which part was to be sung by whom remained a decision for Jackie to make. "You learn the harmony and *then* learn *my* part," he told me, "and when I get there I'll decide which of 'em I'm going to do." Just who would sing what in tunes written for Art and me, or for Jane and me, or for the three of us was no problem—we sang what was written.

Having always rehearsed and believed in rehearsals and because I always had known what part was mine in performance with Gordon, this business of having to learn Jackie's part as well as mine proved quite frightening. More than once I gave serious thought to quitting the show. Once I called Francis Albert to complain, he offered to buy out my contract. But suddenly I recognized that Jackie and his unorthodox methods had provided me with a golden opportunity to learn more about comedy. Fate, as Jackie might have said, had given me one of the world's greatest comedians as a tutor.

Eager to learn, I watched America's comics at work, from the scripted clowns of movies to stand-up topical gagsters in clubs to those who forged successes in the most demanding and material-consuming medium of television. One of the funniest on a stage was Buddy Hackett. When I first saw him as Gordon's opening act, I knew that he was going to go straight to the top. He was not only a comic but an actor, as his work in *God's Little Acre* was to prove.

Another comedian with a flair for acting was Shecky Greene. My favorite comedian-actor was Jack Carter, who would literally leave people holding their sides because they ached from laughter. Dick Shawn was also terrific and had turned in a devastatingly funny performance as Ethel Merman's zonked-out son in Stanley Kramer's zany *It's a Mad, Mad, Mad, Mad World* with an all-star cast of comic geniuses: Milton Berle, Ben Blue, Jimmy Durante, Phil Silvers, Sid Caesar, Jonathan Winters, the gap-toothed Terry Thomas, and one of the masters of screen comedy, Spencer Tracy.

Among my favorite funny people were my friends Peter Lind Hayes and Mary Healy, who had some of their material written by Woody Allen, long before Woody carved his own niche and got an annual blank check from Hollywood to turn out uniquely autobiographical movies. Then there was the pantheon of comedy gods: Jack Benny, Danny Thomas, and Desi and Lucy, all close friends.

When the definitive history of comedy is written, a chapter surely will be set aside for the team of Jackie Gleason and Art Carney, for in bringing to life Ralph and Ed they had created a comedy couple as indelible as Laurel and Hardy, Abbott and Costello, Martin and Lewis, Gallagher and Sheen, and any other comic pairings of stage, radio, screen, and television. They'd been together so long honing their craft and their roles and each was such a consummate comedian that they *became* Ralph and Norton. In truth, they were not acting their characters, they *were* the characters.

Retaining my residence at 13 Sutton Place in the first year of the program, I returned to New York after each show to take Bruce back to school, tend to the house, and soak up the city. Art Carney also went back to the city between shows. One day on the flight up, I suggested we have lunch or dinner in New York. "We'll go to the '21' Club."

"The '21' Club?" he said, looking surprised. "Geez, you know, I always wanted to be a member of that club."

"Art, you don't have to join '21.'" I laughed. "It's not a private club. It's a restaurant!"

With a blank look, he said, "I'll be a son of a gun!"

That was Art, sweetly innocent and with a clear view of what we all did for a living. As we were standing offstage awaiting our cues to go on, I in my Alice costume and Art in his battered Ed Norton hat, white T-shirt, open vest, baggy pants, and suspenders, he bent close to me and whispered, "Do you really think it's normal for grown people to get dressed up like this?"

All comedians are complex, but Jackie was one of the most complicated funny men I had ever met. He was a paradox. He could be enormously generous in giving huge amounts to charities. One of his favorites was giving Christmas gifts to children. But one year he was so depressed and drinking so heavily that he didn't even wrap the packages, handing them out as they came from the store in big brown boxes and plain paper bags. Yet that same year he gave me a magnificent car, a hand-tooled Thunderbird.

I had long noticed how much Jackie and Gordon had in common. Like Gordon, Jackie was easily bored with his work. Some of their reaction stemmed from their ability to grasp the essence of what was required of them and then convey it to the audience. Jackie's way of exhibiting impatience could be seen in his refusal to rehearse. For Gordon it was always looking for something new for the act. These flashes of impatience were, ultimately, pluses for both men; they became better performers. What they shared on the debit side of the ledger was their drinking and their cavalier attitude toward a serious problem that both refused to admit.

"I'm no alcoholic," Jackie once said to me. "I'm a drunkard. There's a difference. A drunkard doesn't like to go to meetings."

They had been drinking buddies whenever Gordon was in New York, hanging out at Toots Shor's. Once, I asked Gordon what they did there for so many hours. "It's just stuff that you don't have to pretend about," Gordon said. Man stuff.

Jackie put it differently. "Sheel, how come you don't like the sauce?"

On the air, Jackie dealt with the subject of liquor in quite an opposite way. Though he made jokes about drinking, the effect was that drinking was not a virtue. He treated it with black humor. The character of Reggie van Gleason was a souse in white tie and tails, quite funny but pitiable. Visits by "Mr. Dunahy" to Joe, the friendly neighborhood bartender, were an "Open, Sesame" to a string of tales whose humor was rooted in stupid things people do and say when drunk. The inebriated Crazy Guggenham, played by Frank Fontaine, was basically a figure to feel sorry for, so constantly drunk that even Joe treated him as an object of ridicule—but humorous.

Ralph Kramden didn't drink at all, save one time when he and Norton set their minds to getting drunk on a bottle of Chianti and proceeded to do so even though Alice and Trixie had switched the wine for grape juice. Even when Jackie sipped what was presumably booze from a teacup during his monologues, he sent a message (unintentional, perhaps) that liquor was not exactly good for you, as he rolled his eyes, jerked his head as if he'd been kicked (drum roll), *then* crooned, "How sweet it is!"

Art Carney also had a taste for booze, but it never seemed to be as central to his being as it was for Jackie and Gordon. Ironically, a number of years after Art and Jackie stopped working together as Norton and Ralph, they teamed up in a TV movie, *Izzy and Moe,* about a pair of real-life Prohibition enforcement officers (Isadore Einstein and Moe Smith) who demonstrated sheer genius in the means they employed to raid speakeasies.

Despite the "how sweet it is" gags, Jackie did not drink during a show, but when it was over, he was like a kid out of school. The drinking began almost as soon as he had his makeup off and continued at dinner and beyond. In his palatial home at the edge of a golf course, the bar was always fully stocked.

Jackie's "girl," Honey Merrill, reigned in the big house. For about a decade, she had been his live-in lover. Never wed to Jack, she took to being a housewife with considerable zest. He did not want live-in help such as a cook or maids and she did all those chores herself, as I discovered upon my first visit to their house. Arriving at the front door, I was greeted by Honey, who was wearing an apron and diamond rings. "I guess I look a mess," she said. "I've been mopping the foyer."

Honey's way of chastising Jackie when he came home drunk was to make him pay for his food. A ham sandwich was $3.50. Chicken was more. "It's a way for me to get 'jolly money' from Jack," she explained as I looked on in amazement at one of those astonishing charades.

Honey had been married before and had children. During the second year of the show, she brought them to live in the house. Kids were not exactly what Jackie preferred to have around him, and Honey's offspring did not cotton much to Jackie. They seemed to delight in provoking him. They defaced his portrait, cut up his neckties, hid his cuff links, and invaded his liquor supply.

This was the late 1960s, of course. Parents everywhere were being confronted by rebellious children and, too often, feeling guilty about setting standards in an era when rules and propriety appeared to have been thrown overboard. I, too, as you'll read presently, was confronting the challenge of being a parent in the decade whose slogan was "If it doesn't hurt anybody, do it." But, of course, a lot of people did get hurt.

The strains at home and of doing a musical every week on TV soon began to show in Jackie. Often he took me by the hand and said, "C'mon, Sheel, let's take a break." By that, he meant he wanted to be somewhere quiet where we could talk. This hallowed place was

Dressing Room No. 1 of the Miami Beach Auditorium, a spacious room with an immense adjustable lounge chair where "the Great One" could lie back and put up his feet. The conversations were never about the show, never about show business. The subjects were my experiences with ESP, UFOs, the Bermuda Triangle, and all the mysteries of life past, present, and future.

I recounted how Gordon was the only person saved on a flight from Mitchell Field on Long Island to Fort Bragg, South Carolina. Gordo was doing special LORAN training for overseas duty. I stayed with my parents because it was only three weeks and there were no hotels available. Every Friday, a Major Brown flew Gordon and two other New York servicemen home for the weekend and back on Monday morning.

I woke up after the second week, screaming, insisting I had to go down there—now today. My parents said that Gordie is coming at three PM as always! No! No! I insisted. When I got to the colonel's house, Gordo was having brunch and wasn't pleased that I wanted to stay the weekend at the base.

"Something bothered me about the plane, darling. I'm sorry."

We were swimming in the colonel's pool when the officer of the day reported that the plane and all the men were destroyed, having hit a tree at Mitchell Field at 3:15. Gordo and I cried together.

Jackie talked about the many ghosts that were supposed to be haunting Hollywood. Jean Harlow was believed to be one of them, as was Carole Lombard and, most recently, Marilyn Monroe. Among the male ghosts, it was said, Clifton Webb still prowled the rooms of his Spanish-style Beverly Hills house just off Sunset Boulevard. A home on Summit Ridge once occupied by John Barrymore was reported to be visited not only the late "great profile" but by his deceased brother, Lionel, and sister, Ethel.

Might there be something about actors, Jackie wondered, that made them especially sensitive in such matters? "Maybe we have some kind of special connection to the force that drives the universe," he said. "Did you ever have the experience when you're acting that everything around you falls away and it's like you're in some special place?"

"Yes, I have," I said. "Just last week, as a matter of fact, when we were doing the scene in the Italian restaurant." In the scene, Alice and Ralph have just had one of their fights, and Alice has gone upstairs to stay with Trixie. Unknowingly, she and Ralph separately go to an Italian restaurant and are seated in back-to-back booths. "I had the feeling then that we were the only two people in the world," I said. "Our connection was so strong that I felt suddenly that there were no cameras, no set, no audience. No Sheila, no Jackie. Just people."

"Yeah," Jackie said, staring into space. "Yeah."

During rehearsals for the first show, we were interrupted by the telephone. "Yeah," Jackie said. "Hi, Peter." Sitting up excitedly, he said to the caller, "Wait a minute." Then he wiggled a finger at me. "Come over here and hold the phone wire!" Bemused, I did so. "Okay, Peter," said Jackie into the phone, "tell me who's here with me." He then thrust the phone toward me.

The voice on the line was foreign-sounding. "It is vooman," he said. "She is five feet, eight inches tall, A size eight or ten dress. Very, very beautiful! She has hurt her back. It is an aggravation of an old injury but she should not vurry about it, it vill go away soon. Am I correct, young lady?"

"Why, y-yes," I said, astounded not only that he knew so much about me but that he knew he was talking to me and not to Jackie. "Who— who is this I'm speaking to?"

"Peter Hurkos," Jackie said, whisking the phone from my hand. "From the look on Sheila's face," Jackie laughed, "I'd say you were right on the money, Peter."

One of the most famous and controversial psychics in the world, the Dutch mystic Peter Hurkos had been consulted by police departments all over the globe in some of their most baffling cases. Just a few years before he described me to myself on Jackie's phone, he had been called in by the Boston police in their manhunt for the Boston Strangler. He'd joined in searches for missing children and even had been consulted by Scotland Yard to assist in their investigation of the Stone of Scone, stolen from the royal throne.

Peter described himself as a "psychometrist" who could divine facts about people or victims of crimes by handling objects they had touched, by being close to them, or by hearing their voices over the telephone. This amazing power had come to him in 1943 after a fall from a ladder had left him in a coma for three days. Awakening, Peter told his doctor, "What you are thinking, don't do it. Something terrible will happen." It turned out that the physician had been planning a trip abroad. He took it and was killed shortly thereafter.

Recently, in Miami, Peter had aided the police in apprehending a murderer by describing the culprit in detail after handling personal articles. Knowing this, I was nonetheless dubious about Peter's performance on my behalf. "Jackie," I said mockingly, "you set this up."

"Swear to God," Jackie said, raising his right hand.

Then I remembered Peter mentioning a back injury. There was no way he could have known about that, no way Jackie could have told him, because Jackie hadn't been present when it happened. In keeping with his aversion to rehearsing, he had not been present when a dog we were using—an enormous Great Dane—would jump up and lick my face. To assure that the dog would act as expected, I was given a small piece of liver to put in my pocket. The dog did just what he was supposed to do. Leaping on me, he shoved me hard against a piece of furniture, aggravating a back problem I'd had since I fell off a fence when I was a child. Even if Jackie had somehow found out about the dog hurting me, he could not have known of the old injury and, therefore, could not have told Peter about it.

Jackie passed the phone to me again. "Ask him anything you want."

"Hello, Peter," I said. "What about our show? Are we going to be a hit?"

"Oh, yes," he said. "The audience will be forty million. But despite this success it will not run the seven years."

In both predictions, Peter proved to be right. The ratings did show an audience of forty million. But, tiring of the routine, Jackie canceled the program in 1970 after a run of four seasons. That amounted to between forty and fifty full-hour performances by jet-setter Sheila MacRae as Alice, whereas Audrey Meadows played the role first in short sketches and then in thirty-nine half-hour episodes.

In all that time, because Jackie was a thorough professional and expected everyone else to be, he went out of his way only once to compliment me more than routinely for a performance. It involved a rare missed entrance cue by Art after Jackie exited in one of Ralph's notorious huffs, leaving me alone on live television and waiting in vain for Art to come on. Stuck, I began ad-libbing about the weather, the view from the window, my mother! After nearly a minute of this, realizing what was happening, Jackie bounded back on stage to bellow: "And furthermore...!" A moment after that, Art finally appeared.

All of this happened with the audience unaware that none of what they were witnessing was in the script. When we were off the air, Jackie hugged me. "Today, Sheel, you joined the ranks of the pros," he declared, calling someone a "pro" being the highest accolade he could bestow.

A few days later, he gave me a jewel box from Cartier engraved with the same words.

Another reason Jackie canceled the show was purely personal. The relationship with Honey had fallen apart and left him upset, dispirited, and uninterested. Instead of doing the show on a regular basis, we did specials, but even those could not engage him. Added to his distraction was a building project. It consisted of a fabulous new house at the Inverary golf course. When he ought to have been paying attention to the show, he was at Inverary supervising the construction.

Soon we learned that there was an extra attraction for him at Inverary. She was a marvelous golfer and an equal to Jackie in the drinking department. When he married her, we were surprised, but on reflection, I understood why. He was a very lonely man and, I think, dreaded being by himself. But I felt quite certain that a marriage built on the shifting sands of golfing, alcohol, and loneliness could not last.

In these difficult times on the show, the rock on which we rested was June Taylor. A brilliant dancer and choreographer, she had been with Jackie a long time, all the way back to Jackie's *Cavalcade of Stars* on the Dumont network. He had a professional and personal relationship with June that seemed incredible. She refused to let him get away with things, berating him for not rehearsing, scolding him for not being attentive enough to his work, chiding him about his drinking. Although she had plenty of problems of her own, including a bout of tuberculosis in both lungs, she was exactly the "pro" that Jackie so admired.

The Taylor whom Jackie *loved* was June's sister, Marilyn, but Jackie was married, and so was she. He hadn't seen her for several years, but I was doing a special with him in 1972 and heard that Marilyn had lost her husband.

"Call her, Jackie," I said. "You two would be so good for one another. You still love her, don't you."

He refused.

So *I* made the call.

I'm delighted to record that my Cupid's act worked out fine. They married and were still together when Jackie died in 1987. I was thrilled to have had some small part in the happiness that Jackie seemed to have found, finally.

Of all my cherished memories of Jackie, the one that catches the essence of him concerns a night on which he appeared to have vanished with all the suddenness and mystery of an airplane being swallowed up in the Bermuda Triangle. Everyone became frantic. Jack Philbin was on the phone to every cocktail lounge, bar, and saloon in the Miami area, and enlisted the help of Ron Wayne (my new husband). At last, when we were at our wits' end, Eddie Deverno, who also worked on the show, said, "I bet I know where he is, Ronnie."

Ron and I found him in an old burlesque house where the women were not young, not pretty, not classy. He had been there through all the shows and now, here was this old burlesque comic regaling them with stories of bygone days and teaching them the fine art of comedy.

At some point, he realized Ron and I were there. Turning, he gazed at Ron questioningly. "What's Alice the Clam doing here with you?"

"I never see Ronnie for days," I replied.

"You forget he's married now. So the two of you can't go out with the Miss Worlds."

"Oh, if only you drank, you'd be a great broad!" he laughed.

Looking at the great clown, I had tears in my eyes as I thought of Kipling's words: "If you can talk with crowds and keep your virtue, or walk with Kings—nor lose the common touch."

As we left that shabby theater in Ron's car, I was relegated to the backseat, as I had been on the long-ago night when I had been allowed to accompany him and Gordon to Peekskill and into the "man's world" that was so much a part of Jackie and Gordon and, I believe, most men.

Later that night, in bed with Ron, I remembered their conversation in the car. Ronnie had said excitedly, "Jack, you did it. We got the numbers from Bill Paley's office at CBS. You've got over forty million in your audience!" As Ron shifted gears on the causeway, Jackie lit up a cigarette without saying a word. Ron queried him.

"Jackie, isn't it great? Hey, you're on top."

Looking straight ahead, with those huge eyes wide open, he answered.

"Great? I've always been great, so where do I go from here, pal?"

Thinking back to that evening when we found Jackie so happy among the strippers and the burlesque comics, I understand what has endeared Jackie Gleason to all of us. As rich and famous as he was, he was, at heart, a kid. And that is why he was exactly the man to bring to life the striving, ever-hopeful, kid-at-heart bus driver of Chauncey Street, and why people will go on and on, watching and laughing and loving *The Honeymooners*.

ELEVEN

Family Matters

DROPPING IN TO SEE ME during one of my hurried visits to Sutton Place between telecasts of *The Honeymooners,* Lucille Ball shook her head in dismay. "You can't go on living like this," she said. "All this running back and forth between Miami Beach and New York, dragging Brucie up and down the East Coast, is nuts. And you're always concerned about what your sis and your mom think. You worry about Meredith and Gar and Hessie. I want you to put this little sign on your mirror."

She handed me a card: "Is this good for ME?"

"And you'd better apply that to your love life."

As always, Lucy was wise. And right. In this second year of my incarnation as Mrs. Ralph Kramden, common sense dictated that I bring some semblance of order to my real life. It was time to let go of the past. As someone said, "The past is a far country; they do things differently there." The future is the same.

Breaking with my past required breaking—at last, finally and completely—with Gordon. Although we had been separated for almost five years, he still did not want a divorce and made it clear that he would not simply grant one. Again and again, he implored me not to take the final step. Each time we talked I came away feeling upset, depressed, and worried about what he might do were I to press for a divorce.

And deep within me there still abided my abhorrence of divorce! The word, the idea of it, sent shudders of revulsion through me. I thought back to the haughty and superior manner I had assumed toward Gene Nelson when he told me he was planning to divorce Miriam. I dwelt on the heartbreak I had felt when I had learned of other famous friends divorcing: Dean and Jeannie Martin; Jerry and Patti Lewis; Doris Day and Marty Melcher; Lana Turner, who had a string of divorces; Esther Williams, and Arlene Dahl, both of whom ended up divorcing Fernando Lamas; Shirley Jones and Jack Cassidy; and, of course, Desi and Lucy.

Now, here was Lucy, disappointed and possibly angry with me for ruining my realtionship with Frank, demanding that I stop equivocating, stop worrying about what Gordon might do if I got a divorce, and start doing what was best for me and the children. "It's bad enough that Gordie messed up their lives," she said. "Don't you make it worse for them."

The MacRae kids, who had romped with the Arnaz kids while their daddies played golf and drank and their mothers played endless, meaningless games during long days of mutual consolation, were grown up now—except for Bruce, who was ten.

True to a genealogy littered with theatrical figures, Meredith was already a promising young actress. In the fall of 1963 she joined the cast of the highly successful sitcom *My Three Sons*. Second only to *The Adventures of Ozzie and Harriet* in popularity, this warm family show starred a cardigan-clad, pipe-chewing Fred MacMurray as a widower coping with raising three boys.

To join this all-male domestic scene, the show's producers were seeking just the right girl for the role of Sally Ann Morrison, a romantic interest for the eldest son. They offered the part to Meredith, who was enrolled at UCLA.

I did not push any of my children to go into our business, and I opposed Meredith's dropping out of college. But convinced that the offer was a great opportunity for her, Gordon gave the parental consent. I was sad that college days were over for an "A" student.

I thought she'd return to the academic world when written out of *My Three Sons,* but Meredith was not off the small screen very long. The next year she showed up as Billie Jo Bradley on another hit comedy, *Petticoat Junction.* This show made its debut in 1963 on the heels of *The Beverly Hillbillies* and marked a continuation of what detractors called CBS's "hayseed period," masterminded by James Aubrey. Once upon a time, Jim had been a dinner-table companion of mine at many a Hollywood soiree. This one took place well before he became a power in TV, and so he found himself at the "B" table with those of us deemed lesser lights in the Hollywood firmament.

Petticoat Junction was set in the backwoodsy town of Hooterville, whose denizens included that marvelous veteran comedienne Bea Benedaret, who had verbally fenced on radio and TV with Jack Benny; the venerable character actor Edgar Buchanan; and the frog-in-the-throat-voiced Smiley Burnett. *Petticoat Junction* would prove to be the parent of another "hayseed" show, *Green Acres,* starring two friends, Eddie Albert and Eva Gabor.

From all of these wonderful actors, Meredith was able to hone the acting talent that, obviously, was inborn. She struggled, however, as do all the children of actors and other famous people, to create an identity of her own and to overcome the inevitable introductions as "Meredith MacRae, Gordon's daughter." Some years later, she created *Born Famous,* a TV talk show around that very theme—the children of celebrities and how they coped with being the offspring of noted parents.

Lately she has been involved in the work of groups whose purpose is to assist the children of alcoholics; she spoke to them about what it was like to be Gordon MacRae's daughter and of the hard times she had endured when his drinking problem became public. In talking about the fifties, she described how hurt and humiliated she felt when the newspapers carried the story of his automobile accidents, in which several people were injured, and her classmates taunted her about them. In addition to these personal appearances, she made television and radio public service announcements to inform those grappling with alcohol addiction that they weren't alone and that there was help available.

As the first of Gordon's and my children, Meredith did not have to come to grips with her dad's drinking problem immediately. She was ten years old before Gordon's addiction manifested itself and so had sweet memories of the untarnished times with the caring and loving father that he had been before he started drinking. Conversely, having known a different father than the one that appeared so suddenly in her tenth year, she felt the pain of Gordon's troubles acutely. She'd known a daddy who was sweet and simple, an uncomplicated "man's man" who loved the out-of-doors, made wonderful movies, cried at sad ones, and went around the house singing and doting on her, Heather, and little Gar. She sensed that to Gordon she was the favorite child, as a man's first daughter often is.

Heather, too, had fond memories of her daddy before the disease of alcoholism overtook him, starting when she was about eight. Very much like Gordon in being open and blunt, she was not exactly reticent in calling my attention to behavior by a daddy who did not meet with her approval. "Mommy," she declared sternly when she was ten, "Daddy's drunk at my birthday party!"

That her father was famous was not especially impressive to Heather, and for understandable reasons. We lived among some of the most famous people in America: Clark Gable, Bill Holden, Bob Hope, Doris Day, Errol Flynn, Gene Autry, Mickey Rooney, and Jerry Colonna, who was Hope's loud-mouthed, bug-eyed, mustachioed comedic companion on radio and TV and in movies.

Despite living in this rarified showbusiness atmosphere while growing up, Heather didn't seem to be much interested in having a career as a performer. A role in *Annie Get Your Gun* at the age of twelve did not strike her as a big deal, and she wasn't very taken with life on the road as she, Meredith, Gar, and Bruce went along with us when we toured. The attention bothered her to the point that when we were in a limousine arriving at an airport or at a theater, she ducked out of view of admiring fans of her father, crouching on the floor and wishing they would all go away. When Gordon called an audience's attention to the presence of his children and they were suddenly hit with a spotlight, she blushed with embarrassment. "Gosh, Mommy," she said, "I just want to be normal."

Inheriting her father's love of the outdoors, Heather would have been quite happy to spend her life working with animals, especially horses, so when she attended a summer camp for children who were fledgling actors, it was the lure of camping, not performing, that attracted her.

Having no idea what she wanted to do after high school, she decided to follow her best friend, Edie Baskin (her father was the Baskin of

Baskin-Robbins ice cream), to Colorado Women's College. One day, she signed up for drama courses. That's when the show business bug bit, its peculiar "venom" causing her to recognize that she had a natural talent for acting and was possessed of a big, capable voice ideally suited for Broadway musicals.

She phoned me. "Mom, it's the end of college for Heather MacRae!" Now it was "Look out Broadway, here I come!" Never mind the old rubric that for every light on the Great White Way there was a broken heart. "Thanks for the warning, Mom and Dad," she said. "I know that an entertainer has a rough life full of disappointments and rejection, but I've got to give it a try." Obviously, confidence in herself as well as voice had been passed on to her through her family's genes.

I recognized her theatrical potential when she had a small part in *Bells Are Ringing* with Gordon and me. Then fourteen years old, but heavily made-up to make her look much older, she played a switchboard operator for Susanswerphone and had a few lines that covered the time between one character's exit and the entrance of Dorothy Greener. A fine actress, Dorothy had been talking to Gordie and it caused her to miss her cue. This left Heather alone onstage. In my dressing room, I heard her say her line, then a line that was not in the script, then another line the author never wrote, and another, ad-libbing until Dorothy appeared.

"Now, that's a born actress," I said proudly to her and Gordon after the show.

"Yeah, that's my girl," Gordon said, beaming.

Soon after arriving in New York, Heather got into a musical. In March 1968, she made her Broadway debut as the female lead in a production with an encouraging title: *Here's Where I Belong.* Based on *East of Eden,* the John Steinbeck saga of the Trask family set in the lush agricultural region of pre–World War I Salinas and Monterey, California, the show did not come anywhere near achieving the immortality of the novel. *Here's Where I Belong* closed after one performance.

I flew up from Florida for Heather's Broadway debut. The next day I found her almost in tears in her room at the Park Sheraton. The floor was littered with morning newspapers whose critics had pronounced the show dead on arrival. "Why can this happen?" she asked. "How can a show close in one night?"

"Darling, they do. They always have and they always will. Bigger

musicals than yours have closed in one night. The flip side of 'hit' is
'flop.'"

Heather soon joined the cast of a hit show that everyone in New York
(and everywhere else) was talking about: *Hair*. Subtitled "The American
Tribal Love-Rock Musical," it was riding the crest of the 1960s rock 'n'
roll, hippies, antiwar, flower children, Love Generation, antiestablish-
ment, pro-drug, "don't trust anyone over thirty" tide of rebellion.

But it was neither the show's radical messages nor its exciting,
unconventional Gerome Ragni, James Rado, and Galt MacDermot songs
that had the nation agog. What had everyone tittering was "the nude
scene." The finale of the first act, the number was titled "Be-In" and
employed the entire cast, some of whom rose nude from a crowd to
stand facing the audience, all rather dimly lit, so that the effect was more
sensational than revealing. Whether to appear nude was each cast
member's choice to make. Heather did so, but when I went to see the
show, as all who had decided that day to be nude rose, a burly actor stood
right in front of Heather, blocking all but a small portion of a leg.

On the night her daddy was in the audience, Heather kept her clothes
on. "There's no way I was going to stand up there nude in front of my
dad," she said with a blush and a burst of nervous laughter. "He'd freak
right out."

After those first two jobs on Broadway, Heather was rarely out of
work. Hand in hand with her successes, as in Meredith's career, went the
ever-present and often overshadowing presence of her father's name.
People who approached her to compliment her about her work
inevitably talked about Gordon. "I was a fan of your father." "Gosh, how
I loved to hear your father sing." "You look so much like your father or
your mother." Performing in their own right and being referred to
constantly in reviews or write-ups as "the daughters of Gordon MacRae"
proved difficult for both Heather and Meredith.

On a cold day in late January 1991, Heather came to see me in an
apartment I had borrowed from my old friends Larry and Norma
Storch. The TV set was on. The war in the Persian Gulf had begun.
Slate-colored clouds glowered down on the rooftops of upper Broadway,
reminding me of Paris.

She brought me a present, a thick collection of theatrical reviews. For
some perverse reason, I and many actors have been afflicted with a
morbid interest in what critics have to say, as though they were gods.

"This is certainly timely," I said of the book. "Have you seen what they did to Stephen Sondheim's new show?"

I didn't have to define "they." The previous evening, *Assassins* had opened. A musical featuring Patrick Cassidy, Shirley and Jack's son, it was built around stories of people who had killed or tried to kill Presidents. Judging by the notices, it was doomed to close once the advance ticket sales had run out.

"Talk about being assassinated! Remember when *Here's Where I Belong* closed after one show and you couldn't understand why? Well, here's the answer. If critics can kill a Stephen Sondheim musical, they can snuff out anything," I mused.

Heather's show had gotten good reviews. *Falsettoland,* by Bill Finn and James Lapine, had been quite successful when seen by those who were its most likely audience. Because it dealt with AIDS, it was not one of those shows that is guaranteed a run of years through theater parties made up of suburban women's clubs and expense-account businessmen keeping out-of-town clients entertained between deals. It was a show about homosexuals and death and, therefore, limited in its appeal. Its closing notice had gone up because the box office ran out of people who constituted the natural audience, not because critics turned thumbs down like Roman emperors in the gladiatorial arena and killed it, but rumor has it reviving soon.

Reviews! Critics! No matter how many actors there are onstage opening night, they know that the most important player in the drama is seated out in the audience. The play isn't over when the curtain comes down. Opening night ends when the reviews come out. It used to be only the newspapers. The advent of critics on TV news shows had changed all that, but there still comes that moment in every show's life when someone comes running into the opening night party with "the papers!"

"Has anyone ever seen a critic in the daytime?" asked P. G. Wodehouse. "Of course not. They come out after dark, up to no good." "A drama critic," said Wilson Mizner, "is a person who surprises the playwright by informing him what he meant." Sir Thomas Beecham said critics were "drooling, driveling, doleful, depressing, dropsical drips." "Critics are like eunuchs in a harem," said Irish playwright Brendan Behan. "They know how it's done, they've seen it done every day, but they're unable to do it themselves!"

Not even my illustrious ancestor Sarah Siddons was immune to the barbs of critics. Of her performance as Lady Macbeth, the reviewer in a February 1785 issue of London's *Morning Post* wrote that "the faces she made were horrid and even ugly." When she came out of retirement in 1816 to play Lady Macbeth again at Covent Garden, a critic said, "Players should be immortal, if their own wishes or ours could make them so: but they are not." He noted that "if Mrs. Siddons has to leave the stage again, Mr. Horace Twiss will have to write another farewell address for her: if she continues on it, we shall have to criticize her performances. We know not which of these two evils we shall think the greatest."

If there is theater (or TV or movies) there will be critics, and actors will rush to them to be judged. Some actors claim that they don't read their reviews. I wait one month. Curiously, it's the "bad" review that somehow finds its way into a scrapbook, a wallet, or a purse, to be dragged out and shown to other actors, much as a wounded war veteran displays his Purple Heart. It's a symbol of rejection, but we're eager for the next play.

The greatest actors and actresses have their bad notices to remind them that no one is perfect. How do actors put up with it? Why do they submit themselves to what they know can be withering criticism? The answers are as varied as the actors. Mia Farrow said that if she couldn't act, she'd probably wind up in an insane asylum. Signe Hasso simply said, "I have to act." Dustin Hoffman: "When I started acting, I felt attractive for the first time." "I'm always acting," said Charles Laughton, "even when I'm alone in a room." Steve McQueen said he took up acting to avoid having to get a forty-hour-a-week job. "But, man, I didn't escape," he complained. "Now I'm working seventy-two hours a week!" Joanne Woodward said, "Acting is like sex. You should do it and not talk about it."

Of course, acting is the only thing actors *want* to talk about.

Before Heather arrived, I had been on the phone with Shirley Jones, discussing the reviews of *Assassins*. Shirley felt quite disappointed and sad for both Patrick and Heather, but we each knew they were skilled actors who understood that there is always the next show. Both would survive with some loving care.

"That's the trouble with being in our line of work," Shirley said. "Sooner or later, some guy walks in and posts a closing notice."

"Yeah, but think of the good times in between," I said, laughing and turning my eyes to the window. The day outside and the news inside invited introspection; perfect day for a mother-and-daughter chat, I thought. Too bad Meredith isn't here.

"Maybe I'll run into Patrick in the unemployment office," Heather said with a wan smile. She glanced at the television screen. "That's where Meredith belongs," she said. "She should be in TV news or on *The Today Show* or with her own talk show where she can use her brilliant mind like Barbara Walters."

The phone rang; my press agent, Barry Landau, had tickets for the memorial service being held that day for Mary Martin. For an instant I remembered Gordon walking out of *The Sound of Music* and my idea about making my entrance in our act by flying in and Gordon groaning, "You mean like Mary Martin in *Peter Pan?*"

There was much I could have said in memory of Mary, but I did not feel up to it. I didn't feel like making my way through a large crowd and the sea of TV news cameras that would be there to catch glimpses of celebrated people. There is always a kind of forced theatricality that accompanies the death of a star.

"No, Barry," I said, "I'll say a prayer in my own way, but thanks, no."

Set aside on the table where Heather and I were having lunch was a sheaf of papers on which, in a hand that only I could ever decipher, I had been scribbling notes for a book I was thinking of writing about my life with Gordon and my years after that as an actress. Heather asked, "How's it going?"

"Fine," I said, "and as long as you're here, I might as well get your thoughts. You know, life with Daddy. Life with Mom. Life with Meredith, Gar, and Brucie. Life with Heather." A familiar, mischievous glint flickered into her eyes. "What?" I asked. "What are you thinking about?"

She laughed. "Are you going to tell about the day you fooled my friend when he called up and you had him believing that he was talking to me?"

I'd spent half an hour on the phone imitating her. When she returned home, I said, "If Darryl calls and says it was really nice to talk to you, just go along with it."

Heather was laughing now as we recalled the episode, but she had been quite cross with me then.

"Write that we all love you, Mom," she said with a toss of her long blond hair, unleashing a big, booming laugh, very much like Gordon's. "You drive us crazy, but we love you."

"That's good," I said.

"You're not going to just tell bad things about Daddy, are you?"

"No, no, no! I'm going to tell how happy your Daddy and I were. We *were* ecstatic together. He was a wondrous creature. We had a wonderful life, but I have to show what happened to this great talent, how drinking ruined it. And him. Maybe it will help others. Other wives. Other children."

"Say this in your book, Mom." Heather said as she stood in the doorway, leaving. "You wanted our lives to be a fantasy. And in many ways, they were. But more importantly, we all knew as long as Mom was there everything would be okay."

A fantasy life? Meredith criticized me on TV.

Yes. I thought as I sat alone in my borrowed apartment and leafed through the book Heather had brought. I *had* tried to turn my children's lives into a fairy tale. I wanted them to know that they were daughters and sons of God's Chosen Boy and his wife, and to look on the good side.

After Gordon's alcoholism surfaced, I had been even more determined to protect them. It was not that Gordon ceased to love them. He simply was out of control when he drank.

Our sons bore the brunt of it, although Gar, the elder, sees it otherwise. Involved in the sound department at Paramount, he looks back and says, "I was the favorite. Dad was okay!"

The truth was that Gar had suffered along with the rest of us, perhaps more so. I remembered how brokenhearted he was when Gordon did not show up for a birthday party. When Gordon later saw Gar's tear-streaked face, he said, "Nothing either good or bad but thinking makes it so." When Gordo had promised to sing at the Cub Scouts, he made me take his place in a jacket and pants. "Go ahead, sweetheart. They're only babies. They won't know the difference, that your husband is drunk." It was a most disappointed audience of eight- to eleven-year-olds.

Christmas, when I had all my children with me at Sutton Place, Gordon asked to visit to help them decorate the tree. He said he had given up drinking. I believed him. Drunk, he fell down two flights of stairs, cutting his forehead. The kids were picked up by Sammy Davis, who gave them the best time—and he pleaded with me not to give up on Gordie on Christmas Eve.

When he was drunk, he was capable of striking the kids. There were terrifying, ugly outbursts in which the happy, sensitive man I had known became gruff and violent and was up to throwing the telephone at Gar. I saw Gordon grab Gar and shake him simply because Gar had misplaced the keys to the car. Only my wrestling him away kept Gar from being hurt.

Our younger son, Bruce, had a relationship with his father that was quite different from Gar's. Gordon mistreated Gar. For Bruce, he just wasn't there. The "Winston Churchill look-alike" babe-in-arms whom Oscar Hammerstein had adored on the set of *Oklahoma!* was born in 1954, and so never knew a totally sober father. While Gar, Meredith, and Heather had their feet planted solidly on a father who was a rock, for Bruce, Gordon was as ephemeral as clouds.

Realizing that I had to become Bruce's underpinning, I kept him close to me, first at the Waldorf Towers and then at Sutton Place. I enrolled him in the best school I could find and got Jackie Gleason to agree to let me bring him to Miami Beach on weekends. I wanted to spin around him a cocoon made of all the security, happiness, and love I could bestow by being protective and indulgent. I wanted him to have exactly the life of fantasy that Heather described and teased me about.

Only once did I fear that maybe I'd gone wrong. It happened when a policeman came down from the roof of our house to appear quite unexpectedly in my bedroom. "Sorry to startle you," he said, "but there's been a burglary at Otto Preminger's home, just next door. In investigating, I found the door to your roof garden open."

"We're all right, thank you," I said. "Ron, wake up!"

"Well, ma'am," he said, "there is one thing that bothers me. I noticed that you've got some plants up on the roof."

"Yes. My son gardens as a hobby."

"Is your son in at the moment, Mrs. MacRae? Aren't you Alice?"

"He's in his room. It's five AM."

"May I speak with him, please?"

"Is he in trouble?"

"Well, you see, it's not against city law to have a garden on the roof. But the problem's a little more serious than that. There are marijuana plants growing up there. If I could talk to your son, Alice!"

Yes, Bruce admitted, there were marijuana plants. Yes, they were his. "It's my garden. Mom said I could do what I want on the roof."

"You're wrong, son," the officer said. "You are culpable by law. But seeing that you've been honest with me, I'll just go up on the roof and root out the plants. Then you'll give me and your mother your solemn word that it won't happen again."

"It won't, officer," Bruce said, repentently.

"And your mother?" asked the officer.

"It won't happen again, Mom," Bruce said.

I was not pleased to learn of a flourishing marijuana garden above my head, but I was quite proud of how Bruce had handled the situation— and a week later, he had some in his room! Ron thought it was wrong so eventually I let him parent Bruce. I guess I wasn't a good father.

Gordon was slipping deeper and deeper into alcoholism. The years were a roller coaster of emotions for Bruce. On one day Gordon was a wonderful father, everything a little boy could wish. Later that day he would become just the opposite, if he were around at all. In the interim, of course, he had been drinking.

Bruce had gone through a series of raised expectations and dashed illusions. He was living with us while I was working on the Gleason show, so I made plans for him to fly over to the Bahamas for a day of fishing, the one thing that he and his father were both crazy about.

Gordon was to meet him at the airport.

I was pleased with the idea that they were spending a day together and, I hoped, drawing closer. During rehearsal of *The Honeymooners,* I was called to the telephone.

"Mrs. MacRae," said a man on the line, "this is the Nassau police."

My heart stopped. An accident, I thought; their fishing boat has capsized. No. No. That's negative.

"We have an eleven-year-old boy here at the airport who says he's your son. He says he's been waiting since ten-thirty this morning for his father."

It was now past six in the evening.

"Do you know where your husband is, so we can try to contact him?" asked the policeman.

"No, no," I said bitterly. "Just put Bruce on a plane and send him back to me. We'll pick him up."

What could I say to Bruce? What I had been saying to him all his life? That Daddy was really a wonderful person and he didn't intend to be mean? That Daddy had an illness called alcoholism and that he needed understanding and patience and love? Bruce was not Heather, who could bluntly accept that Daddy was drunk. He was sensitive and shy, totally bewildered, and less and less willing to accept the excuses I made for a father he did not really know.

Graced with a talent for music and excellent on piano and organ, Bruce became quite a brilliant composer.

When he showed me a song he'd written for Gordon, a lovely piece entitled "Forever Young," I suggested to Gordon that he include it in a forthcoming appearance at the Fairmont Hotel in San Francisco.

Still hoping I could find a way to build a bridge between Gordon and Bruce, I saw the song as an opportunity. I suggested that he take Bruce along to be his piano accompanist when he did the song in the show.

"Yeah, the song's pretty good," Gordon said, "and, yeah, I guess he can come."

I was thrilled.

Bruce was anxious, not only because he was to be with his father onstage but because he had never had the experience of playing with a big band.

"It will be fun, Brucie," I said. "As for the orchestra, Van Alexander is conducting. He's an old friend of ours. He'll help you. Everything will be fine."

Waiting eagerly in New York to hear how it turned out, I entertained happy visions of my scheme to bring father and son together.

They were sharing a suite at the Fairmont and would be with one another constantly. Surely, at some point a spark would ignite between them, and, I hoped, with nurturing, it could be kindled into a bonfire.

"Be sure to call me after the first rehearsal," I said to Bruce as he boarded the plane to the coast. "Let me know how it's going. And never mind what hour it is. You phone me."

The call came late at night.

"Mom, it was awful," he said. "He never introduced me to the guys in the band. They were really mean."

I remembered my own experiences with the boys in the band when Gordon and I were newlyweds. The ribbing. The snickers. The off-color jokes. At the time I had thought the musicians had been intentionally cruel.

"I think maybe you misunderstood them," I said to Bruce urgently. "You haven't worked with a band before. You don't know what musicians are like. They get to be a little cynical and clannish. Go up to them and introduce yourself. You'll see a difference once they know you're Gordon MacRae's son. And don't be afraid to tell them it's your first time and you need a little help."

"Mom, I want to come home," he begged. "Now."

"Don't do that, Brucie. Stay. It will be okay. I promise you it will be all right."

He remained in San Francisco, and the song went over quite well, reaping very warm applause from the audience.

"Thank you. It is a nice song," Gordon said.

What he didn't tell them was that the composer was his sixteen-year-old son, until a few days later.

To make matters worse, late that night Bruce received a phone call from the hotel manager. "Can you come down to the lobby, please, Mr. MacRae? Your father's here and he's, uh, I'm sorry to say it, drunk. And he's got two shows to do."

"I'm sorry, sir," Bruce said politely but coolly, "but it has nothing to do with me."

A moment later, he phoned to tell me he'd be on the first New York–bound plane in the morning. "Don't ask me again to stay," he pleaded. He took a deep, pained breath. "I just can't stand him, Mom."

Sooner or later, everyone faced with a loved one's addiction to alcohol comes to the point Bruce had reached, that awful time when he or she just can't stand it anymore.

Reaching that moment of truth had taken me a very long time. At great cost to myself mentally and physically, I had devoted myself to being Gordon's guardian. I thought I could save him. I believed that I could hold it all together.

I kept saying to myself and anyone who would listen, "I have a wonderful life," but it was not true. The wonderful life I had known with Gordon was over.

The reality was that I was the wife of a man addicted to alcohol and to gambling. Mercedes McCambridge called me out of the blue: "You are not the reason for his drinking. Go on with your life."

We had become exactly the opposite of what we had been. He had been the strong one—the captain of the ship. Gradually, because of his problems, I had been forced to take the helm.

Gower Champion had noticed the change long before I did. "Somewhere along the way," he had said to me, "you and Gordon switched places."

I still loved Gordon, but, like Bruce, I had reached the point at which I simply could not stand it anymore.

When, at last, I divorced him in April 1967, Meredith, Heather, and Gar took the decision with stoic resignation. They had long accepted it as inevitable, but Meredith was the most distressed.

Bruce was relieved.

I cried all the way down to Tijuana, while signing the papers, and all the way back to New York.

So much for my vaunted scruples against divorce, I thought.

Join the ranks.

Welcome to the club.

Adieu, Malted Milk Kids.

Good-bye, at last, to Mr. and Mrs. God's Chosen Boy. Farewell to the Hollywood Mother of the Year.

TWELVE

Doors Opened, Doors Closed

THERE WAS A POPULAR SAYING in the 1960s: "Today is the first day of the rest of your life." There was also a smash-hit musical that reflected that philosophy perfectly. It was *Mame,* starring my friend Angela Lansbury. The show's book was written by Jerome Lawrence and Robert E. Lee and was based on a bestselling novel, *Auntie Mame,* by Patrick Dennis. Music and lyrics were by Jerry Herman. While every song was a gem, two were right in keeping with the sixties: "It's Today" and "Open a New Window." I thought they enunciated precisely what I was feeling about separating from Gordon, and certainly they matched my mood a year later, after the divorce.

Angela's tour-de-force performance in the title role was backed up by a wonderful cast that included a knock-'em-dead comedy turn by Bea Arthur as Mame's hilariously jealous actress-friend, Vera. The show appealed to the secret longing in the hearts and souls of audiences to have a relative like Mame, who declared, "Life is a banquet and most poor bastards are starving to death." Who wouldn't want, however

210

secretly, an aunt whose approach to life was summed up in Mame's declaration: "Open a new window, open a new door, travel a new highway that's never been tried before!"

Sitting in the audience, I didn't have to wish that I had someone like Mame in my life. I did. My mother. Just as Mame Dennis threw her arms, heart, and home open to Agnes Gooch, who had found herself inexplicably pregnant, Winifred Baker Stephens had an open-door policy for our house in Roslyn, Long Island, when I and my sister Paula were growing up. We never knew what hapless soul would be sharing our home. There was an effete runaway from the Salvation Army who tried to cure my mumps by shaking a tambourine and praying. A sea captain and his wife lodged with us, rent free, and then continued their wayfaring voyage on the road of life early one morning with two of my mother's suitcases crammed full of Mother's clothes.

One summer's day, there appeared a pair of gaudy girls whom Mother introduced to Paula and me as "models on their way to New York." Paula, who had a tendency to view life with a suspicious and careful eye, knew better. "They're barflies from Bloder's Tavern in Glenwood Landing," she whispered to me in our room. Paula's assessment of the "models" proved more accurate as the girls continued on their way—taking along Mother's new fur coat.

Our twice-a-week helper-around-the-house was outraged. "You girls don't know how loved your mother is in this town," she said to Paula and me. "If you ask me, she's got too generous a heart. Everyone takes advantage of her."

I never knew anyone who had more friends than my mother. When Paula and I brought boyfriends to the house to meet her, they were quite likely to spend more time talking with her than with us. Glenwood hadn't seen the likes of her—bright, charming, sophisticated, talkative, optimistic, brimming with a zest for life, yet tough when she had to be. In my view, being twelve years old and terribly interested in the news with its grim forebodings of war in Europe, my mother was the one best suited to deal with Hitler. Put Winnie Stephens and Adolf in a room alone, I said, and Mother would put the little Nazi paperhanger who looked like Charlie Chaplin in his place.

She had done just that to one of my teachers. I'd come home from school carrying a book about Karl Marx. "What is this?" she asked, leafing through it. "They're teaching you Communism at school?"

"Yes," I said. "My teacher says Communism is wonderful."

"Really? Isn't Communism as a subject a little advanced for twelve-year-olds?" she asked.

"It's an advanced school," I said proudly. "They're making all kinds of changes in the classes. We're going to be allowed to learn about the things we're interested in. There's going to be an assembly when it's all going to be explained. I'm going to read from *The Communist Manifesto.*"

"Is that so? It sounds very interesting. I shall be there."

As promised, she came to the assembly at which the grand new design for the education of her daughters and all the other pupils was to be unveiled. Silent and attentive, she waited as the staff of the school spoke glowingly about free-form learning, skipping grades, unstructured classes, and a shift from the three R's to courses in the liberal arts, including Marxism.

"Excuse me. I'd like to get this quite clear," said Mother as she rose in the midst of the audience of parents. I shrank as far down in my chair as possible, embarrassed and a bit afraid of what she might say. "You say you are planning to deemphasize subjects such as arithmetic?"

"That's correct, Mrs. Stephens," said the principal, Arthur Keesler.

"But what will happen when my daughter Sheila is grown up and married and has a family and has to balance her checkbook?" A burst of parental applause greeted the question. "Mr. Keesler," she continued as the clapping subsided, "you're a German, aren't you?" Nervous laughter rippled through the auditorium.

"I am," said the principal, "but what has that to do with this teacher."

"You let her teach Karl Marx?"

The audience laughed.

"As an educator," the principal said, "I believe that the students should become familiar with all the world's great philosophies."

"I see," Mother said, her voice rising. "Does that mean also your curriculum will include the teachings of Jesus Christ? I do believe, being quite familiar with both philosophies, that the words of the carpenter from Nazareth will outlive those of Herr Comrade Marx."

The teacher who had sent me home with *The Communist Manifesto* under my arm took me aside a few days later. "Sheila," she said gravely, "you never told me *your mother* was such a radical. She knew about the Oxford Movement!"

A dark cloud occasionally obscured Mother's blue skies. My father had the affliction of alcoholism. It never caused him to waver in his love or his duty to his wife and daughters, but Mother, like me with Gordon, often had to be both mother and father. She never complained, for complaining, in Winnie's view, never accomplished anything. She believed that things would work out well. But she also understood that a satisfactory outcome depended on doing something about whatever problem one faced. As she saw it, life could be hard at times, but that didn't mean you had to go around with a long face.

Sometimes my father simply shook his head in bemusement over his wife's behavior, but they remained deeply in love up to the day he died. Weathering life's tribulations and my father's bouts with alcohol, they came through with flying colors, due in no small measure to Mother's toughness and optimism. I believed that had she died first, my father would have had a very difficult time. If he passed away before her, Mother could be expected to grieve, adjust to the loss, and get on with the rest of her life. But she didn't. Her health declined precipitously, although flashes of the old spark could still be seen. So could some glimpses of the old feistiness, as on a day when she was quite frail and being contrary and we were all determined to take her along in the car for a ride in the country. She refused to get out of her rocking chair. Gar put the top down on the car and lashed the chair and her into the backseat. There she sat like a queen, quite delighted with herself.

Mother had believed wholeheartedly in living joyously. She hated being bored. If she were invited to a party, she became the life of it. "A person who is invited to a party is expected to bring joy to it," she lectured Paula and me. Years before Mame Dennis declared life to be a banquet, my mother had been hostess to many a feast.

Settling down in Florida after my divorce, I made up my mind to take a few leaves from Mother's book of living and to ensure as best I could that my children and I would proceed with our lives as joyously as possible. The timing certainly was right. It was the 1960s, mythologized as the selfless decade when it was, in fact, a self-indulgent period.

Like almost everyone at that time, I was carried along by the current. My approach toward the children was lax. After all they'd been through, I wanted them to be carefree and happy. Our home took on the aspects of a beach party in keeping with the new openness that seemed to be sweeping through the country and all of society. As Gordon MacRae and

Doris Day and their music had embodied and symbolized the America of the late 1940s and early 1950s, the cultural icons and music of my children's generation, in their twenties and teens, were Elvis, the Beatles, the Rolling Stones, and Simon and Garfunkel, who were leading America's kids to a rock beat. Their slogan was "sex, drugs and rock 'n' roll." It was, as Heather sang with the "tribe" in *Hair,* "the dawning of the age of Aquarius," and I embraced it.

In *Mame,* young Patrick Dennis's unrestrained aunt resided at Beekman Place, only a few blocks away from the house behind the red door at 13 Sutton Place which I had promised Miriam Hopkins I would love and where I was determined to open a few new windows and doors of my own. The doing had taken a little longer than I'd excepted, thanks to JP, who had wanted too much control, Francis Albert Sinatra, who was in too much of a hurry, and Gordon MacRae, who couldn't let me go. By the spring of 1967, I had broken with all of them. I had also accepted the wise advice of Lucy Ball, relinquished the house with the red door, and committed myself to living in Miami Beach for the full run of the new *Honeymooners,* however long that might prove to be.

Like a hen on a new nest, I settled down comfortably with Ron Wayne and we opened our wings to my children. Teenage Bruce took up permanent residence. Meredith, Heather, and Gar were more transient. The girls were grown-ups pursuing their careers, and Gar was at school, but they all came down to Florida from time to time to see me.

As they were welcome in my house, so were their friends. One was a troubled girl named Debbie who had drifted into Miami Beach on a footloose journey in search of herself. Bruce had met her on the beach. Being a rebellious member of the "Hair" generation, Bruce took one look at Debbie—dirty, hungry, and totally lost—and, feeling sorry for her, brought her home with a dog.

Clearly, what Debbie discovered as she settled into our house was an existence far beyond anything she'd known in her life and probably more than she ever imagined life could be. "My god!" she gasped when she saw me straightening out my clothes closet. "Look at all these fabulous *dresses*! Do you *wear* these?"

"Most of them are for my nightclub act."

"They must be worth thousands," she said. "Can I...can I touch one? I won't hurt it or mess it up or anything."

"Of course you may," I said, laughing lightheartedly when what I wanted to do was cry over this waiflike, wandering girl.

"It's so beautiful," she sighed as she took a gown from the closet and stepped before a mirror to hold it in front of her. "And you have so many more." Still pressing the dress against herself, she did a turn, making the skirt flare. "Fabulous," she sighed, like Peter Sellers rifling through my wardrobe at the Waldorf. "Just... fabulous."

Months later, she was gone. And so were a half dozen of my gowns. Seated disconsolately on my bed as I stared at the looted closet, I heard an echo of my sister's voice from so long ago, after the "models on their way to New York" had absconded with our mother's fur coat. "Sheila, you're just like Mother," Paula said. "Don't take in everyone you see."

More out of pity and a need to understand than from anger and disappointment, I went looking for Debbie. When I found her after about an hour, she was drifting along a seedy street notorious for drugs and drug addicts. She was high on speed, the amphetamine pills having been bought with the proceeds of a "no questions asked" sale of the gowns to a secondhand clothing store a few blocks away.

Whom to blame? Was it Debbie's fault that she was hooked on drugs? Had her parents failed? Should I take Bruce to task for bringing her home? How could I do that when I was the one who had thrown open the door to Debbie? How about blaming American society for creating an atmosphere that drove its children to drugs? That was a common explanation for what was happening to the country's kids. If our children thought they needed to "escape" by taking drugs, there had to be something amiss in America.

"Where do I go?" asked the singers in *Hair*. "Will I ever discover why I live and die?" Their answer was to seek escape in one another and as a group. The new window and the new door that Auntie Mame exhorted people to open had led them to mind-numbing narcotics—pot, hashish (there was a song extolling it in *Hair*), speed. Timothy Leary's LSD, peyote, hallucinogenic mushrooms.

There seemed to be no escaping the influx of drugs. Angela Lansbury took extreme steps to extricate her two children from the sixties drug scene in Malibu where, she said, drugs were "as common as bubble gum." She packed up the kids and moved them to almost totally drug-free County Cork, Ireland, and lived there until they had outgrown any likelihood of temptation. Jackie Gleason's lover, Honey, was having problems with her children. While Honey and I crossed paths at our mutual psychologist's in search of help with our children's difficulties, Jackie didn't put much store in any of it. "Tell your troubles to a bartender," he cracked. "Who ever heard of a shrink giving you one on the house?" For Jackie and Gordon and so many others of their generation, the drug of choice was still alcohol.

One of Jackie's buddies when he went out carousing had been Ron Wayne, his show's producer. With great looks, a beautiful voice, and immense charm, Ron could have gone on to success in any area he might choose after Jackie stopped doing the show. But he wanted to continue as a television producer. Unfortunately, the choices open to him were limited. The era of the big TV variety show was ending. Only two remained on the air, Carol Burnett and Dinah Shore, each with a full staff. There simply were no jobs for Ron.

In addition to dealing with that reality, Ron had just gone through a painful divorce that required high alimony and child support for his daughter Elizabeth, which I paid.

Elizabeth was very fond of me despite having been told by her mother that "Sheila is against Jesus, and bad."

During this challenging period, I was especially concerned about Bruce, the youngest and most impressionable. Of all my kids, he was the one who had been shortchanged the most by Gordon's alcoholism. He discovered in Ron the father he had missed in Gordon, and in Elizabeth, a baby sister to love.

It was Bruce who asked one day, "Why can't we divorce Daddy and marry Mr. Wayne?"

For me, Ron was a remedy for loneliness. He was caring, kind, sexy and funny.

We married in 1967, with only Marge and Irv and my kids there.

A small ceremony, it was not announced publicly and was held in virtual secrecy in the garden of No. 13 Sutton Place because I was afraid that news of me marrying would have a disastrous, even fatal, effect on Gordon.

That same year, Gordon returned to Broadway, joining with Carol Lawrence in taking over the roles originated by Robert Preston and Mary Martin in *I Do! I Do!* A musical version of *The Four Poster* produced by David Merrick, it was a show with only two characters, a husband and wife, and one setting, their bedroom. It's hit song was "My Cup Runneth Over," a celebration of the couple's three children and the joys of married life.

Gordon also had remarried. His new wife, Elizabeth Lamberti Schrafft, came from Lincoln, Nebraska. She was the opposite of me. While I had been the girl with the English accent who went on to become Sheila of the Waldorf and to be described as one of the jet-set sophisticates of the sixties, she was at heart the sort of small-town lady who always had an appeal to the small-town boy in Gordon.

Wishing him happiness and contentment as he started a second family, I thought I could shut the door on him and proceed with my own life unfettered by tormenting visions of him being alone, remorseful, and resentful of me for having left him, divorced him, and remarried. I prayed he would experience bliss and peace and that, finally, he would exorcise the twin demons that had plagued his years with me—the alcoholism that had ruined his career and the gambling that had drawn both of us down into the horrible vortex of gambling debts and federal tax liabilities.

While I had divorced Gordon, I couldn't so easily separate myself from having been married to him or from the fact that we had also been partners in the business side of show business. I quickly learned that I was still being held responsible for the awful state of our financial affairs.

There can be no more chilling words than "The United States of America versus..." When I saw them preceding my name on legal papers concerning our back taxes—"The United States of America versus MacRae and MacRae"—I shuddered with fear and shame. With tearful and unbelieving eyes I stared at the paper. The United States of America was suing *me*!

The case grew out of an Indian lands deal that involved not only Gordo and me but a long list of Hollywood names: John Wayne, Kirk Douglas, Doris Day, Dorothy Dandridge, Billy Eckstine, and others less famous. In the complicated transaction, the land in question belonged to the Indians and was being acquired by us for future development under a federal program designed to let private entrepreneurs exploit mineral rights. For those who took part in such a deal there were inherent tax benefits. The law required principals to visit the land at least once, a clause that, unfortunately, Gordon did not fulfill. The result was an IRS review of our entire financial structure and a suit against him and me for taxes, not just for those growing out of the land deal but for those due from other properties. Among those were oil wells on which I believed taxes had been paid. They hadn't been; Gordon had lost the money gambling.

When I began my incarnation as Alice Kramden, a sizable portion of that money was still owed. To meet my obligation in paying it, I was sending Gordon two thousand dollars a week to be combined with his share. But a few months after I became Alice, Jackie's secretary rushed into a rehearsal and drew me aside. "Sheila, I had a call from a friend of yours on the Coast. She wants you to call her right away."

The caller was Gordon's secretary, Shirley Vaughan. She had also been my secretary when Gordon and I were married. Before that she was Oscar Hammerstein's. "Sheila, I shouldn't be doing this because Gordon would be angry if he found out," she whispered into the phone. "But I feel I owe it to you." She gulped for breath. "Did you know that your house is being sold for taxes? It's being auctioned off tomorrow and everything in it."

"That's impossible!" I cried. "I've been sending Gordon two thousand dollars a week for the taxes. What happened to it?"

Shirley didn't answer. She didn't have to. We both knew where the money went. Gordon had lost it gambling.

I had treasures in that house: personal items, jewelry, oil paintings, irreplaceable pictures of my children. My heart sank.

"If you can wire me ten thousand dollars," Shirley said, "I'll get everything out and ship it wherever you wish."

A miracle worker, she rescued everything. Fortunately, Jackie Gleason had a warehouse in L.A. for her to put it all in. Despite an offer from Irv and Marge Cowan to buy the house, there was not enough time to save it.

More bad news broke. This time it concerned some insurance policies which Gordon and I had taken out on one another years before. A letter from the holder of the policies arrived to inform me that they had followed my instructions and transferred the policies to the new Mrs. MacRae and "any issue she might have." I'd given no such instructions, signed nothing that permitted the company to take the action they were informing me about.

Barely able to contain my anger, I called Gordon to demand an explanation. "Well, I signed your name," he said. "I figured you wouldn't mind. I have a family to think about, you know.'

"If it were only me, Gordie, I wouldn't mind," I said as calmly as possible, "but I do care about the four children who were supposed to be the beneficiaries of those policies. This is so unfair."

"Well, what's done is done."

It got worse. When dividends on our oil investments were due but did not come, I inquired of the investment firm. I was told, "We must refer you to the owners, Mr. and Mrs. Gordon MacRae."

"I *am* Mrs. Gordon MacRae," I answered.

"Our records show that you signed your rights over to the current Mrs. MacRae."

Again, I called Gordon. "I was in a real bind," he said, "so I sold them to Liz."

"Gordie, don't you remember when we bought those wells that we agreed they were for the kids?"

"I remember, but people were breathing down my neck for what I owed them and that was my only way out."

"Sue him!" Lucy Ball said, more outraged than I. "Sue the ass off him."

"No, no, Lucy," I told her. "I couldn't do that."

"Well, if I had a husband who did a lousy thing like that to me, *I'd* sue him."

"I know you would, Lucy, but I'm not you. I don't have your toughness."

She laughed. "Yeah, you always were a softie."

"If all this weren't so bad," I said, starting to laugh myself, "it would be funny. Just think about it! I finally got up the gumption to leave Gordie, *then* divorce him, and a few years later, as far as the government's concerned, because Gordie and I always filed joint tax returns, I'm *still* Mrs. Gordon MacRae. The way they look at it, I owe them. I could be married five times since Gordie and I'd still be Mrs. MacRae. I'd still owe. What is this, Nazi Germany?"

"Nope," she said. "Just the good old U.S. of A. It's like that old joke about the Ways and Means Committee. 'If you've got the means, they've got the ways to get it from you.' Knowing you, hon, you'll get through it and someday you'll look back on what happened and have a big laugh about it."

As grimly depressing as all this had been for me, there were funny moments. The scene: my dressing room in Boston. I was getting ready to go on. A knock on the door. "Come in," I shouted.

The door swung open and into the room stepped two looming, broad-shouldered, pug-faced men in heavy overcoats and snap-brim hats. They looked for all the world like characters from *Guys and Dolls*. One said, "We come for duh dresses."

"Beg pardon?" I said.

"Duh dresses. We come for duh dresses."

"I don't understand. What about the dresses?"

"You're Mrs. MacRae?"

"Yes."

"Well, duh boss says if we don't get duh money he's owed, we should take duh dresses."

"There's some mistake," I said, forcing a laugh. "Look, I've got a show to do."

"Lady, duh boss said if your husband dint come across wit duh dough he owes, we was to come and pick up duh dresses. He dint. So we's here to get duh dresses."

"But I need the dresses," I pleaded. "I have to have them for the show."

"Wull, I guess you'll have to do your show widdout dem."

"Look, what's the hurry?" I said. "Will another hour hurt? Why don't you both go out front and watch the show, and after it's over, we'll settle this matter. The dresses aren't going anywhere, and I certainly am not. You guys have a couple of drinks on me, catch the show, and then I'll take care of whatever it is your boss is owed. All right?"

"Yeah, I guess that'd be okay," he said as he turned to his silent partner. "Okay wid you, Johnny?"

"Sure," Johnny said. "What could it hoit?"

As my financial woes mounted, the Gleason show flickered from the nation's television screens in 1970. He never had a weekly show again, and he might have faded into the pages of TV history, save for the syndication of the thirty-nine *Honeymooners* filmed episodes he had made with Audrey Meadows. They kept Jackie on the screen decades after he had played Ralph with me, the last Alice Kramden. I had hoped that our singing-and-dancing Ralph and Alice would also become available so future TV generations could enjoy them.

With the end of the show, I was, of course, out of work. And still owing my share of the former Mr. and Mrs. Gordon MacRae's tax debt. It was my first time as an unemployed person. I was in my forties. What to do? What could I do? Go on the road.

I had to face up to the fact that Gordon's management of our money had been not only ruinous but fraudulent. Thinking about the amount of debt facing me, I fixed my eyes on the woman in my mirror, remembered Lucy's confident prediction that I would pull through, and said, "Honey, you'd better get your ass in gear and get back to work."

Ron and I put together a TV talk show which included Meredith and Heather. Syndicated to local stations, *The Sheila MacRae Show* for Metromedia was not much of a success. We also put together a couple of other pilot shows, using money that was borrowed in my name. This was a terrible business decision. The shows didn't sell, and, to make matters worse, there was a sharp downturn in the stock markets that caused the bank to call in the loan. We were wiped out. The only way out was for me to go on the road with my act. In nightclubs, I could earn very good money, many thousands a week.

This required almost constant traveling and resulted in strains on my marriage. Ron loved Florida but, quite aside from my need to earn the large amounts of money that were available by working on the road, I felt more at home in the East. On top of all this were demands being made on Ron by his former wife. He faced large alimony and child-support payments. Because I was working I paid them, though Ron's mother warned me not to.

Frustrated and anxious, I talked over the situation with my old friend Marge Cowan. She and her husband Irving were being quite supportive and sympathetic. They gave Ron the job of running their hotels. Marge thought I should remain in Florida with Ron. "I can't do that," I replied, almost in tears. "I have to work. We have no money. I've got debts to pay."

It was a familiar dilemma. Do I stay with my husband? Or do I follow my career?

Into this most confused time walked Jack Heller. An actor who was producer of a touring company of Murray Schisgal's hit *Luv,* he was looking for a "name" and somebody who was good in comedy. We tried it out in Jacksonville and then headed out on tour, playing in large cities for five weeks from coast to cost to very enthusiastic audiences. Much of the credit belonged to Jack. He had precise ideas about doing comedy and being true to the script. He saw comedy as a ballet, following Mike Nichols's direction.

It was hard but I began to discover what Jack found in the work, the joy of working itself. I had great respect for him and learned a lot about comedy, but it was my son Bruce who recognized that I was falling in love with him and that the result was going to be a divorce from Ron.

He was right. Long stretches of being away on the road, our mutual financial difficulties, and our differences over living in Florida took their toll. There was no acrimony or bitterness. Ron and I parted as friends—and still are.

While my money problems made it necessary for me to work constantly, I didn't perform only for money. I played many benefits. I felt an obligation to entertain servicemen who faced the grim reality of a war in Vietnam that was increasingly unpopular on the homefront. Regardless of how people felt about the war, I thought, those who were in uniform deserved a little cheering up when they returned.

I also gladly accepted a bid from the warden of a prison who had decided I was just the person to entertain his inmates. I happily journeyed with Jack through a bleak and snowy Minnesota landscape to a grim and forbidding gray-walled maximum security institution with machinegun-toting guards looking down from towers at every corner. A huge steel door swung open to admit me. "Do you want a personal bodyguard on the stage with you?" the warden asked.

"Lord, no," I answered. "I don't want these men to think I'm afraid of them. I hope they laugh, though."

"Okay, then," he said, "let's go introduce you to Charlie. He's a dandy electrician. He'll take care of setting up lights and anything else you'll need."

Charlie was a charming, elderly black man. "Pleasure to meet you, ma'am," he said, doffing a baseball-type cap. "Just tell me what you need and I'll fix it right up."

"I saw a small couch that would come in handy," I said. "It's in the little waiting room outside the warden's office, you know?"

"Ma'am, I ain't been out there in twenty-five years." Only then did I realize that Charlie didn't work for the prison. He was an inmate. "But if you wants that couch, I'll get a couple of the men and fetch it for you. I'm sure no warden's going to say no to a lady."

He broke into a broad grin. "You know, ma'am, there's men in this place that ain't laid eyes on a woman in an outfit like that. I told 'em all that they'd better act like gentlemen or they'll have to answer to me. Now, they may yell at you and shout things, on account of they don't get actresses, but they won't mean any harm by it. Understand? It'll be just 'cause they're happy that you took the time to come and put on a play like *Owl and the Pussycat*."

I started to cry.

Charlie looked worried. "I say somethin' wrong, ma'am?"

"No, Charlie," I sobbed, "it was one of the nicest things anybody ever said to me."

As Charlie'd promised, the moment I set foot on the stage of what was usually the prison's movie theater, the men went crazy. "Hey, babe," yelled an occupant of a front-row bench, "you are really *stacked.*"

"Come on down here and sing to me," shouted the man next to him.

"Hey," I said, laughing as the room exploded with groans and whistles, "if I thought you could handle it, I would."

From a corner of the stage, Charlie yelled, "Atta girl," and winked.

They loved the show, though I assumed that they would have gone just as crazy over having their day brightened by anyone who walked onto that stage. Thanking the warden for having invited me, I couldn't leave without putting in a good word for Charlie. "He was such a dear. I couldn't've done the show without him." I also could not leave without knowing why Charlie was in prison. "I didn't want to come right out and ask him." I said to the warden.

"Oh, Charlie's in for life," he told me. "Rape and murder."

"Oh, no, that's impossible," I said. "Charlie would never have done such a thing."

When I told the story to Jack Cassidy, he literally fell on the floor laughing. "Only you, Sheersie," he howled. "Things like that could only happen to you!"

Jack's career had really taken off since Shirley Jones proudly showed him off as the love of her life in Boothbay Harbor. Following the completion of *Carousel,* they'd headed the cast in an American National

Theater and Academy European production of the show. They were paired again in a 1968 ANTA musical, *Maggie Flynn*. When they weren't otherwise occupied, they toured with a nightclub act. For British television they did a show called *Date With Shirley and Jack*.

Since earning his first TV-performer paycheck in the early 1950s on one of Gordon's shows, Jack Cassidy had found a very lucrative income in television, whether it was with Ed Sullivan or Lucille Ball or on *Gunsmoke, I Spy, 77 Sunset Strip*, or on a string of game shows. Probably his finest hour in TV drama was his portrayal of the sadistic Confederate prison commander in *The Andersonville Trial*. Fans of Peter Falk's *Columbo* series were familiar with Jack's skills as an actor. He played the murderer on the show three times, a record for repeat appearances by a guest star on the mystery series. In the movies, he portrayed a detective in 1971's *Bunny O'Hare,* an effeminate courier in *The Eiger Sanction* (1975), and a boozing John Barrymore in *W. C. Fields and Me* with Rod Steiger (1976).

Broadway honored him in 1963 with a Tony for his portrayal of a dashing Hungarian lover and philanderer in *She Loves Me*. The next year, he starred opposite Carol Burnett in *Fade Out—Fade In*. In 1975, he returned to the Broadway stage, starring with Janet Leigh in *Murder Among Friends*. His role was a self-admiring and arrrogant actor marked for death by his wife and his agent.

"The agent wants to kill you?" I teased. "It's usually the actor who wants to kill the agent."

Critic Clive Barnes of the *New York Times* wrote that Jack was brilliant and marvelous. "He walks on the set wearing his ego like a cloak and his mind like a dagger," the review went on. "His timing is impeccable, and with the right pauses, rhythms, and expressions, he can make the most harmless lines sound wickedly and bizarrely funny."

The dean of theater critics, Walter Kerr, hailed Jack in the *Times*'s Sunday Arts and Leisure section for "unassailable aplomb." It was just the right phrase to describe Jack, I thought as I read the column.

I had always felt very close to Jack. I often thought I felt his presence even when I knew he was hundreds or thousands of miles away. Frequently on those occasions, the earring would fall from my right ear. It was quite inexplicable, but whenever it happened, I would hear from Jack. It became a joke among our friends. If the earring dropped, someone would say, "Uh oh, I guess we'll be getting a call from

Cassidy!" Good-humored jibes aside, Jack and I were psychically attuned.

In 1976, he was living alone in a top-floor apartment in Los Angeles. It was a lovely place, just like him. An actor's rooms, it had places set aside for show business memories—his Tony Award, photos of him in his many roles, carefully placed pictures of Shirley, Shaun, Patrick, and David. It was a man's domain.

Jack Heller loved Cassidy and the feeling was mutual. Heller and I invited Jack to our new house in England and planned to go and spend a week with him in Palm Springs.

But I felt something else in Jack's apartment. "There's a feeling I'm getting, Jack," I said, "and I don't like it as much as the last place."

With amused eyes and crinkling dimples, he said, "Oh, come on, Heller, she's getting into one of her spooky moods. Sheila, as long as I've known you, you've been picking up bad vibes about places and things. You and Gleason! What a dopey pair of sobersides you two could be. Ghosts and goblins. ESP. UFOs. Your 'psychic sixth sense.' Your trouble, darling, is you didn't ever have a sixth sense about the men in your life!" He took me in his arms. "She should've grabbed me when she had the chance, Heller."

My Jack said, "You two would really have meant trouble."

"So sit down," he said, letting me go to drop into his couch and light a cigarette. "Fill me in on all the trade gossip. You two, show-biz talk! "How are the careers going?"

We talked away the afternoon, as we'd done so often when he visited me at Sutton Place. We caught the red-eye for New York, an actress in pursuit of a job and a mother looking forward to a happy Yuletide holiday with her kids.

Two weeks before that Christmas, December 12, 1976, Jack smoked a last cigarette and went to bed in his apartment. The hot remnant of the cigarette fell onto a couch which smoldered for a time then went up in flames that quickly engulfed everything. Overcome by smoke and trapped in the conflagration, he died in his bed. His agent, Rowland Perkins, identified Jack by his jewelry. The Los Angeles medical examiner confirmed the identification through dental charts.

Jack was only forty-nine years old.

"A Man of Many Roles," the *New York Times* headlined its obituary the next day. "Yes, yes, yes," I sobbed as I read it.

And no finer role, nor one for which he was more suited, I thought, than friend.

Shirley Jones asked Jack Heller and me to undertake the melancholy task of removing Jack's possessions from his home in Palm Springs. Neither of us will ever forget the experience.

We were asleep in Cassidy's bed with the air conditioning turned on. Jack thought I had switched it on. Within minutes, we were freezing. "Sheila, I can't take this," Jack said. "I'm going to shut it off, okay?"

At that moment the air conditioner turned itself off. But a few minutes later it went on again. "It must be defective," I said.

"Maybe," Jack said. "Or maybe it's Jack's ghost."

"Don't joke about things like that," I said.

"Ah yes. You believe in spooky things, don't you? ESP and all that hocus pocus."

Because we could not finish the packing that day, we decided to spend the next night there. But sleeping proved impossible. All night long, the air conditioner kept going on and off. Then the lights started flicking on and off, and I called the police.

When morning dawned, the maid arrived. But after a few minutes of fussing in the living room, she rushed to me looking very upset. "I'm sorry, Mrs. MacRae," she said nervously, "but I can't work today. That man is getting on my nerves."

"What man?" I asked.

"Mr. William Orr," she said.

"But Bill Orr isn't here," I said.

"Well, the man sure looks like him. He's got a little beard, right?"

Bill Orr did indeed wear a goatee. So did Jack Cassidy! At times they looked like brothers.

"I swear to you, Mrs. MacRae, that it was Mr. Orr I saw in the rocking chair just now, or Mr. Cassidy. Oh, God!"

Rushing into the living room, I found it unoccupied. "Show me the chair," I said.

The maid pointed to a rocker. "That one."

I recognized Jack Cassidy's antique chair, recently purchased.

"That does it," I said to Jack Heller. "We're leaving. Jack's spirit is here and he doesn't want us disturbing his things."

My companion laughed. "Sheila, Jack loved you. There's no reason to believe his ghost would harm you."

The story was dismissed by some to whom I told it. The strange events were easily explained, they argued. Besides, I was in a vulnerable state of mind. Maybe so. But I do believe our souls are immortal. Was Jack's spirit present in that apartment? Perhaps, one day, I shall have the opportunity to ask him.

In my relationship with Jack Heller and with the new phase of my career going well, we reached Indianapolis. There, disaster struck. I slipped and fell backward from the stage, fracturing four ribs, breaking my pelvis, and exacerbating my old childhood injury. The pain was excruciating, and it didn't go away. Nothing helped. My union sent me to the doctors. Working was out of the question, they said.

This proved a disappointment to Jack and me. Our tour was over.

A friend who appreciated that there are times when just being there is enough, Carol Channing called. "You know the expression 'having a monkey on your back'?" I asked her. "This feels as if there's a wolf on my back, gnawing on it." I turned for help to a clinic in Seattle that specialized in intractable pain but found no lasting relief. I tried ancient oriental remedies, spending hours chanting and doing yoga. I prayed and returned to Christian Science.

My mother had been a firm believer in the notion that when God closes one door He opens another. The door he opened for me in the midst of the agonies of my back injury led me into the world of writing. Immobilized and often flat on my back in tears from pain and boredom, I started filling the hours by developing ideas for plays and other theatrical productions. Having always been fascinated by the life and times of William Shakespeare, I mused on what might have happened if Will had had an affair with Good Queen Bess. Might there be a play about ill-matched lovers out of time with a deep passion for one another? History did not record what happened in their frequent meetings when she was fifty-three and he was twenty-eight. In Shakespeare's words, slightly twisted, "the play's the thing wherein I'll catch the queen and the playwright" being amorous.

I also toyed with the historic fact that women had not been allowed to become actors in Will's day. Boys played the female parts. When the strictures against women in the theater were abandoned, great actresses played Shakespeare's females. I wrote *Shakespeare's Boys*, where women assumed the roles that only boys filled in Shakespeare's day. I envisioned these actresses gathered together in some mystical future place where their talk was the theater, the Bard of Avon, other playwrights, their roles, their lives, and their loves—my renowed ancestor Sarah Siddons, Maud Adams, Liz Taylor, and others engaged in "girl talk" and talk of their trade. In my pain and discomfort, I envisioned and jotted down dramas and comedies, even a film musical.

Occasionally, friends broke into my solitude to exhort me to get out of my bed and back into life. I resisted. But as another Christmas approached, Jeannie Martin, who had always given wondrous Yuletide parties, demanded that I attend that year's festivities. "All right, I'll come," I said. "But I'll just be sitting there, you know. Don't expect me to get up and do a Highland fling!"

"Of course not, my darling," she said. "I'll see to it that you have a proper chair from which you may reign like a queen."

The first person to approach me was Gene Kelly. The star of so many MGM musicals had always been one of my favorite Hollywood people. I loved talking to him about them, but one number I quickly learned not to discuss was his most famous and enduring, *Singin' in the Rain*.

"If I hear one more chorus of that damn song, I'll scream," he said. "I've had a head cold ever since."

He looked in a fine fettle to me that evening as he bent to give me a kiss on the cheek. "Where've you been lately?" he asked. "We've missed you."

I explained why I'd not been out and around.

"Why didn't you let me know?" he said. "I would have dropped in to visit."

"I was following the advice of my grandmother. She told me, 'If you have a pimple on your bottom, don't go around looking for sympathy. Nobody's interested in somebody's else's troubles. They all have their own.'"

"Well, your grandmother was wrong. How are you now?"

"Getting better."

"How soon till you'll be performing again?"

"I haven't been thinking about performing much."

"You're not giving it up?"

"I've been doing a lot of writing."

"That's great. Anything I'd be interested in? You know, I'm running Francis Coppola's Zoetrope studio now."

"I've been working on a musical."

"Tell me about it," he said, sitting before me on the floor.

"It's an old-fashioned musical called *Come Home for Christmas,*" I began. "It's set in a little town in the Midwest in 1898. I even got Ralph Blaine and Hugh Martin to write the songs."

"They did the music for *Meet Me in St. Louis,* correct? 'The Trolley Song,' 'The Boy Next Door,' 'Have Yourself a Merry Little Christmas'! I want to see everything you've got," he said, rising excitedly. "When can you send me the script? And a tape? Have you got the songs on tape?"

"Gene, I'd rather do it the old way," I said. "Remember how it was? You all sat around and read the script? If you're really interested, I'll hire some singers and audition it, like MGM."

"That's fine with me," he said. "I'll set it up. We'll do it at my house." The audition was arranged for early January. When I arrived with the little troupe that would perform the musical numbers while I narrated the action and described dialogue, Ralph and Hugh were already there. Gene threw open the door. "Francis is coming," he exclaimed.

I was shocked. "Francis" to me was Frank Sinatra. I really didn't expect that. "Why is *he* coming? I'm so nervous."

"I may be running the studio," Gene said, looking mystified, "but the Zoetrope studio is still Francis Ford Coppola's outfit."

Relieved that Francis Albert Sinatra was not coming, I was delighted to see this other Francis. Always a great family man, he arrived with his wife and kids. Also with him was the business manager of Zoetrope. "We can't start yet," said Francis, stroking his beard. "We have to wait for John."

"John who?" I asked.

"John Travolta," he answered. "When he heard about this audition, there was no keeping him away. He's just wrapped *Staying Alive* and is looking for his next project." He and Francis are great friends.

When John Travolta arrived, he immediately enveloped me in his arms. "Sheila, I hope you've written me a great part," he said as I winced with the jolt of pain his hug sent down my spine.

"Take it easy, kid," Gene said. "The lady's got a bad back! You'll put her in the hospital again."

The audition went very well, interrupted over and over by Francis Coppola jumping to his feet and shouting, "It's great! I love it!

Fantastic." When the audition was done, he announced an immediate meeting in the kitchen between himself, Gene, Zoetrope's business manager, and me. "It's going to be a thirty, maybe forty, million dollar picture," he said for openers.

The budget I had in mind was less than half that, I told him.

"Impossible," he said. "If we're going to do it, we'll do it right! and we *are* going to do it, believe me."

I was afloat with excitement, gliding through the air like Billie Burke as the good witch Glinda in *The Wizard of Oz*. Then my bubble burst. Beset by financial troubles and some personal ones, Francis went broke. Zoetrope was thrown into bankruptcy and with it, as a company asset, went my musical for several years.

Francis Coppola eventually came back in a big way with a third *Godfather*. He used relatives in his movies. Among them were his sister Talia Shire in all three *Godfather* films, his father, Carmine Coppola, who provided the *Godfather* music, and his daughter Sofia in the third *Godfather*. That the offspring of stars and the other people who made motion pictures should also go into show business was, I suppose, inevitable.

Parents in all walks of life hope that their kids will think enough of them to emulate them, so I was pleased to see scions of many of my friends trying their wings: Tina and Frank Sinatra, Jr.; Carrie Fisher, the daughter of Debbie Reynolds and Eddie Fisher, breaking through as Princess Leia in the *Star Wars* films; Jamie Leigh Curtis, daughter of Janet Leigh and Tony Curtis, also with a blossoming movie career; Chris Lemmon, Jack's son; Gregory Peck's boy, Tony; David Cassidy, Jack's first son, and Shaun and Patrick, the children of Jack and Shirley; Lucie Arnaz and Desi, Jr.; and, of course, Meredith and Heather MacRae.

Tragically, Dean and Jeannie Martin lost a son. Dean Paul Martin, a captain in California's Air National Guard, was killed in March 1987, when his jet fighter crashed in the San Bernardino Mountains during a blizzard. Jeannie had been a friend for thirty years, always ready to share a laugh or a good cry and never failing if the time came when more than laughter, tears, or a pat on the head were needed. I was heartbroken when their marriage went on the rocks and desolate when she lost their son. Dean was never the same again. Jeannie was never remarried.

We have always been close friends since we founded a group called

SHARE and decided to concentrate our efforts on aiding young people. It means "Share Happily and Reap Endlessly." The charter members were Jeannie, Miriam Nelson, Mrs. Sammy Cahn, Marge Chandler, Joy Warner Orr, and Robert Blythe.

I can't believe it all began in 1954 and has well over one hundred members who devote all their time to fund raising.

As I struggled to recover my health, I went to New York, primarily for a visit, and was invited by Gena and Hy Hollinger to stay in their apartment. Despite the circumstances—still not fully back to health, broke, and with no clear idea of what I'd do with the rest of my life, I was delighted to be in New York and wanted to remain there because I felt that it was the most likely place for me to find work.

Presently, I got a call from Jay Bernstein, a producer who wore safari clothes and a large necklace that was adorned by a big tooth. "Sheila, we're doing a new musical called *Nora,* and I'd like you to be in it." The show was based on Ibsen's *Doll's House,* which had been tried before as a musical, unsuccessfully. But Jay was offering me twelve weeks of work, so I was not inclined to debate with him about the wisdom of producing another singing Nora.

During my encampment in the Hollingers' apartment, Marge and Irv Cowan were producing a Broadway show for Peggy Lee. It was to be a solo performance similar to Lena Horne's recent success. Because they were eager to return to their beloved Florida, they asked me to take over as one of the associate producers. I was thrilled. I'd been a fan of Peggy Lee, and Gordon and I had been close to her for years. She was, I believed, one of the most brilliant cabaret performers ever and among the greatest singers. And I had a huge success doing my own interpretation of Peggy in my act.

Unfortunately, Peggy did not adapt well to the demands of the show. She wanted to do the entire show seated on a chair. She was opposed to any suggestion that she simply couldn't treat a Broadway stage as if it were a nightclub. She resisted all pleadings to move around the stage. While she had written a marvelous score, what she chose to say to the audience was a grim recitation of the troubles she had faced in her career.

I tried to cajole her into talking about the happy times. She wouldn't have any of it. I wanted to bring in Bob Fosse to help with the staging.

Any idea I presented was rejected amid bitter accusations that I was trying to close the show. As a result of her refusal to make changes, the show was a disaster. The reviews were horrendous. Acerbic critic John Simon called it "a singing wake."

In this period of the energetic and enervating 1980s, I lost another friend, "the Great One" who'd come into my life so late but with a lasting effect. Jackie Gleason, from whom I had learned much about comedy and acting, died of cancer on June 24, 1987.

Fittingly, the man who contributed so much to making television the prime source of entertainment in America received lengthy tributes on that evening's news programs and in specials that showed clips from his shows that demonstrated the genius of his comedy. When I prayed that night, it wasn't just for Jackie's immortal soul but to give thanks that I had known him and for all that he did for me in choosing me to be Alice, in being a magnificent teacher, in sharing my interest in exploring things unknown, and in giving me lots of laughs on the show and off.

I spoke at a memorial service held at the Museum of Broadcasting in New York. "I'm standing in the middle of Jackie's dreams. He wanted to be famous. He was. He wanted to be a great actor. He showed us all that he was. We all hope for fine friends, good colleagues at work and someone to love. Jackie had them in abundance. He married two wonderful women. He was the father of two lovely daughters. Yes, Jackie was a man of amazing achievement. We called him the Great One. And that he was. But inside that great man was still a five-year-old boy, ready for fun. So, Jackie, wherever you are, I know you're enjoying yourself."

Jack Carter spoke after me. "Thanks a lot, Sheila," he said. "How do I follow that?"

The year before Jackie passed away, another show business legend and close friend of mine had died. Desi Arnaz succumbed to lung cancer. Though he had been overshadowed by Lucy and had been seen by the public as little more than a straightman and foil for her antics, Desi was a remarkable performer and actor in his own right, as well as a brilliant businessman who contributed much more than his name in the creation of Desilu Studios.

"All my life I've worried about what I'd do when I got too old, too fat, and too ugly to be in front of a band," Desi once told an interviewer at the height of Desilu's success. "Now I don't worry. We're learning to produce television shows." Besides the *Lucy* programs, Desilu—with

Desi at the helm—turned out such winning TV series as *Our Miss Brooks, December Bride,* and *The Untouchables.*

If there's one lasting contribution of the Desi Arnaz–Lucille Ball collaboration to television history, other than *I Love Lucy,* it was inventing and perfecting a system that used three cameras rather than one, a process that was adapted for use throughout the industry. And in filming their shows rather than presenting them "live," they also made it possible for a show to be repeated. Before Lucy and Desi there had been no such thing as the "rerun."

When Lucy and Desi divorced in 1960, she bought out his interests in Desilu, making him a rich man. After that, he was not as active in show business and faded, more or less, from the public's attention, save for the reruns of *I Love Lucy.*

About a year after Desi's death in 1986, Lucy suffered a mild heart attack. She rebounded with her usual vigor and good humor, but the next year she was stricken again. Around noon on April 18, 1989, she complained of chest pains and was rushed to Cedars-Sinai Medical Center, where she underwent seven hours of surgery for the repair of her aorta and aortic valve. Dr. Robert Kass announced to her millions of worried fans that her condition was guarded and that the next twenty-four hours would determine how well her recovery would go. Again, she bounced back.

Encouraged by the hopeful reports of her recovery, I called her. "You know, honey," she said brightly, "my kids used to look at my red hair and call me the Henna Thud. I told 'em that one day the Henna Thud would die and they wouldn't have her to kick around anymore. Well, I guess old Henna Thud gave them a real scare this time, huh?"

"You scared all of us, Lucy."

"As for you," she said, "I still haven't forgiven you for taking your impression of me out of your nightclub act."

"It was wrecking my voice. Besides, nobody but you could ever be Lucy."

"Yeah, but your version of her sure was funny!"

A few days later, early in the morning of April 26, 1989, she was gone. She was seventy-seven. As Sammy Davis, Jr., put it so well: the good ones die young.

In 1991, CBS, the network she had almost single-handedly put on top with *I Love Lucy,* broadcast a TV movie-biography called *Lucy and*

Desi: Before the Laughter, based on the years before their smashing success on television. "Total trash," said their daughter Lucie (when she went into show business, she'd swapped the "y" at the end of her name for "ie" to avoid confusion between her and her legendary mother). "If there is reincarnation," she went on, "both my mom and dad are going to come back and haunt CBS."

She was absolutely right. The show had been an insult to Lucy and Desi. "Don't trust anybody in show business," Lucie said. "They're all scum."

Not all. Many of the show people I've known were and are first-rate human beings. These passed away in the eighties: Gordo, Geraldine Page, newfound friend Dick Shawn, Sammy Davis, Jackie Gleason, Florence Jensen Simmons (my second mother), Barbara Stanwyck, Irene Dunne, Mary Martin, Gower Champion, and Lucy.

THIRTEEN

Friends, Lovers, and Me

PEOPLE BELIEVE THAT EVERYONE in show business knows everyone else. It's not true. When meeting a famous person for the first time, actors and actresses can be just fans.

I was bowled over by Archibald MacLeish at a New England party, showing off my dog-eared copy of "Poetry and Experience," his series of lectures.

Next weekend, I traveled to Buffalo in hopes of getting Dr. Theodor Reik to appear with me on television in Philadelphia, explaining how *Of Lust and Love* was my nightly read.

And so, as the summer stretched out, the races at Saratoga turned out the most overwhelming experience. Staying with friends, I was introduced to Albert Finney. I had, of course, seen his films and his Broadway plays *Joe Egg* and *Luther*—raw and arresting performances.

Born in England in 1936, the son of a bookie, he'd trained for the stage at the Royal Academy of Dramatic Art and made his debut in 1956 with the Birmingham Repertory Theatre, spending the next four years playing Shakespeare. In 1960, he exploded onto the London stage as a rebellious youth in *Billy Liar* and onto the screen in *The Entertainer* (as Olivier's son) and *Saturday Night and Sunday Morning*. Three years later he established himself as a movie star in the boisterous and bawdy title role in *Tom Jones*. He was a powerful and dynamic actor with a wide range that ran from the handsome and rakish Tom to Agatha Christie's foppish Belgian-born detective Hercule Poirot in the movie version of *Murder on the Orient Express*. As Poirot, Albert was so thoroughly into his character as to be virtually unrecognizable. I admired all his roles and had no argument with anyone who saw him as the new Laurence Olivier.

My ties to Gordon were long ago. And to JP. I was divorced from Ron. The affair with Jack Heller was over. I was deep in my financial troubles, now recovered from my back injury, incurred when a speeding drunkard knocked me into the Sepulveda Dam. Whether Albert Finney knew any of this at the time I don't know. "Intense passion is a wonderful antidote," he said. "You're not married, are you?"

"I'm separated," I smiled, "but I am almost involved with someone."

He answered with a knowing grin. "Who isn't?"

Our paths crossed again at the trendy California spa, La Costa. He was there buying horses. I was working hard to get back into shape at the health spa. He telephoned, asking me to join him at the restaurant later that night. Taking my hand, he said, "We're going to see more of one another."

The only way to describe my feelings is to use a very old word. I felt as if I were going to *swoon*. That night we danced and sang songs from *Guys and Dolls* to one another. "You and I could be more than friends," he whispered. I was totally mesmerized.

I felt strongly attracted to him and perfectly connected to him. He had a brilliant mind and a keen sense of humor. He was a gentleman. But he reminded me too much of Gordon. I tried not to fall in love. Unsuccessfully, I must say.

In many aspects the affair was thrilling. We met often in many places. And I could not escape the sense that I was reliving my experience with Gordon. But Finney had an excess of energy, talent, and ladies, so I retreated to the safer relationship of friendship.

My life always takes unexpected turns, and that winter, I toured in *Absurd Person Singular* that took me from Delaware to Toronto, Chicago, and Detroit. I costarred with the one of the most delightfully debonair actors of films, television, and the British stage, Patrick Macnee. He and I had forged a friendship instantly.

Also in the cast were the elegant Betsy von Furstenberg and Judy Carne, working on a comeback after a difficult period in her career following her skyrocket to fame on *Laugh-In*. They had an important scene together that played very well until we reached Chicago.

Judy missed her cue and came onstage a few seconds late. Furious, Betsy, who was holding a drink, splashed the contents into Judy's face, a bit of business that was not in the script. Judy responded with a string of sexual epithets that, likewise, were not in the play. Neither was the punch that Judy threw at Betsy. Nor the brawl that followed.

Unaware that the fight scene was for real, the audience roared with laughter.

My immediate reaction, aside from horror, was concern for Judy and Betsy. Moving upstage, I dropped to my knees as if in prayer. "Please," I begged as the curtain dropped, "is there a doctor in the house?"

A man and woman rushed forward.

"Oh, doctor, thank goodness," I said to the man.

"I'm not the doctor," he said, turning to the woman. "My wife is."

To make matters worse, my sister, Paula, had come to see the show with her daughter. Unaware that the play did not contain the language they had been forced to listen to as Judy unleashed her verbal attack on Betsy, Paula wagged a finger at me as she visited in the dressing room. "Was that language in the London play?"

With the debacle behind us, Patrick and I were relieved to arrive at the next stop on the tour, Detroit. But as we checked into our hotel, out of the corner of my eye I glimpsed a familiar figure. It was JP.

I felt faint.

"Sheila, what's wrong?" asked Patrick. "Are you ill?"

"I can't talk now," I said. "Take me to the bar."

Patrick squinted. "You don't drink."

"Please! Please!" I spurted out the whole tale.

Patrick listened quietly to the end. "Darling, darling," he said stroking my trembling hand, "you're making much too much of this."

"I can't stay in this hotel," I cried.

"I'm afraid you must," he said. "All the hotels are full. There's not a room to be had."

All my hopes and plans for not having to confront JP were dashed by mutual friends who were also in Detroit. Shirley Eder and her husband, Hy Slotkin, invited me to a party for our opening night.

"You must come," she said. "And guess what? Your friend JP is in town and will be there!"

I explained my dilemma to Patrick. "Of course you will go," he said. "These are your friends. Besides, I shall be there with you. I shan't leave your side for a moment."

"Very well," I said, "but you must make an excuse for us to leave early."

Soon after we arrived, the dreaded moment came. "Hello," I said as JP approached me. "How are you?"

"Very well," he said. "Apparently you're doing fine, too. Everyone tells me you're a big hit in the play."

"She is really divine," Patrick said. "She plays my wife."

"I see," JP said. "The perfect wife?"

"Actually, I play a British bitch," I said.

JP smiled. "Type casting?"

I felt tears welling. "You'll have to excuse me," I said, "I have someone I have to call on the phone."

"Did you hear that, Patrick?" JP said. "She has someone she has to phone. Dare we ask whom?"

Fighting back the tears, I hurried from the room.

Patrick caught up with me.

"Will you stay with me in my room?" I blurted.

"That's a wonderful thing to contemplate," he said, smiling. "But don't you think it would be simpler if you just locked your door and turned off the telephone?"

I did, but I found the little red light glowing, signaling messages, all from JP. "Call me." "Why don't you call me?" "Aren't we friends?" Others were in the form of notes slipped under the door.

Then I heard him at the door. "Come on, Sheila, open up. I know you're in there."

It was six in the morning. I couldn't have him standing in the hall knocking loudly and attracting attention. Opening the door, I found him with a suitcase in his hand.

"I'm leaving," he said.

"Oh, Shirley said you'd be here for a while."

"So you discussed me!"

"The subject was unavoidable."

"Well, I'm going. Call me in New York."

Next day, I related the events to Patrick.

"You know, Sheila, I have a marvelous therapist who could do wonders for you."

When my birthday came, he presented me with a gift of a four-hour session with the doctor. "In spite of your problems," he said when we were finished, "you seem to have your life fairly well together."

"Not entirely," I said, "but I'm working on it."

A major problem that only prayer could solve was simply finding acting jobs. I needed money, but more importantly, I had to have work.

In early 1990, while I was appearing in Dallas, Texas, I got a phone call from Ron Howard, whom I and everyone else remembered as Ronny Howard, the tow-headed little Opie on *The Andy Griffith Show* of the 1960s. Later, the national love affair with little Ronny turned into an adolescent crush when he became a teenager and starred in *Happy Days.* From there, he went into directing and producing, zooming to the top of the ladder in 1985 with a movie box office bonanza, *Cocoon.* With his partner, Brian Glazer, under the banner of their production company Imagine, he then turned out another big-screen winner in 1989.

A warm, funny family picture, *Parenthood* had starred Steve Martin, Mary Steenburgen, and Dianne Wiest. Filled with family values and lots of adorable kids, the film seemed perfect for adaptation as a television series.

"To my mind you're just the person to play Ed's mother," Ron said to me. "Could you come out here so we can talk about it?"

I thought Ed Begley, Jr., to be perfect for the lead—witty, young, appealing, and an actor!

Ron was planning thirteen shows. A decision on whether there would be more would depend on the ratings. Not unaware that the money was attractive, I jumped at it.

Arriving at the studio for the first day's shooting, I saw Ed and stopped my car to chat with him only to hear the blaring of the horn of a Rolls Royce behind me. The impatient driver was JP.

I sprang from my car to his.

"What the hell are you doing on this lot?" he asked.

"I'm involved in *Parenthood,*" I said proudly.

"Doing what?" he asked. "Producing?"

"No! Acting!"

"God," he groaned. "Are you still doing that?"

Dashing to my car in tears, I could not believe that after more than twenty years he still had a hold on me. Fortunately, that day's shooting did not involve me to a great extent. Had I had more to do, I'm not sure I could have done it.

Even before the film *Parenthood* had been completed, NBC executives had looked at a rough cut of the movie and immediately recognized the makings of a TV version that could be the keystone of the network's Saturday night programming in the upcoming 1990 season. For a while, they even considered scheduling it twice a week, but the show started with a one-hour pilot on Monday night, August 20. This was well ahead of the customary kickoff week for new fall shows. The plan was to repeat the original program a month later in a second premiere week. Network executives believed this "double pump" technique would garner many more viewers than the usual method of a new show having one debut.

The reviews were heartening. *Time* magazine, in looking at all the new shows being offered by the three networks, saw few "rays of light" but judged *Parenthood* to be superior because it cut "closer to the bone than most family sitcoms" and because it did such a good job of duplicating the hit movie. In the Sunday *New York Times,* Caryl Rivers liked the reality of the kids on the show, compared to the kids in other sitcoms. "Now and then, though," said Rivers, "you happen on a show that makes you say to yourself, 'Yeah, that's it. That's how it is.' Watching the pilot of NBC's *Parenthood,* I said to myself, 'Whoever wrote this has real kids—and they're taking notes.'" Kay Gardella in the *Daily News* noted that the show "manages to strike a note of reality." David Bianculli of the *New York Post* observed that Ron Howard as the "parent" of the program "ought to be proud. It's a winner, and has the look of a durable, likable hit." *Variety* said Sheila MacRae is wasted.

The reviewers liked us, but what about the audience? What did the ratings show? They, too, looked good. But then things went amiss. Instead of an hour, NBC decreed that each episode would be a half hour. For the writers, it was a daunting task. Because the show had been planned as an hour in length, it had a large cast. The idea was to have an ensemble. Squeezing them all into a half hour and making sense of what was going on proved impossible. From the original Saturday-night-at-ten slot, the show was moved back to eight. The core audience for the show was adult women, ages eighteen to fifty-four. History had demonstrated that an adult female audience just wasn't there early on Saturday evenings, and it wasn't there for us. The network did not see itself at fault, however. Rather, it said that the show had failed because it had no "breakthrough characters" and wasn't "funny enough." Utter nonsense.

In December, after six half-hour episodes, NBC put the show on "hiatus." The term usually applies to a vacation period for a show that's going to be renewed. In this case, the suspension of production was for the purpose of assessing whether it would continue.

Coming at the Christmas holiday season, the break permitted me to take a much-needed vacation with all my kids in the Caribbean. When I returned in January, a decision still hadn't been made on the future of the show. It didn't come until the end of the month. Canceled. I read about it in the morning newspapers. The official word didn't reach me until late afternoon by telephone from the West Coast.

"That seems a little rude," said a friend who was with me when the call came.

"That's television," I said.

"What now?" he asked.

"Now, if you will excuse me," said I, picking up the phone, "I've got to call my agent about getting a job again."

In the boom times of the 1980s, when it seemed there was no limit to how far American business could go or how high the stock market could zoom, the "in" term that defined what Calvin Coolidge had called "the business of America" was networking. "Who do you know?" was the watchword in getting ahead, even more so than in previous periods of the country's long history of "old school ties" and "old boy networks." In tapping friendships, Wall Street and the Ivy League were laggards compared to show business. Theatrical grapevines had sprouted in Shakespeare's day. Now, the scuttlebutt was relayed instantly by phone and fax as showfolk traded news about who was casting, what new shows were in the works, who was putting together a road show version of what show, what studios were gearing up for what new pictures, where the jobs were.

I really have no complaints about the demise of *Parenthood*. Being on the show served me well. I was able to pay off more than $160,000 in business debts and back income taxes. Having done so, I was broke again. But I was also free again.

When I went out to Hollywood for *Parenthood* in 1990, it had been forty-one years since a pair of Malted Milk Kids in their twenties had set foot on the Warner lot. The movie capital had undergone a dramatic change. "Nobody makes pictures in Hollywood anymore," someone said. "they make deals. No one writes movies. They write deal memos. Moguls don't run things anymore. The Japanese do."

Since going to Hollywood in what some might call "the good old days," I had made and kept scores of friends in all aspects of the business, from major stars to stagehands. Status never mattered to me. I liked the fact that Doris Day's women friends were chosen from a stratum below hers. I never saw her in a close friendship with a female star who was entitled to equal billing. Her best friends were the wonderful character actress Mary Wickes, with a Hollywood career that started in 1942 as a harassed nurse in *The Man Who Came to Dinner* and continued into the 1990s with *The Father Dowling Mysteries* as the rectory housekeeper, and Kaye Ballard, a great comedienne.

Joan Crawford seemed to me to be unduly conscious of a person's standing, whereas Ava Gardner, Rita Hayworth, Mary Martin, Carol Channing, Lucy, and so many other great women stars could not have cared less about a friend's name recognition.

Neither Frank Sinatra nor Jackie Gleason nor Gordon cared about their friends' status, although, in retrospect, Gordon might have been better able to cope with his problems if he had had pals who did not share his compulsions for wagering and drink.

In my meandering way, I see that this chapter has gone back and forth. As Lawrence Durrell wrote: "Events in human memory do not come in sequential form but appear here and there like quanta in the universe." That's what happened.

In 1990, I was visiting the Cowans and looked out their window to see the Diplomat Hotel closed. I thought of Jackie and *The Honeymooners* and the first season in 1967, when Margy Cowan said that she had a call from JP. "He asked me if you were seeing anyone."

"What did you tell him?" I asked.

"He didn't give me time to reply. He said he was coming down to see you."

The evening he found me was stormy. Literally. A hurricane was pounding Miami. Snug and safe from the weather but nervous over the prospect of seeing JP, I was having dinner with Marge and Irv at the Celebrity Room and anticipating the opening of Peggy Lee's show when JP arrived.

He made straight for our table.

"Can we talk?" he asked, and for the next hour, he reminded me nonstop of how we were and could be.

"No," I said, "we can't."

He flushed with anger. "What is it you really want?" Then I recited the usual complaints of lovers—"Can't *you* do *this*. Then *I'll* do *that!*"

What I wanted was to get away. Rising abruptly, I dashed out, plunging into the storm. The wind was fierce and the rain slashed into my face like a million knives as I ran in a beaded gown that was bound to be ruined by the soaking it took as I fled to my car. Very nearly hysterical, I sped away, not knowing were I was going and not caring, wanting only to get away.

With the hurricane increasing in ferocity, I made a made dash over the bridge between Miami and Key Biscayne. It was a dangerous and foolhardy thing to do. It seemed so crazy that TV cameras took a picture of my car—the only one on a bridge that could have been swamped by wind-driven, surging waves that could have swept the car and me away.

Eventually, I made my way to Ron Wayne's apartment. "What's happened?" he asked, taking me into his arms.

As I explained what he occurred, I found him comforting and understanding. I talked and he listened, and my anxiety gradually faded and my thoughts turned away from JP's demanding attitude to the gentle, caring, considerate man sitting beside me and holding my hand. We kissed. Presently, we made love for the first time.

The next day, Marge Cowan telephoned. "Where were you last night? We were terribly worried. You just ran away? Don't do that to me!"

Then she told me what JP had said after I rushed out. It was typical of him. "She'll be back," he had said. "You'll see. She always comes back."

He was wrong. I did not go back.

In February 1984, on as bleak and rainy day as New York City can conjure, while heading for a meeting at "21," I thought I was exactly where I wanted to be—an independent woman, happy and at work in

New York. I was wearing my favorite leopard hat, a red cape, and, despite the gloomy day, my customary dark glasses. The only thing on my mind was the future. Suddenly, as I rounded the corner from Fifth Avenue onto 52nd Street, I found myself thrust back into my past.

Directly ahead of me in front of "21" was JP. Now, suddenly, I was in the rain again—a steady, wind-gusted, dismal Manhattan rain—and there he was in front of "21." He had one foot in a limousine and was talking to someone. As always, he looked tan, healthy, and strong. He turned his head and saw me. "Fellas, I'll see you guys later," he said, smiling toward me. "I just fell in love."

He raced to me and hugged me, sweeping my wet umbrella aside. I tried to keep my hands from shaking as I looked into his gray eyes. We talked rapidly of other things.

"I read about you in the newspapers," he said.

"Yes, I'm in a play."

"Something with some Puerto Ricans. Yes?"

"It's by a playwright who's being called the Venezuelan Noël Coward."

"So, this guy, this new Noël Coward, is he your lover?"

"No, he isn't. His name is Isaac Chacron." I pronounced it. "E-e-t-z-a-k."

"Listen. No matter how you say it, it's Isaac. He's a Jew. And don't tell me he's not your lover!"

"He is *not* my lover."

He shrugged.

I wanted to touch him, but I forced myself not to. "Please come to see me in the play."

"No. Never. One of us has to be sensible."

"Well, I'm separated."

"You're always separated. I don't want to see you again unless you can be sensible."

"What does that mean?"

"Look, I don't want to talk about it. It's raining. I'm getting wet." He walked back to the limo. "Call me. I have a locked box in my office that you might want to see. Come."

Pulling my cape tightly around me as I dashed for the door of "21," I thought, "This is like a scene in a Hitchcock movie. What was it he said? 'The true romantic insists on imposing *illusion* on *reality* almost as an obsession.'"

I sat on a chair in the lounge. I picked up a menu and wrote on the back of it. "Which was the reality? Us? Which was the illusion? The rain? I remember being at a party with him. It was the only time he'd ever defended me. Usually he tried to tear me down. It was a memorable night. He had castigated a woman who attacked me verbally at the party. They were both quite drunk. He stopped in front of her and said, 'Listen, you bitch, what she's got, you couldn't spell, and what she has, you used to have.'"

I twisted around and gazed at the door, hoping I would see him coming in, coming back to me. He wasn't. To myself I said, "A love affair is the culmination of a dream. It's like mountain climbing. The accidents happen on the way down. It's the euphoria that leads to the slip."

The owner of "21," Pete Kreindler, sat beside me. "Sheila, when are you going to give this up? Come on!"

Crying, I retreated to the ladies' room and gazed into the mirror at my tears. Down the years, the attendants in the ladies' room at "21" have gotten used to crises. This day was no different. The woman handed me a Kleenex. "Memory," she said, "is a book of your soul."

Picking up my gray umbrella, I left without going to my meeting. Walking in the driving rain, I thought, "We came together accidentally. It's always an accident. What were we doing standing there? Only making plausible eyewitness reports that pass as truth." Exhausted, I wanted to go home and sleep. I wanted to stop this, but could I?

"Memory is a book of your soul," the woman in the ladies' room had told me. How right she was. I remembered New Year's Eve years ago during the three months of JP's ultimatum when we were not to see one another or be together even casually. I was invited to celebrate at the Lake Success home of Susan and Herman Marinoff, lovely friends. I was planning to go with my two Jacks—Cassidy and Carter.

When JP found out I was going, he phoned. "This party on New Year's Eve," he said, very upset. "I don't want you to go."

Just as upset, I answered, "Well, I'm going."

Throughout the evening, we scrupulously avoided one another, but after midnight he appeared at my side and asked, "Do you want to dance with a drunk?"

"I've done it before," I said, thinking of Gordon.

"How can you do this?" he asked. "How can you joke and smile and dance when I'm hurting like hell."

"I'm a good actor."

"Not that good."

"Now you're putting down my acting!"

Staring, he said, "I hate you looking happy!"

Although it would be a few more weeks before I called him to tell him that I was not going to divorce Gordon and we had the argument that ended our relationship, those angry words at that New Year's Eve party were a confirmation that our love affair had come to the end.

Yet as my running into him outside "21" showed me, it could never be completely over between us, just as I'd never gotten over my love for Gordon.

When it came time to welcome another New Year—1986—and everyone round me was singing the lovely Scottish refrain of old times, I joined in *Auld Lang Syne* and thought wistfully about Gordon.

It would be grand to see him. I thought, but he was very ill and far, far away, much too distant for me to kiss him as I'd done on so many New Year's midnights in the golden years of a most extraordinary love.

While the last notes of Robert Burns's anthem of things past faded away, I recalled other lines that he might have written for Gordie and me:

O, my luve's like a red, red rose,
That's newly sprung in June.
O, my luve's like the melodie,
That's sweetly played in tune.

FOURTEEN

Last Silver Song of a Lark

IN THE TWENTY YEARS AFTER I left Gordon and fashioned my own career, marrying and divorcing again, finding new romances, acting and writing, Gordon had not fared well. The years of drinking had destroyed his voice. Alcohol and time had also spoiled his beauty. The world of movies that he had known had vanished like the gorgeous palaces in Will Shakespeare's *Tempest*, an "insubstantial pageant faded."

The grandiose theaters which had shown Jack Warner's lighthearted musicals had been either demolished or cut up into little pieces so their owners could show three, four, or five, even ten pictures at a time in tiny boxlike auditoriums having all the magic of a bus station. The stars of the films weren't stars at all in the Jack Warner sense; they were instant celebrities with megamillion dollar contracts, production deals, a piece of the profits taken right off the top, marketing tie-ins, total script approval, and the freedom to write, star in, and direct just about anything they wished. The studios were rarely making movies themselves. They bought film "concepts" from independent producers, packaged them, distributed them, collected the money, and often cooked the books so that a movie with gross receipts of hundreds of millions of dollars showed up on the ledgers with losses.

In the age of rock 'n' roll, the big bands were gone, and their hit songs were being hawked on TV as nostalgia packages aimed at senior citizens.

Movies starring Gordon and Doris Day were shown on television with cuts for commercials in the wee hours of the morning.

Doris Day was reclusive in Carmel, California. An ardent champion of animal rights, she had surrounded herself with dogs and cats and other creatures and stepped into the limelight rarely. She had done so with a ravaged-looking Rock Hudson, who was fighting not only against AIDS but to keep his affliction a secret and, ultimately, to die in peace.

Others who had toed the line for Jack Warner in Gordon's day were also gone from the scene—dead or retired. In show business if you're not on, you're forgotten—until the obituary appears. For many of the old stars, when the news media announced that they had died, the common reaction was, "I didn't even know he (or she) was still around!"

In January 1985, Gordon was still around, living with his wife, Liz, and child in her hometown of Lincoln, Nebraska, but he was not the Gordon MacRae the public remembered. His entertainment career was finished. The golden voice of screen, radio, records, and stage had been stolen away forever by cancer of the mouth and jaw, the result of a lifetime of smoking cigarettes and drinking.

Living alone on Central Park West in New York City, I had been thrilled to learn that his cancer had gone into remission, but the day came when Heather telephoned to inform me that he had been stricken again, that he was hospitalized in Lincoln, that he was being moved to Los Angeles, and that she was going out to stay with him. She did not have to tell me that he was dying.

As I put down the phone and gazed out my window at the bleak, cold stretch of the park on that brittle afternoon, I thought it was sad that he was so far from all the places he loved. Although his movie roles often cast him as "the boy next door" and the embodiment of small-town America, he was never comfortable in what he called "the middle of the country."

He preferred the coasts, where he could see the ocean, where he could fish and scuba dive as we'd done so many times. Together we had fished at Lake Louise, at June Lake, and in the Indian Ocean and explored the water of Baja California. My thoughts flashed back to camping in the Sierras with Bill Orr.

Now, the vigorous, outdoorsy, vibrant man who'd always preferred tramping across a sunny golf course to the spotlights of a movie studio was confined to a hospital bed in Nebraska.

Lying awake that night and the ones that followed, I found myself thinking not about Gordon dying but of Gordie alive with joy and zest; not the man racked with sickness but the cocky and seemingly self-centered youth who'd declared from the stage of the Millpond Playhouse "I am Albert Gordon MacRae" as if the name were magic. The words that came to me about him were not "sad" or "tragic" or "pity" but adjectives that captured Gordie's essence: happy, devil-may-care, optimistic, hopeful, loving, and faithful.

Clearly, I heard him proclaiming the old and cherished Christian Science maxims he'd learned as a child. "Truth removes properly whatever is offensive." "Let go and let God."

Presently, Heather accompanied him to Los Angeles for diagnosis and whatever treatment could be given to him at the UCLA Medical Center. I went to L.A., staying at the home of two of my dearest friends, Larry and Norma Storch, who always seemed to have a room for me if I needed a place to stay. There I received a call from a woman saying she was Gordon's nurse. "He wants to see you, Mrs. MacRae," she said.

"You've got the wrong Mrs. MacRae," I answered. "The Mrs. MacRae you want is named Elizabeth. I'm Sheila."

"No," said the nurse emphatically. "He told me to call you. 'Get Sheersie,' he said."

I rushed to him. Though heavily medicated for pain, he was in good spirits, joking and teasing and taking me to task for what he regarded as my past sins. "You were always after me about gambling," he said. "What was the big deal? Hell, I was only having fun."

"You were no good at it," I said. "That was the big deal."

"And the drinking!"

"That you were good at."

"Yeah, I drank. But I *wasn't* an alcoholic."

"Oh no?" I said with an ironic laugh. "Then how is it you're on the board of the National Council on Alcoholism?"

"Well, that's just one of the things you do, you know? Like doing benefits. It doesn't mean *I'm* an alcoholic."

"I see," I said. "That explains it." I was thinking, "Still denying it, even now!"

He quietly accepted his condition with grace and good humor. Following a conference with the doctors at which they discussed surgery to remove a portion of his tongue, Heather wheeled him back to his room. Presently, she heard him singing in the bathroom. "Daddy," she called out to him, "what is that song?"

He answered by opening the door and singing, "Life without a tongue . . ."

When I visited him at Meredith's, he groused, "Those two cops you sent over are holding me prisoner."

"Cops? *What* cops?"

"Our daughters! They're like the Gestapo! They've taken away my liquor, my cigarettes, my candy, *and* my money. I had a thousand dollars and Meredith took it away for 'safekeeping.'"

Meredith was right, but I did not care. If he wanted those things. I was not going to say he couldn't have them. "Give them back," I ordered. "And the money." When I visited him again, he displayed the thousand dollars. "I want to go to the club and blow this. Don't be a spoilsport. Just you and me. C'mon."

Having been in love with and married to him for twenty years and never having been able to deny him anything, and despite all the heartaches and woes he'd imposed upon me after I left him, I gave in. "Okay," I said. "Come on." His eyes lit up.

The spirit was willing but the flesh proved weak. We stayed for a few minutes, then he said, "I'm tired, Sheersie. Take me back." After I'd helped him out of his clothes and into bed, he reached out to hold my hand. With effort and obvious pain, he lifted his head. "Sheersie," he sighed, "why did you go and leave me?"

"You know why, Gordie. It wasn't the same between us. The Gordie I married, I—I just could find anymore."

His hand tightened around mine. "Maybe if you hadn't left me I wouldn't be dying."

I dissolved in tears. "You were *gone,* Gordie," I sobbed. "You were somebody totally different. You, you . . ." Unable to go on, I buried my face in my hands. "To me back then," I sobbed, "you were...were already dead. My Gordie died in 1963."

For the rest of my life, I shall regret those words, his and mine. They'll haunt me to the end. What I had said was true. Gordon *had* vanished from my life. The magician had disappeared, lost to me forever in a netherworld of alcohol where I could not go. I might have continued with him, as he had begged me to do, but I would have been deceiving myself if I had stayed in the belief and hope that I could help him. Had I stayed, I would have made the tragic mistake of too many women who love their men so profoundly that they go on accepting the drinking, the absences, the physical and mental abuse, the battering of body and soul when what they should do—*must do*—is leave.

As the cancer worsened, Heather was with him constantly, a loving and ministering angel. One day she called me in near panic. "Mommy, I think he's delirious," she cried. "He keeps mumbling, but I can't make out what he's saying."

I could hear him in the background. "Put the phone close to him." I said. His words were not intelligible. But he wasn't delirious. I said, "Gordie, it's Sheersie. I'm going to sing along with you. So from Gian Carlo Menotti, I sang: "What is death but a sweeter change. There's no party, there's no end..." It was Gordie's favorite lyric and I couldn't finish the song.

That afternoon we were back on the road again, playing outdoors and in tents, Annie and Frank, Sky and Adelaide, Essie and Tom, Ella and Jeff. We were doing our club act in Vegas, the Sands, Tahoe, the Coconut Grove, the Fairmont, the Deauville and, of course, at the Empire Room. It was the last time our voices joined, the last he sang for me, the last silver song of a lark.

He died on January 24, 1986.

That night I awoke feeling his presence. Turning in bed, I found him lying beside me. He had on his favorite plaid pajamas.

My first thought was that I was dreaming. I was not. I screamed. Of course, sleeping was impossible. Breathless and trembling, I got out of bed and went into the living room. When I returned he was gone. I moved from the apartment within a week.

At sixty-four years of age, he was, of course, much to young to go. "Star of Movie Musicals" was the headline of the obituary that appeared in the *New York Times* the following morning. "Mr. MacRae, who was self-taught in both singing and acting, lent his rousing baritone voice, clean-cut good looks, and boy-next-door personality to sixteen movies," the obituary said. Recalling Gordon's four films with Doris Day, the *Times* quoted its movie critic, Thomas H. Pryor, as having written, "These two complement each other like peanut butter and jelly."

There was to be a religious service, the *Times* noted. In lieu of flowers, the article said, contributions could be made to the National Council on Alcoholism. The service was to be held on January 27 at the Sheridan Lutheran Church in Lincoln.

Elizabeth Lamberti MacRae made it clear to me that she did not want me there. "If I have to," she said, "I'll hire guards to keep you away. This is going to be *my* show."

She had left the message on my telephone answering machine. I still have the tape.

Outraged, Anne Meara insisted that I attend. "I'll go with you," Shirley Jones vowed defiantly. Marge Cowan said, "If she hires guards, I'll hire men to accompany us and they'll have bigger guns than her guards!"

I did not attend the funeral. I did not want to create a scene that might embarrass my children.

But I *was* there, in a way. My children saw to it. A photo of me and Gordon that Bruce carried in his wallet, taken when Gordie and I were young, was slipped into the coffin by Meredith's husband, Greg Mullavey.

Accompanying the *Times* obituary were two photos of him. The smaller showed him with a slight but rather quizzical smile. It was taken in his sad, troubled later years. In the other, he stands beneath a tree in Nogales, Arizona, with Shirley Jones as Laurey looking lovingly at him as Curly, cocky in cowboy hat and chaps and with an arm raised in a boyish gesture. It was from the scene where he and Shirley sang "People Will Say We're in Love."

Taking up a quarter of a page, the *Times*'s story on Gordon's life had been accurate and complete in the basic facts, but it didn't and couldn't catch Gordon's essence. Probably no article could, especially one on the life of a singer. The songs can be listed, the movies and shows named, and bits of reviews recited, but where is the music?

In this, my story of Gordon and me, the music has also been absent. Words can't capture the sound of a voice. Nor the effect of that voice on the listener. With that in mind, I hesitated to write a book about my life.

After all, as the monkey climbs higher, the more you can see its backside! Is autobiography an extreme act of conceit? Perhaps that's why so many of them are written by actors and actresses. When Samuel Goldwyn was approached to write the story of his years as one of the great movie moguls and starmakers of all time, he replied with a typical Goldwynism: "I'm never going to write my autobiography as long as I live." That was my feeling, but then I realized that my story would also be Gordon's. And his was a tale well worth telling.

Alas, in this book I have not been able to give you all of him because his voice is not here. Words on the pages of a book cannot give you that. But movies can. When I began telling our story, I noted that motion pictures are made possible by a quirk of the human eye that permits a series of still pictures to spring into movement, an optical illusion. A favored few are called upon to take part in the magic. Although a movie in itself may not be memorable, each frame that big unspooling coil of celluloid called motion picture film which is captured in the gate of a camera and a projector just long enough to fool us into believing that we're seeing real people moving and dancing and talking and sing-ing...lasts forever.

Gordon was in sixteen movies. I hope that, given the chance to see one of them—or all of them—you will.

Two, *Oklahoma!* and *Carousel,* shed upon him something more than wordly fame and riches. They bestowed upon Albert Gordon MacRae a grace which we all seek and hope for. Immortality.

FIFTEEN

Move On

WHEN I LEFT GORDON, friends told me I was a fool to leave a great, lucrative act I helped create and that I might never do well on my own. I had been content to spend my youth as a wife and mother and harbored no other aspirations. In due course, I had expected to fade into old age as Gordon's wife. Not once in all my Hollywood time or on the road with Gordon had I considered the possibility of being without him. Gordon had been the magician who pulled the rabbit out of the hat. I was the pretty girl who stood next to him, proudly pointing the audience's attention to him and his bag of tricks. I was happy in the role.

But because of his drinking I had been required to become his guardian, mother to our children, and arbiter between us and the agents, producers, and others who were angry with him. There had been no room for me.

I had been Mrs. Gordon MacRae, a mother, a bevy of famous females through impressions, Ella Peterson of Susanswerphone, Essie Whimple, gun-toting Annie Oakley, sniffly-nose Adelaide, and Sheila of the Waldorf.

After leaving Gordon, I had sought that same love with JP, with the

Chairman of the Board, as Ron Wayne's wife, as Jack Heller's partner, and in affairs with Bob Fosse and Albert Finney and others.

In those years, I became the actress Jack Warner did not want me to be, Alice Kramden, a nightclub act, a federal tax case, an invalid, a writer of plays and movies, a producer, and a vagabond graced with the gift of good and caring friends.

But good fortune smiled, and in 1984, in association with Irv and Marge Cowan, my friend Nora Hayden was working on plans for a movie titled *P.K.* She asked me to produce it.

I mention the film here because it demonstrated to me that life is full of new and challenging opportunities for those who are open to them, not matter their age, and we never know what's just around the corner.

For me, as I plunged into my new role as a film producer, the surprise was a charming, handsome, thirty-year-old English actor whom I shall name Richard Leonard Marseden. He auditioned for a part in the picture, and for solely artistic reasons he did not get it. But he insisted on a dinner date and we talked for hours.

Neither of us expected that we would become lovers, but as I look back, I now understand why it happened for me. I was not married. I had more freedom than at any time in my life. He was urbane, witty, and a gifted actor. Talent had always attracted me.

He proved to be exquisitely romantic in a charmingly old-fashioned manner, covering the bed with roses and gardenias and little presents. As a lover, he seemed to have emerged from the most erotic passages of Henry Miller or *The Joy of Sex*.

At this time I received an early-morning phone call from my agent. "I think I have just the thing for you," he said. "It's a wonderful play called *The Crows* and you'd play seven parts, from a seven-thousand-year-old woman to a woman of the future."

Written in verse, it also had an avant-garde musical score based on Elizabethan madrigals composed for the synthesier by William Hayden Wayne, usually addressed as Hayden.

I had always worked well with composers, writers, and artists, but at the second rehearsal, Hayden and I clashed over the song that I was to do at the beginning of the play, "Will You Remember Me?"

"We're not dealing with a fifteen-piece orchestra," he said, roaring onto the stage. "This is synthesized music."

"I know very well what it is, Hayden," I retorted. "Do you think that because I'm *older,* I don't know about synthesizers? You're a pain, Hayden, and I don't think I'll do the song."

To my amazement, when I returned home that evening, I found him waiting quite impatiently in front of my house. Tall and blond, he might have been me were I a man. "Look," he said, "the producer wants you in the play. So we are just going to have to work this out between us. We'll get together in the morning and see what we can do about it."

His bossiness rankled. "I can't sing in the morning," I said as rudely as he had spoken to me. "I'm *not* some twenty-year-old and I can't—"

"You're copping out," he snapped. "Stop acting like a diva. Something's bugging you and it's not the music. Ten to one it's a man." He strode away. "I'll see you downtown at nine o'clock sharp."

I do not know what was colder that morning, the temperature of the rehearsal room or the atmosphere between us.

"Now just sit and listen," he said. "And by the way, who is the man?"

As Hayden played my song, I felt as if I had been transported to another time and place. It was wonderful. The ice melted.

"Now get up to the mike," he said softly, "and sing it as I want to hear it. Stand close to me."

We sang together. Now this was a man who knew exactly what he wanted...one whom I could trust.

During the third week of rehearsal, he woke me up at seven in the morning with a phone call. "Sheila, marry me?"

"No," I said. "No, no, no, no, no, no, no, no, no, no..."

"Well, that was eleven noes, wasn't it?" he laughed, and I saved that morning's tape.

Complications arose: days were spent with Hayden, creating, laughing, with inexhaustible energies...but Richard was still in my bed and my apartment. Hayden and I ran to plays on the weekend, concerts, out-of-the-way restaurants.

Even before I met Hayden, the relationship with Richard began to sour. More and more he was using cocaine and other drugs—*with* liquor. I also had felt he owed it to himself to have children... to marry. From the outset, I said, "You're too young..."

Even if I had not fallen in love with Hayden, the time was imminent for Richard and me to part. Oh, how I wished Hayden and Richard were one—one fantastic man!

Richard left for London in a week—and years later I was happy to hear he'd straightened out, married, become a father, and had a successful career as a writer-producer.

As for me, it was time to try to shoot *P.K.* and finish in three weeks. The cast for the film was incredible: Jackie Mason, Dick Shawn, Sammy Davis, Jr., Anne Meara, Louise Lasser, Kaye Ballard, Sandy Baron, Irwin Corey, Virginia Graham and Larry Storch, and then Dick Shawn passed away before we had edited *P.K.*—and we had many problems that put the film in limbo. I have high hopes that we can finish it this year.

I had barely stopped shooting on *P.K.* when a new project presented itself. Another film, *Golden Days*, was to be produced in Budapest. For Hayden and me, they *were* golden days beside the Danube and then in London, recording the music. Then we traveled to Munich and Milan and spent a final week in Figina Cerenza, near Lake Como, recording the voice of José-Luis Rodrigues from Venezuela—a talented singer. We all worked in a restored castle, and afterward, Hayden and I spent time lying naked in the hot Italian sun on our balcony—not speaking for hours on end, but finishing each other's thoughts and planning to write together forever. We both knew that this perfect microcosm of time would always be the best—that the synergistic love we felt was rare.

We drenched ourselves in a mutual love of Shakespeare that for me resulted in the writing of a play, *Elizabeth and Will*. On the surface it dealt with a love affair between the playwright and his monarch, Queen Elizabeth.

A story of the passion between an older woman and young man, it was also the story of Hayden and me and Richard and me!

But a problem presented itself. Hayden wanted to be named as coauthor. I refused.

Although he had made me happier and more creative, I saw in our relationship only a potential for trouble and heartbreak. Although I had said no to his marriage proposal eleven times, I could not think of him gone from my life. I was as obsessed with him as I had been with Gordon and J.P. A life without his strength, decisiveness, and talent seemed unimaginable. Yet we were at odds over everything and working together became difficult.

The tense relationship reached a climax during a trip to California to see Heather in Stephen Sondheim's *Merrily We Roll Along*. Hayden changed his mind about us staying in La Jolla for a few days after the opening of the show as we had planned.

"I don't want to be here," he declared. "We're leaving. Pack your bags. You know Hessie is great!"

With the good-natured resignation that had gotten Heather through so many parental disappointments, she gave me a hug and a kiss. "It's okay, Mom," she said. "I understand. You saw it twice."

As Hayden packed our bags into the car, a longtime friend of mine sidled up to me in the hotel lobby. A theater veteran, George Furth had written the book for Liza Minnelli's *The Act* and, earlier, the script for *Company* and *Follies,* Steve Sondheim's quintessential portrait of life in show business. "I see that nothing's changed in the saga of Sheila MacRae," George said. "You have your controller with you."

I laughed. "What do you mean, 'controller'?" A phrase Anne Meara had used!

"Sheila, in all the years we've known one another, you have always let somebody else run your life. Frankly, why a talented, smart, and capable woman permits the men in her life to turn her into a cypher has been a puzzle to me."

"I must love it!"

As I listened to George's harsh indictment, I could not be offended. I had posed a similar question concerning Gordon as I grappled with the how and why of his enslavement to alcohol and gambling. Ultimately I learned that he had an addictive personality and that he could deal with and overcome it only when he accepted the truth. As in so many things, the Bible pointed the way. "Ye shall know the truth and the truth shall set you free."

The truth is—as I tell my story—I see some things were lots better and some very much worse.

The story is: as Gordon had been controlled by drinking and gambling, I was addicted to men. As they dominated me, they dominate the pages of this book.

I thought about George's words as Hayden and I drove to L.A.

Breaking off my relationship with Hayden was not easy. I would not answer the phone, so he came in person.

"I know why you're doing this," he said. "You're depressed over Gordon's death. Deep down inside you wish it had been me who died. You're angry at me for being alive. You won't face that."

Hayden Wayne and Richard Leonard Marseden will always have a special place in my heart. Through those passionate young men, I came to realize that I could still desire and be desired. I felt like a warm, overripe peach—good feelings for a woman at any age.

Maybe you are asking yourself whether you've seen *Golden Days*. I can tell you that you haven't. Because of innumerable problems, it was never released. Chief among them was the refusal of the Hungarian government to let the film be taken out of the country. That was in 1986 when Hungary was Communist. In the wake of the downfall of Communism and the welcome installation of democratic government in Budapest, I hope that *Golden Days* will come to the screen at last.

And I know *P.K.* will be finished and *Elizabeth and Will* will open on Broadway.

When this happens, there will be entries in a diary that has had its fill of sad, glad, and funny moments.

From my diary, November 9, 1991:

I can't believe it! It's been twenty-six years since the big New York blackout and JP's ultimatum to me to get a divorce from Gordon or else! Well, I got the divorce. But not because JP had demanded it. I did it for me.

In a few weeks, the year will be 1992. How did it get here so fast? The magical year 1992 was a time when Gordon and I were to write the words with which all fairy tales are expected to end. "And they lived happily ever after!"

When our financial problems burst upon us in the 1960s, I told Gordon that I would work until 1992. "By then," I said, "all our money woes will be past. We'll be able to forget about the IRS. We'll be free to be ourselves. World travelers together!"

But I lost Gordo. His dark side overcame him.

Before the spirit of the man I'd loved died all those years ago, long before his body perished, we had talked about growing old together, enjoying our grandchildren. We dreamed together of Africa. The Himalayas. Scuba diving in the Great Barrier Reef. Taking in the world.

Could I do those things alone? Or with someone else? "Why not?" my children asked.

Truthfully, I could think of no reason not to do so. Until today. Letters have arrived. Official-looking envelopes, they hold answers to my inquiries about all the vital issues that become important at a certain point in one's life. They deal with the future. How much Social Security might I expect to collect? What pensions were mine from the unions I joined so I could be in show business? Proceeds of annuities? Funds to finance the waning years after so many seasons of hard work as Gordon's partner offstage and on.

During the seven years of working with Gordon, we had earned between nine hundred thousand and a million dollars a year.

Now that it was payback time, how much might I expect?

The answer was stunning. Nothing!

I do not exist prior to 1966. All the contracts had been in the names of Mr. and Mrs. Gordon MacRae but had been paid into a corporate entity bearing Gordie's name.

The letters state that the payments due from Social Security and union pensions for those seven years are being paid. But to the second Mrs. Gordon MacRae.

Reading the letters in my dressing room at the studio where I am acting in the ABC-TV soap opera *General Hospital*, I asked aloud, "Gordie, how am I going to get over this?"

As clearly as if he were standing beside me, I heard his answer. With the old optimism of the young Scot I had married, he said, "We get through by the grace of God and a good infield."

The names of my good infielders have been sprinkled throughout this book. As Gordon would say, they were always there for me in the clutch, saving the game for me when it was the bottom of the ninth, bases loaded, and I was behind in the count.

Therefore, in the time-honored rule of show business—"Never cut the credits"—and in keeping with another hallowed tradition in which stars of equal magnitude are billed alphabetically, I gratefully acknowledge them here:

Van and Beth Alexander, Louis Ambrosio, Shirley Baskin, Vera Brown, Martin Broones, Carol Channing and her good infielder Charles Lowe, Gena Collins, William Conn, Marge and Irv Cowan, Bill and Phyllis Dorman, Gloria and Mike Franks, Albert Finney, Hattie and Sam Friedland, Charlotte Greenwood, Elizabeth Forsyth Hailey, Oliver Hailey, Nora Hayden, Jack Heller, Hy Hollinger, Marty Ingels, Shirley Jones, Arthur Keisler, Barry Landau, Jean LaTourette, Robert Lewis, Jeannie Martin, Anne Meara, John Meyers, Miriam Nelson Meyers,

Gloria Monty, Meg Mortimer, Greg Mullavey, Bill Orr, Jack Philbin, George Peppard, Professor Sam Schoenbaum and his wife Marilyn, Bob Schulman, John Schulman, Florence Jensen Simmons, Francis Albert Sinatra, Florence Small, George and Lynn Stewart, Jerry Stiller, Norma and Larry Storch, Alan Surgal, Bettina and Alex Swan, June Taylor, Marit Tenzaghi, Elizabeth Wayne, Ron Wayne, Pauline Weinstein, Ann and Jack Warner, Bonnie and Paul Zindel. And, of course, my mother, Winifred Baker Stephens, my father, Lewis Albert Stephens, my sister, Paula Stephens Pigott, and her husband Maurice, and the MacRae children, Robert Bruce, William Gordon (Gar), Heather Allison, and Meredith Lynn. Finally, but by no means least, my grandchildren, Michael, Caitlin, Jeremy, Josh, Allison, and Zachariah.

Epilogue

The past catches me off guard, as it did not long ago when JP and I ran into one another at NBC.

I recognized his look. Surprised. More than a little upset, as if I had known he would be at the Rockefeller Center studios.

"Well, hello there," I said, forcing cheeriness to mask my nervousness.

Releasing the door, he got on the elevator and stood near but not close. I looked down at my shoes, hating how I felt and sure that he sensed it. He had always boasted that he was able to see right through me.

"Were you at the Christmas party?" The chilly tone of voice was all too familiar. His meaning was quite clear. *"What the hell are YOU doing here?"*

I looked directly into his eyes. "Yes, I was there."

"Funny! I didn't see you."

"I was—uh—standing on the periphery."

He grunted. "Periphery! You must be in one of your writing moods again. What is it? More of that poetry you used to spout at me all hours of the night?"

"Not poetry. I'm writing a book—and—and —you're in it!"

He squinted incredulously. "A *book?*"

The elevator stopped. The door slid open. The magnificent art deco lobby of the RCA Building beckoned, offering escape.

"Yes, a book," I said, stepping out. "It's the story of my life. I've got an agent, and a man who's written lots of books is working with me."

"Does this book have a title?" he asked, following me from the elevator.

"I was going to call it *Thirteen Sutton Place*. But my agent, Mel Berger of the William Morris office, said it sounded too much like a mystery."

"That's you, all right." He paused to light a cigarette. "Mystery and paradox."

We went through a revolving door into the chilly evening. Rockefeller Center's Christmas tree sparked with cheery lights above the skating rink.

A sleek black limousine waited at the curb. His, I presumed.

"Then I thought of another name for the book," I said. "I suggested calling it *Apples of Gold*. But my collaborator didn't like it."

"He's obviously an author with good taste," JP said, leaning against the car. *"Apples of Gold?* What the hell does *that* mean?"

"It's from the Bible. The Tree of Life. Adam and Eve."

"I get it," he said, opening the limo door. "I assume you are the lady Eve." His eyes drilled into mine. "Who am I? God—Adam—or the snake?"

"Take your pick."

"Oh, by all means, the snake!" He flicked the ash from the end of his cigarette. "Make me the thing that Eve pointed to *after* she enjoyed herself."

As the limousine slid away from the curb, tears welled, aching behind my eyes.

"You know you'll never finish it, Sheila," he shouted, leaning through the window. "You're not a closer."

"You are so wrong," I answered, knowing he couldn't hear me. I tightened my scarf against the cold—in my head a Sondheim song: "Just keep moving, if you've been there. Then it's gone! Move on!"

And that is what the Hollywood Mother of the Year has learned since she wrote the diary entry that begins this book!

Move on!

What would I change in my life if I could? One thing.

Gordon would not be an alcoholic.

If I could have altered that, there would be a different ending to this story. Gordon and I would still be together.

Amen!

Index